GLOBAL JIHAD

GLOBAL JIHAD

A Brief History

Glenn E. Robinson

STANFORD UNIVERSITY PRESS

Stanford, California

STANFORD UNIVERSITY PRESS
Stanford, California

Printed in the United States of America on acid-free, archival-quality paper

Library of Congress Cataloging-in-Publication Data

Names: Robinson, Glenn E., 1959- author.
Title: Global jihad : a brief history / Glenn E. Robinson.
Description: Stanford, California : Stanford University Press, 2021. | Includes
    bibliographical references and index.
Identifiers: LCCN 2020013814 (print) | LCCN 2020013815 (ebook) |
    ISBN 9780804760461 (cloth) | ISBN 9780804760478 (paperback) |
    ISBN 9781503614109 (epub)
Subjects: LCSH: Jihad—History—20th century. | Jihad—History—
    21st century. | Islamic fundamentalism—History—20th century.
    | Islamic fundamentalism—History—21st century. | Islam and
    politics—History—20th century. | Islam and politics—History—
    21st century. | Political violence—Religious aspects—Islam.
Classification: LCC BP182 .R63 2020 (print) | LCC BP182 (ebook) |
    DDC 303.6088/297—dc23
LC record available at https://lccn.loc.gov/2020013814
LC ebook record available at https://lccn.loc.gov/2020013815

Cover design: Rob Ehle
Typeset by BookMatters in 10.5/14.4 Brill

For Julia, Emily, and Abigail,
the reasons I embrace with pride
the appellation Abu'l-Binat

Contents

Preface

FROM AL-QA'IDA'S 9/11 TERROR ATTACKS IN THE UNITED STATES to the ISIS "caliphate" and its reign of violence in the Middle East, Europe, and beyond, global jihad has captured headlines, impelled vast national policies, and seized the imagination of people around the world in recent years. This book is an interpretive study of the global jihad phenomenon, designed to assemble in a short, accessible volume an understanding of the global jihad movement in recent decades. To produce this history, I have drawn from both primary documents in their original Arabic and the best secondary works of scholarship on this phenomenon. I make two broad and novel arguments. First, and most important, I construct a typology that suggests global jihad is best understood as four quite distinct iterations, or waves, each stemming from a unique set of crises and each having significantly different ideological answers detailing the way ahead. The four chapters describe and analyze every wave in turn, from the 1980s to the present.

In the conclusion, I offer a second broad argument that situates global jihad among the universe of violent political movements of the past century. I argue that global jihad is not sui generis, or unique unto itself. Rather, and no doubt provocatively, I argue that global jihad can be more usefully understood as a variant form of a "movement of rage," as opposed to more typical revolutionary or anticolonial movements. While relatively rare, movements of rage across different cultures and continents share distinctive sociological and ideological features. Seeing global jihad in this light rebuts both those who argue for its historical uniqueness (or even the exceptionalism of Islamist movements writ large) and those who argue that global jihad is just another form of revolutionary movement. Revolutionary movements—be they of the Left (e.g., Marxist), the Right (e.g., Fascist), or the broad Center (e.g., National Liberation)—are all based on Enlightenment ideals that their struggle will produce human progress, a better society that is more equal, freer, or more advanced. As with other movements of rage, the ideologues of global jihad do not make an Enlightenment case for their cause, as I show in my discussions of the four waves. Rather, global jihad is profoundly nihilistic (in the political, not philosophical, sense of the word) and apocalyptic in its ideology and behavior.

This book was written while I was on an abbreviated sabbatical at the National Centre for Peace and Conflict Studies at the University of Otago in Dunedin, New Zealand, and at the Middle East Institute at the National University of Singapore during the first five months of 2019. Both institutions proved to be wonderful hosts, and I would specifically like to thank Richard Jackson at Otago and Teo Michelle Agnes, Bilahari Kausikan, and Helen Lee at NUS for making those wonderful (if too short!) stays possible. The faculty and graduate students at both institutions proved to be terrific sounding boards for some of my ideas, and I hope I proved equally helpful in their research.

I offer my profound and humble gratitude to the many scholars who read through an earlier version of this manuscript and offered invaluable feedback: Martin van Bruinessen, F. Gregory Gause III, Mohammed M. Hafez, Thomas Hegghammer, Richard Jackson, Mehran Kamrava, Marc Lynch, William E. Shepard, Robert Springborg, David Waldner, Craig A. Whiteside, and the anonymous reviewers at Stanford University Press. Their inputs have made this book that much better, and none should be blamed for any mistakes or interpretations I have made. While all thought my typology of the four iterations of global jihad was an insightful addition to the literature, it is fair to say there was a decidedly split verdict on my argument about global jihad as a variant form of a movement of rage. I hope my more robust discussion, in response to some of their skepticism, will win over the remaining doubters, but I will leave it to the readers of this book to judge the final outcome.

A special debt of gratitude goes to Elizabeth K. Robinson, my copy editor of long standing, as well as my soul mate. She read through the whole manuscript twice, making the writing that much clearer and more accessible. She also painstakingly constructed the bibliography while I made final edits to the manuscript.

I have utilized a common form of transliteration from the Arabic, which is a simplified version of the professional standard recommended by the Middle East Studies Association in its *International Journal of Middle East Studies* (IJMES). Most 'ayns and hamzas (glottal stops) are represented with an apostrophe ('), and both long vowels and short vowels are kept to a simple *a*, *i*, or *u*. The exception is Arabic (or Farsi) words that have already made their way into the English language, in which case I adopt the common spelling. Hence, Usama Bin Laden, rather than 'Usama bin Ladin, Khomeini not Khomayni, and Musab instead of Mus'ab. I have also adopted a common use rendering of the word "Shia" as both singular and plural noun as well as adjective to avoid switching between Shi'i, Shi'a, and Shi'i, respectively. Unless otherwise noted, I have done the translations myself. The one big exception to this rule is that in chapter 4, I have used Brynjar Lia's excellent translation of the key parts of Abu Musab al-Suri's book *Call for Global Islamic Resistance*. Although I have smoothed out the language in a few places, Lia did such a good job that I saw little reason to change it.

Last, but not least, I have dedicated this book to my daughters, Julia, Emily, and Abigail. In the more machismo strains of Arab popular culture, one man questions another's manliness by hurling the epithet *abu'l-binat!*—"father of girls!" Given how proud I am of my daughters and all that they have achieved, I will gladly wear the term with honor.

Introduction

THE BIRTH OF ISLAMISM
AND JIHADISM

FOR A WORD THAT GENERATES A GREAT DEAL OF POPULAR MEDIA attention and usually terrifies the imaginations of the ill-informed, the word *jihad* is remarkably poorly understood in the West. The word comes from the common Arabic root *j-h-d* (most Arabic and Hebrew words have a three-letter root from which related words are constructed), with the verb form meaning "to make an effort" or "to struggle." It is not exclusively or even mostly a religious word. Indeed, forms of the word are used commonly in nonreligious phrasing, typically around the notion of trying really hard to do something.

In religious terms, jihad has two meanings popularly accepted today, both of which have generally positive connotations to Muslims. First, it can mean "jihad of the sword" (*jihad al-sayf*), religiously sanctioned armed violence carried out in defense of Islam, Muslim territory, or Muslim lives—all of which are seen to be beneficial attributes. Religious jihad has a second popular meaning: to struggle against forbidden temptations. It is a personal struggle to lead a more upright, pious life (*jihad al-nafs*). This latter definition is often referred to by Muslims as the "greater jihad" (*jihad akbar*) in reference to a (contested) *hadith*, or saying, of the prophet Muhammad. In this book the word *jihad* is used overwhelmingly in the context of *jihad al-sayf,* jihad of the sword, where ideologues call for armed violence to advance a political agenda under the banner of Islam. Such violence is rarely sanctioned by proper religious authority.

1

Thus, according to Islamic jurisprudence, the calls for violence described in this book are almost always illicit.

Global jihad is a new phenomenon, dating back only to the 1980s, although its intellectual origins can be traced to a century ago. The early part of the twentieth century was a time when the Muslim world was riven by conflict and competing intellectual currents. The rise of European industrial and military power in the nineteenth century had by this point in history overwhelmed the Muslim world, establishing colonies, protectorates, mandates, spheres of influence, and other forms of imperial domination from Morocco to Indonesia. Western dominion throughout Asia and Africa in many ways was like every other conquering army over the course of history, where sheer power and force of arms were sufficient to conquer and mostly pacify vast stretches of land and peoples. And, like in previous cases of conquest, there were many examples of local populations both fighting European conquerors as well as working with them. The difference in this case was that the British, French, and other European powers brought with them in conquest not just raw military strength but institutions of government, education, law, and society that produced extraordinary wealth, efficiency, and opportunity that appealed to many in the subject populations.

Exporting the seeds of Western modernity around the globe was no humanitarian mission or "white man's burden." It was, first and foremost, a means to make colonial domination sustainable. Educating a class of indigenous civil servants in modern, scientific methods could provide the kind of rational bureaucracy that would make a colony run efficiently for generations to come. Building a railroad infrastructure was typically about getting local raw materials to European markets for processing into finished goods for resale. Having a functioning legal system protected private property and the underpinnings of this new system. European domination was less about the rule of law than it was about rule through law. Liberal governmental structures at home in Europe were rarely for purposeful export to colonies. Still, those democratic institutions and their philosophical foundations could not help but seep into local systems and consciousness in a beguiling way.

In other words, European domination of the Muslim world was a complicated affair, marked by brutality and supremacy but also containing within it the seeds of powerful and appealing new forms of society and economy.

European modernity, exported through the barrel of a gun, was both ruthless and enticing at the same time. Not surprisingly, there was a vast spectrum of response by Muslims (and other subject populations) to this new form of domination. While some Muslims saw the promise of European modernity and sought to embrace it fully, many more sought instead some hybrid form of synergy between a revered religious heritage and culture as well as the appeal of selective European legal and economic institutions and practices. Still others saw no good coming from such new and foreign practices, and sought to reject them root and branch. It was an intellectually turbulent time.

One of these many and varied responses by Muslims in this stormy period was to construct a new discourse and social movement that today we call Islamism. Islamism arose from the educated urban middle classes and sought to construct a form of modernity that was strongly anticolonial, that rejected much of European sensibilities, and that promoted the ascendancy of Islam in the public square. Islamist arguments centered mostly on the nature of the state, of what a modern nation-state should look like that was focused on Islam (or at least their interpretation of Islam). It is important to remember that Islamist debates on the proper nature of political power in the modern era did not represent traditional, time-honored deliberations in Islam. The very idea of nation-states and the institutions of the modern state—not of empires, which had dominated the Muslim world—were mostly new concepts throughout the Muslim world, brought via European colonialism. Indeed, those ideas were relatively new to Europe as well, where they had grown organically out of European realities and battles in the previous two centuries. Marrying new concepts of a modern state to a belief that Islam must dominate the public square in any proper Muslim country was an intellectual challenge for Islamists in the twentieth century that had not been germane to previous generations of Muslims.

The premier organizational response coming out of Islamist circles from these debates was the founding of the Muslim Brotherhood by Hasan al-Banna in Egypt in 1928 (on which more below).[1] While Islamism represented the first intellectual precursor for the later emergence of global jihad, with its strident politicization of the religion of Islam, it failed to fundamentally change the nature of politics in the Middle East during the four decades following the founding of the Muslim Brotherhood in 1928. Most Muslims in most parts of the Muslim world simply did not accept the kind of arguments about politics and religion that Islamists were putting forward, least of all the political elites who mostly followed a type of secular politics. The Muslim Brotherhood and similar organizations were somewhat influential but were hardly momentous and consequential groups throughout much of the twentieth century.

Frustration by some Islamists at the failure of political Islamism to foundationally change the nature of politics in the Muslim world and to push forward an agenda of creating Islamic states led to the emergence in the 1960s of a second intellectual precursor to global jihad: arguments for the use of violence under the banner of jihad to overthrow local regimes, capture states by force, and implement some version of an Islamic state (there is no consensus over what such a state should look like). But that effort largely failed as well, despite the occasionally dramatic event, such as the assassination of President Anwar Sadat of Egypt in 1981. The group that pulled off the assassination was crushed, its leaders executed, and its lesser members imprisoned. It would take years to rebuild. The inability of local jihadism to capture state power anywhere in the Sunni Muslim world represented a starting point for much of the intellectual effort concerning the idea of global jihad in the waning years of the twentieth century and the early years of the twenty-first century. They asked themselves: What is preventing local jihadis from capturing power and advancing their various political causes in Egypt and elsewhere in the Muslim world? Global jihadis believed that there was a *systemic* problem at the global level that had to be addressed, through violence under the banner of Islam, before their success could be assured. Neither the political work of Islamists nor the violent actions of local jihadis represented sufficient leverage to change the system and achieve their broader aspirations.

Of course, broader debates about the relationship between religion and politics go back to the beginning of Islam. Muslims have debated how best to form and manage a proper political community ever since. As with similar debates within Christendom, opinions have ranged far and wide as to the proper relationship between faith and polity, and to the nature of the polity itself. While secularism has many supporters in the contemporary Muslim world, there is a broad tradition within Islam that rejects a wall separating mosque and state. The idea of secularism in the Muslim world has walked a tightrope for centuries between its pragmatic partial adoption by various

rulers and the "dogmatic no" of orthodoxy.[2] The point here is that debates over
the proper relationship between religion and political power—between *din
wa dawla*—has a long history in Islam, as it does in other religious traditions.

But Islamism was a new phenomenon in multiple ways, including in the
kinds of demands it made on the political system and on society as well as in
the sociological community from which it arose: an urban, educated middle
class, which itself was a new phenomenon with shallow historical roots. Islamists, like everyone else, were trying to make sense of the organizational
and institutional political arrangements embodied in the modern state, while
at the same time trying to rid their lands of foreign occupiers (a much more
old-fashioned kind of goal) and preserve their own cultural and ideological
traditions. The Islamist movement, born a century ago, has proved to be exceptionally durable as it captures the political sentiments of several hundred
million Muslims around the world. Put another way, gauging by various elections and public opinion surveys, there are about as many adult Islamists in
the world as there are people living in the United States.

Since the term *Islamism* is often thrown around without much precision,
let us define exactly what we mean by the word. The term encompasses a
broad array of people and groups over the past century, so generalizations have
many historical exceptions. That said, Islamism may be defined as *a sociopolitical movement seeking to create a modern version of an Islamic state, typically
through political (nonviolent) means.* There is a lot to unpack in that definition,
so allow me to focus on the four principal components of the definition. First,
Islamism is a sociopolitical *movement*, particularly in recent decades. In its
first years of existence, Islamism was confined to a relatively small segment
of society, but since the 1970s, it has typically represented around 25 percent
of the adult population of Muslim-majority countries and has been well institutionalized.[3] Often, Islamism has been the single largest sociopolitical
movement in Muslim-majority countries.[4] Second, Islamists seek to create a
modern state and society. This is how Islamists are different from traditional
Salafis, the "ultra-orthodox" within Islam. Salafis seek to recreate an imagined Islamic polity from the seventh century. Indeed, historically, the ultra-
fundamentalist Salafi Muslims are apolitical, wishing to focus on piety, not
politics.[5] Islamists, by contrast, seek to merge political modernity with Islam,
to create an ideal state that reflects a modern interpretation of Islam. Third,

that state is to be *Islamic* in some essential sense, although frankly there is no consensus on what a modern Islamic state is supposed to look like precisely.

Finally, Islamists have focused on using *political, nonviolent means* to achieve their goals. This is the fundamental difference that sets Islamists apart from jihadis: Islamists believe in grassroots, bottom-up, political work, while jihadis—both local and global—believe in the *necessity* of violence, of top-down direct action against the state. I do not mean to imply that Islamists have never resorted to violence; they have. But Islamists do not view violence as a central, necessary component to achieve their political ends, while jihadis do. Jihadis believe that political means have been blocked, typically by a corrupt and apostate system, while Islamists are typically willing to "get their hands dirty" working nonviolently within the political system if allowed to do so. The centrality of violence to their program is what sets all types of jihadis apart from Islamists.

The quintessential organizational expression of Islamism has been the Muslim Brotherhood. But even after its founding in Egypt in 1928, the Muslim Brotherhood and Islamism more broadly remained relatively marginal to the broader strokes of Muslim history. I do not mean to suggest that the Brotherhood was wholly unimportant during its first four decades of existence, but rather that there were more important intellectual and political currents. For example, nationalism was far more important and consequential in the Middle East and the broader Muslim world than Islamism was during much of the twentieth century, especially before the 1970s. This was a time and a political culture when it was possible to mock the Muslim Brotherhood and its leader, as, for example, Gamal 'Abd al-Nasser in Egypt would do, without fear of serious political consequences.[6] It was only in the 1970s that Islamism truly found its voice and became a major political force in the Muslim world.

The overall failure of Islamism to either seize political power or fundamentally change society gave rise to the ideology of *jihadism*, for radicals to argue that Islamism's emphasis on political work had failed and would never lead to the construction of an Islamic state in Egypt or anywhere else.[7] Indeed, the argument about the failure of political work to advance an Islamic state, and thus the need for armed action under the banner of Islam, began to arise at the same time in the 1960s in both the Sunni world (especially Egypt) and the Shia world (especially Iran). In both places, the intellectual foundations to justify armed jihad against the state were being built by ideologues who would later become synonymous with modern jihadism. For example, contemporary Sunni jihadism was founded in 1964 when an Egyptian by the name of Sayyid Qutb published a slim volume that radically reinterpreted an old Muslim concept that referred to the moral darkness in Arabia immediately prior to the coming of Islam. For Qutb, that old depraved period of *jahiliyya* was being recreated by current Muslim regimes and broader societies. Only a generational struggle based primarily on armed jihad could save Islam and Muslim society from steep moral decay. While Shia ideologues, including Ayatullah Khomeini, did not rely on the concept of *jahiliyya*, they too constructed ideologies calling for the use of radical action to overthrow the monarchy in Iran and advance Shia interests elsewhere.[8]

The rise of violent jihadi movements in the 1970s to implement the visions of Qutb, Khomeini, and others focused overwhelmingly on removing what were seen to be corrupt, repressive, and apostate secular regimes throughout the Muslim world. Jihadi groups to this day remain mostly focused on these local issues. But these local jihadi groups also largely failed to bring substantial changes to the political order. They would assassinate a president or prime minister from time to time, slaughter some hapless tourists perhaps, but their violence did not meaningfully change the apostate nature of local regimes or cure other evils in the eyes of radical jihadis. Out of this failure was born *global* jihad—that is, ideologues and groups dedicated to using violence to address *global, systemic causes* of the major problems facing the entire Muslim world, at least in the eyes of this new generation of jihadis.

Thus, just as local jihadism was born from the perceived failures of Islamism, so too was global jihad primarily born from the perceived failures of local jihadism to address the perceived systemic causes of the woes facing Muslims around the world. And just as there has been little consensus among Islamists or among jihadis about a range of issues, global jihad had distinct variations and viewpoints. In fact, beginning in the 1980s, global jihad saw four distinct iterations, or waves, each emerging from a particular crisis and each with its own ideology and program for achieving a global end. Those goals varied considerably: the first sought to create a Jihadi International to liberate occupied Muslim lands; the second focused on driving the Americans out of the Muslim world; the third wave aspired to recreate a new and radical caliphate to defeat apostasy throughout all of the lands once ruled by Muslims; while the fourth aimed at mounting a global, leaderless jihad to keep alive hope during a desperate time. This book tells the story of those four waves of global jihad: their origins, their evolution, and their quite distinct ideologies.

This brief overview of the intellectual precursors of global jihad should make clear that global jihadism did not simply emerge from whole cloth in the 1980s; it had an intellectual history that dates back a century. With this brief outline in place, I now explore in greater detail the intellectual and political evolution that would lay the foundation for the later development of global jihad, and provide an introduction to the phenomenon of global jihad as it began in the 1980s in Afghanistan.

THE FOUNDING OF THE MUSLIM BROTHERHOOD

Modern Islamism began in organizational form in 1928, when a twenty-two-year-old Egyptian schoolteacher named Hasan al-Banna founded the Society of Muslim Brothers, more commonly known as the Muslim Brotherhood (al-Ikhwan al-Muslimin).[9] In its early years, the Brotherhood was more of a youth group and social club than a political organization, although it did promote an all-encompassing view of the role of Islam in society. Like most Islamists to follow, Banna was not a cleric. Rather, he was a teacher who received his training in Cairo at the secular Dar al-'Ulum academy before accepting a teaching position in Ismailia, in the Suez Canal Zone. It was in Ismailia where Banna founded the Brotherhood shortly after arriving. Ismailia, and the whole of the Suez Canal Zone in 1928, were still very much under British control. Britain had long dominated Egypt, first indirectly throughout much of the nineteenth century, then directly with its invasion and occupation of Egypt in 1882. Britain's "protectorate" over Egypt lasted until formal independence was granted in 1922, but Britain remained a hegemonic force inside Egypt until the 1950s. Britain's domination of Egypt was particularly strong in the Suez Canal Zone, which London viewed as its strategic lifeline to India and all of its colonial interests "east of Suez."

Like so much in Egypt during this time frame, the Muslim Brotherhood was impacted by European intellectual currents—from the serious, including the prominence of fascism (with which the Brotherhood shared a focus on tradition, conservatism, and discipline), to the superficial, as the Brotherhood's motto of "Be Prepared" ("prepare yourselves": *'addu*) was lifted straight from the Boy Scouts.[10] But although they were influenced in various ways by European thinking, Banna and his followers were strongly opposed to British imperialism in Egypt and believed that a vigorous and strong interpretation of Islam was necessary to rid the country of foreign control as well as corrupt cultural influences. Banna's nationalism was a key feature of his ideology, beginning with his participation in the 1919 "revolution" against British control.[11]

By the late 1930s and early 1940s, the Brotherhood had become more overtly political and militant. It formed its own armed militia, the "Special Apparatus" (*al-jihaz al-khas*), which was answerable directly to the leader of the Brotherhood, Banna himself. Indeed, as the Brotherhood grew and became more politically involved, it also became more secretive and almost cultish in orientation. That cult-like secrecy and allegiance to the leader were key features of the group that allowed it to maintain organizational integrity and coherence; however, those features also generated plenty of critics who grew to distrust the Brotherhood's intentions. That organizational duality of the Brotherhood is as true today as it was in the 1940s.

The late 1940s and early 1950s proved decisive for the Brotherhood in Egypt, particularly as Egyptian nationalism against British imperialism grew. The Brotherhood's small armed force participated in the war in Palestine in 1948, arguably faring better than the Egyptian military, which performed disastrously. The Brotherhood's intense criticism of the regime for its poor showing in Palestine got it banned by the Egyptian prime minister, Nuqrashi Pasha, who was almost immediately assassinated by a member of the Brotherhood. Regime security forces took revenge by assassinating Hasan al-Banna in February 1949. In an atmosphere of intense anti-British sentiment and popular support for groups opposed to British control, the government in Cairo lifted the Brotherhood's political ban in 1950. The organization quickly became active in anti-British demonstrations and made common cause with military officers, who overthrew the Egyptian monarchy and established a republic in 1952. That alliance soured quickly because the Brotherhood opposed the secular policies implemented by the new military regime in Cairo.

A key issue for the Muslim Brotherhood under Hasan al-Banna (and after) is its relationship with violence. Does the Muslim Brotherhood endorse political violence as an important and necessary instrument to achieve its political ends? Or, rather, has the Muslim Brotherhood mostly eschewed the use of violence to achieve its political ends? Certainly during its first quarter-century in existence, the Muslim Brotherhood had a complicated relationship with violence. Banna and his cohorts were not pacifists, either in reality or ideologically. They created their armed wing (the Special Apparatus) for a reason and periodically engaged in violence, mostly against the British or those Egyptians whom they viewed as doing the bidding of the British. They were stridently anticolonial in outlook and viewed violence directed at British control as legitimate. In addition, on ideological grounds, the Brotherhood adopted the word *jihad* as a central animating feature of its program, without ever really defining what type of jihad it had in mind. It is fair to conclude that Banna was no pacifist, as he accepted that violence may sometimes be necessary for the good of the cause or community. Licit violence against the enemies of Islam (as Banna viewed it) was acceptable.

On balance, though, it is also fair to say that Banna was no revolutionary either; he viewed the work of the Brotherhood as essentially a force for evolutionary change, not revolutionary upheaval. For Banna, the slow Islamization of society was consistent with an Islamic reformist or revivalist world view, and the Brotherhood could play a vanguard role in the slow deepening of belief and religious life in Egypt. As Banna himself said, "The Muslim Brotherhood does not believe in revolution, and does not rely on it in achieving its goals and if it happened, we will not adopt it.... Our task is to create a new generation of believers who can reformulate the Islamic umma [community of believers] in all aspects of life."[12]

The point of my argument is this: Although Islamists in general and the Muslim Brotherhood in particular have engaged in violence in Egypt and elsewhere throughout the past century, violence per se is not foundational to their project; it was not so in the group's founding and it is not so today. As Banna suggested, if the Brotherhood is successful, it will mean that it changed society at the grassroots level through reformist means, that it convinced Muslims to reembrace Islam as a solution to all of their problems, and that it did not engage in revolutionary violence. As noted earlier, the question of violence is the primary difference that separates Islamists from jihadis: the centrality of violence to their political programs. For Islamists, violence is not essential, even if it occurs from time to time for specific reasons. For jihadis, violence is absolutely essential; it is the *only* means to achieve their desired ends.[13] The famous jihadi ideologue 'Abdullah 'Azzam (see chapter 1) captured the centrality of violence for jihadis with a saying he was fond of repeating: "jihad and the rifle alone: no negotiations, no conferences, no dialogues."

Despite the efforts of both Banna and the Muslim Brotherhood, Egypt was no closer to establishing an Islamic state in the 1960s than it was in 1928 when the Muslim Brotherhood was formed. The durability of anti-Islamic regimes (in the eyes of radical jihadis) mandated a change of course, a rejection of political and social work that most Islamists favored and an embrace of violent jihad to advance the cause of Islamic rule. Not unlike political elements in the United States, France, and elsewhere, the 1960s proved a particularly fertile decade for building the intellectual architecture for armed jihad to advance political agendas under the banner of Islam. It is in the 1960s and early 1970s that Islamists and jihadis fundamentally split from each other, even while both grew more powerful with the tectonic postindependence political changes sweeping the Muslim world. Islamists more firmly embraced a nonviolent path, particularly beginning in the early 1970s, while jihadis split from the Muslim Brotherhood to advocate for the necessity of violence as the only means to confront regimes seen as intrinsically hostile to Islam. The most important intellectual architect laying the foundation for the centrality of armed violence in politics also emerged, like Hasan al-Banna, from the Egyptian countryside: Sayyid Qutb, the father of modern Sunni jihadism.

SAYYID QUTB, JAHILIYYA, AND THE FOUNDING OF MODERN SUNNI JIHADISM

Sayyid Qutb was born in 1906 to a relatively prosperous family in the Asyut province of Upper Egypt. His family was pious but not overly so, and their politics more nationalist than Islamist. While Qutb is said to have memorized the Qur'an as a boy—a difficult but common challenge, especially during earlier eras in the Muslim world—his education was secular. A good student, Qutb moved to Cairo to finish his education as Hasan al-Banna had done: at the Dar al-'Ulum academy, the premier teacher training college in Egypt. Again doing well in his studies, Qutb was offered a job by the Ministry of Education upon completion of his education, first as a schoolteacher and then as an administrator within the ministry. Ministry jobs in particular were highly sought after, so it was a mark of Qutb's growing prestige that he was invited to work there. He worked for the Ministry of Education for a quarter century, until his radicalism made continued employment by the state untenable.

During Qutb's first four decades of life, he betrayed no signs of radical Islamism. He was a well-educated man familiar with the West, quite a fan of European literature and classical music. Although he was pious, his politics were much more in line with the Arab nationalism of the day. He wrote extensively on a broad range of subjects, from poetry to literary criticism to Qur'anic commentary. Throughout his adult life, Qutb wrote prolifically, and much of his work was not particularly political. His work for the Ministry of Education was valuable enough that he was selected to study in the United States for nearly two years, from 1948 to 1950, to examine the American educational system. He spent much of his time living in Greeley, Colorado, a planned Christian utopian community aligned with the Temperance movement, built astride the Denver Pacific railroad tracks. Greeley was a "dry" municipality when Qutb was there.[14] He also spent time in Washington, DC, in New York City, and at Stanford University in California.

Qutb's time in the United States represented a clear step on his slow path toward radicalism. He had already established an interest in the relationship between Islam and the good society when he published *Social Justice in Islam* just prior to his journey to America; after his sojourn to the United States, Qutb revised the book to make it more militant in its arguments.[15] Despite his comfort with European culture, Qutb was shocked by what he found in America. For Qutb, US culture was degraded by sex and debauchery, materialistic in the extreme, and beset by racism. Whatever was good in America was overwhelmed by the superficial and the artificial. Qutb was a small and dark man, so was likely the subject of overt racism himself while in the United States; he was also an Arab in the United States during the founding of the state of Israel, which he viewed as an obvious injustice but which the US government and many Americans supported. Ever the prolific writer, Qutb published his observations of America, which can be read as ludicrously superficial. His descriptions of young American women read as Freudian-repressed sexuality.[16]

Soon after returning to Egypt, Qutb joined the Muslim Brotherhood as editor-in-chief of its weekly newspaper. As his political critiques grew sharper, he left the Ministry of Education. These were heady political days in Egypt, with its growing nationalism against continuing British control over the coun-try, and with rising political sentiment against the monarchy and political establishment in Cairo. Qutb, like most of the Muslim Brothers, supported the 1952 military coup that overthrew the Egyptian monarchy and brought Gamal 'Abd al-Nasser and the other Free Officers to power.[17] The new regime in Egypt did not immediately have a strong sense of ideological direction, outside of being nationalists opposed to British domination. But over the first several years in power, two trends began to solidify: that secular Arab nationalism would be the dominant ideology of the regime, and that Nasser would be the primary leader of the new republic. The regime's decision to take a decidedly secular and Arab nationalist direction instead of an Islamic one caused Qutb to quickly lose his enthusiasm for the 1952 change.[18] Relations between the new regime and the Muslim Brotherhood deteriorated rapidly, and an assas-sination attempt in 1954 on Nasser by a member of the Brotherhood landed Qutb and the rest of the Brotherhood leadership in prison, where he spent the next decade of his life.

These turbulent years in the first half of the 1950s, especially the "betrayal" of Islamist goals by the new Nasserist regime, marked a second step in the radicalization of Sayyid Qutb. His writing became more militant, as was seen in his reworking of the books *In the Shade of the Qur'an* (*fi zilal al-qur'an*) and *Social Justice in Islam*.[19] Qutb's most radical phase occurred during the last few years of his life and was represented by his publication in 1964 of the small volume *Milestones* (*Ma'alim f'il-tariq*, literally "signposts along the road").[20] *Milestones* drew in part from Qutb's previous work, especially *Social Justice in Islam*, which itself became noticeably more strident in editions published after the repression of a revolt by imprisoned Muslim Brothers in 1957. Qutb published the book in 1964, the same year that he was released from prison, which had occurred at the personal intervention of Iraq's new president, 'Abd al-Salam 'Arif. A member of the ruling secular Arab nationalist Ba'th party, 'Arif was an odd choice to champion Qutb's cause to Nasser, his fellow pan-Arabist.

Qutb's most potent surge in radicalism can be largely explained by his experiences in prison in Egypt, where the torture of Muslim Brotherhood members and nearly everyone else was an everyday occurrence. In Qutb's view, the regular torture, degradation, and humiliation that he witnessed violated the very core tenets of Islam. He saw Islam as a religion of egalitarian justice, of brotherhood, where God's rules applied to all men equally. The fact that prison officials engaged in the regular humiliation of their fellow Muslims, lording their position of power over others based on no legitimate grounds, underscored for Qutb just how broken Egypt's system was. It needed to be eliminated, root and branch, in order for Islam's highest purpose—"the liberation of humans from servitude to other humans"—to be realized.[21] It was the publication of *Milestones*, and its call for the radical removal of the anti-Islam Nasser regime—by armed jihad if necessary—that got Qutb rearrested, tried, and hanged in 1966.[22]

Milestones was for jihadis as Lenin's *What Is To Be Done?* was for Communist agitators: a justification and guidebook for revolutionary change. In particular, Qutb made two momentous ideological innovations in *Milestones*, both of which greatly influenced the jihadi movement for decades to come. First, and most famously, Qutb radically reworked the concept of *jahiliyya* into a justification for the armed overthrow of Muslim regimes.[23] *Jahiliyya* (a noun) is a concept that every Muslim schoolchild learns growing up. Historically it has meant that period of moral darkness and decay on the Arabian Peninsula immediately before the coming of the light of Islam. *Jahiliyya* has typically been translated as "ignorance" or even "barbarism" but it should be understood in the context of the orthodox Islamic dichotomy of good versus evil, of light versus darkness, of knowledge versus ignorance. That is, in the period before the prophet Muhammad and his revelations, the world was an ignorant place, beset by polytheists praying to a multitude of gods, or none at all, and of having no civilization worth the word. Like a pharaoh, man could rule arbitrarily and capriciously over other men, making up the rules as he desired. Moses, a man of God who lived by God's rules, not his own, had been forgotten. *Jahili* (the adjective form) society was an ignorant, venal, unjust place that had turned its back on God. In Qutb's view, modern Egypt had transformed into just such a place.

The coming of Islam, in this Manichean, black-and-white duality, changed darkness into light, ignorance into knowledge, and man's arbitrary and capricious rules into God's laws. *Jahiliyya* represents the opposite of Islam. But it also represented a period of time, an era, an epoch even, before the coming of Islam. It did not represent a characteristic of modern society or regimes.

Building on the work of the Pakistani ideologue Abul A'la Mawdudi (in fact, going even further in his reinterpretation of Islam), Qutb reinterpreted *jahiliyya* to mean not just a period of time but a characteristic of whole societies and regimes that have turned their backs on Islam, even though Islam is knowable to them. For Qutb, the purposeful ignorance of contemporary *jahiliyya* is even worse than historical *jahiliyya*, as modern Muslim societies well know of the Qur'an and God's law (shari'a) and yet still choose to knowingly cast off Islam. Qutb's many years in prison exemplified contemporary *jahiliyya*, where prison guards who would call themselves Muslims acted in barbaric ways, ignoring God's word and implementing the policies of their leaders, who themselves purposely chose to ignore the laws and sensibilities of Islam. This was the arbitrary and capricious rule of the Pharaoh, not the Moses-like implementation of God's law in Qutb's view.

Qutb's was a systemwide critique, not an accusation against a single person. *Jahiliyya* applied to whole societies and whole regimes. Regimes that knowingly chose to live in *jahiliyya*, and thus reject Islam, must be removed. Since they are corrupted, *jahili* societies are in no position to remove authoritarian and equally corrupted regimes—that is, regime change could only come through armed jihad led by a vanguard (*tali'a* or *jama'a*) of righteous Muslims. Qutb was not subtle in his conclusion that Nasser's regime in Cairo—not just the man but the entire regime system—had rejected God and Islam, and thus must be removed through radical action to start the process of creating a pure Islamic state and society. Qutb seemed to realize that this was a generational struggle and not one that would see victory in a year or two. His concept of *jahiliyya* is sometimes wrongly confused with *takfir*, the process of excommunicating a Muslim.[24] *Takfir* has become a favorite tactic of many jihadis, as it allows them to justify armed violence against a ruler whom they have declared an apostate through *takfir*. This is not what Qutb was talking about, however. *Takfir* is an old process, much like excommunication in the Catholic Church, which was sparingly used historically and based on a system of trial and evidence of a person having left Islam. It is a *personal* system of adjudicating an individual's potential apostasy, not a means to declare whole categories of abstractions (societies, regimes) to be apostates. Qutb's notion of *jahiliyya*, by contrast, *only* applied to these large abstractions (societies, regimes) and was not a means to evaluate the level of legitimate piety of an individual Muslim.[25]

With his radical reinterpretation of *jahiliyya*, Qutb constructed for fellow jihadis a conceptual framework that could justify armed violence in pursuit of radical regime—and societal—change. His vision was not essentially global but rather a radical call for change within Egypt and the Muslim world through revolutionary violence. Qutb was also clear on the ultimate source of corruption: Muslims turning their collective backs on Islam to adopt the alluring, corrupting ways of Europe and America. *Jahiliyya* was a Muslim problem for Muslims to solve, but the source of that cultural contamination was the West, especially America. Unlike later ideologues, Qutb's solution to this problem did not involve attacking the source of corruption itself—the West—but rather focused on those Muslim regimes and societies that needed to be cleansed of non-Islamic influences, to abandon *jahiliyya* and return to Islam.

Qutb's second ideological innovation was to understand jihad in a radically new way: not as episodic event but as permanent revolution, much in the same way that Leon Trotsky saw revolution in his world. In orthodox Islam, each legitimate armed jihad has a beginning when it is called for by an appropriate authority, and it has an end—win, lose, or draw. No armed jihad is supposed to last forever. Clearly drawing on Trotsky but without accreditation, Qutb redefined armed jihad as a kind of permanent revolution—not as an event but as a way of life, of perpetual preparation and action. As long as *jahiliyya* was present in the Muslim world, jihad-as-struggle was a permanent necessity to rectify it, including armed jihad when appropriate.

Indeed, Qutb saw the fight against Nasser's *jahili* regime as taking many decades to defeat. But even then, the jihad-as-permanent-revolution would not be over. Nor was jihad-as-permanent-revolution an issue of defensive or offensive jihad, as both of those forms were also episodic by nature. Historically, a defensive jihad ended when the battle was won, and an offensive jihad ended when the subject population had been subdued and converted to Islam. However, *jahiliyya* was so extensive that all elements of jihad must be put to use, strategically implementing the right form of struggle for the circumstances, perhaps even lasting until the End Times. Qutb's jihad-as-permanent-revolution was not focused on any restoration of the Caliphate, a notion that did not concern Qutb. He never wrote about a restored Caliphate in his voluminous writing career over several decades. Armed jihad was to be a potentially permanent mode of action, a sort of state-of-nature.

Jihad-as-permanent-revolution could not, by definition, emerge out of *jahili* segments of society, which, according to Qutb, impacted most people. Rather, it had to come from a *vanguard* of strong and pious Muslims who understood the extent of the problem and the actions necessary for prosecuting this multigenerational struggle. The notion of a pious vanguard leading a permanent revolution had no real precedent in Islamic discourse. Again, Qutb appears to have drawn on Marxist thought—this time Vladimir Lenin—to come up with his vanguard strategy.[26] Qutb's notion of jihad-as-permanent-revolution was not fully thought out, and Qutb himself did not use that phrase. While he generally avoided the word *revolution* (*thawra*), he did speak of the permanent (*da'ima*) conditions that made such struggle necessary. The idea was less half-baked than cut short, as his execution in 1966 at the age of fifty-nine prevented him from developing it further. Qutb was not generally thought to subscribe to the theological practices of Salafi Islam, but it was a Salafi conceptualization of *tawhid* (the oneness of God) in the hands of 'Abdullah 'Azzam that provided a fuller theoretical rationale for why armed jihad must be viewed as a permanent revolution. 'Azzam built on and completed Qutb's argument as to why armed jihad was a necessary and enduring requirement for Muslims (see chapter 1).

Although global jihad has been specifically a Sunni phenomenon in recent decades, jihadism itself cuts across the sectarian divide in Islam. At nearly the exact same time that Sayyid Qutb was constructing an ideology and rationale for armed jihad to overthrow regimes in the Sunni Muslim world, the Shia world was witnessing a similar ideological phenomenon and indeed would be far more successful in implementing regime change under the banner of Islam.

AYATULLAH KHOMEINI AND THE FOUNDING OF MODERN SHIA JIHADISM

The Shia world produced its own versions of Islamism and local jihadism— from the revolution in Iran to the emergence of Hizbullah in Lebanon. The timing of the Shia political and militant revival matches that of its Sunni cousins, as both came of age beginning in the 1960s. Indeed, while the *vocabulary* of Shia Islamists and jihadis is quite different from that used in the Sunni world, the underlying *problems* they describe and the political solutions they advocate are strikingly similar to what we see among their Sunni brethren. Shia ideologues, like Sunni ones, were concerned primarily with injustice born from neglect of Islam, and of proper and legitimate forms of authority in an Islamic polity.

The political interpretations of Shia Islam were revolutionized by a hand-ful of activists—both clerical and lay Muslims—in the 1960s and 1970s. It was a remarkable transformation of interpretation by a small number of po-litical ideologues. These ideologues came out of a position of both political and interpretive weakness. Outside of Iran, the Shia were often persecuted minorities in a world where about 85 percent of all Muslims are Sunni. In the small number of countries that had Shia majorities, such as Iraq and Bahrain, Sunni communities often still held the reins of political and economic power. In Lebanon the Shia have likely constituted the largest single religious group (known as "confessional" groups) since the country was established but filled out the lowest classes of peasant farmers and southern Beirut's slum dwellers, with little political or economic leverage by comparison to smaller groups, such as Maronite Christians or Sunni Muslims. Constructing an interpretation of Shi'ism that encouraged activism, even revolution, was no easy task for Shia ideologues as Shia orthodoxy had developed a strong tradition of political quiescence, of not getting too involved in political fights or questioning the legitimacy of political leadership.

The generation of Shia ideologues that came to prominence in the 1960s directly challenged the dominant quietist political interpretations of Shia Islam and sought to use Shi'ism itself as a vehicle for political change. This generation of Shia activists included, most famously, Ayatullah Ruhollah Kho-meini, an Iranian cleric sent into political exile in Iraq by the Shah of Iran in 1964. But it included many others with radically activist interpretations of Shi'ism, including such clerics as Mahmud Taleqani and Mohammed Beheshti in Iran and Musa al-Sadr in Lebanon. Chief among lay ideologues was Ali Sha-riati. With a PhD from the Sorbonne in Paris, Shariati was a charismatic and masterful orator, drawing large crowds of university students with his unique mixing of Shi'ism and Marxism, very much akin to the Liberation Theology movement in Catholicism in Latin America in the 1970s. Arguably, Shariati was the most famous and important critic of the Shah from an explicitly Shia religious perspective during much of the 1960s and 1970s, until his premature death in 1977.[27]

Perhaps the most important example of this new reinterpretation of Shi'ism revolved around the centuries-old tale of the death of Imam Husayn Bin Ali, grandson of the prophet Muhammad, on the plains of Karbala in modern-day

Iraq. The facts of his death are not much in dispute. Given his bloodline, Husayn was viewed as a dangerous political challenger by the nascent Umayyad dynasty in Damascus. He refused to pledge his allegiance to the new Umayyad leader, Yazid, and set off from Mecca to Kufa (in present-day Iraq) in 680 CE at the invitation of the local population to lead them. Husayn's caravan was intercepted by Yazid's army, Husayn and most of his companions were killed, and Husayn's head was taken back to Damascus for display to Yazid and others.[28] Although the facts of his death are not challenged, the *meaning* of Husayn's death became an open arena for contestation in the 1960s. For many traditionalists, Husayn's death was a cautionary tale: even the righteous grandson of the Prophet could be killed when he spoke up too forcefully. The caution urged by traditional Shia clerics was to not expect justice in this world but instead to focus on saving your soul for the next life, where justice prevails. Do not waste time on a political fool's errand in this life; otherwise, you might lose your head, just like Imam Husayn. This interpretation of Husayn's death privileged quiescence and demobilization.

Shariati, Khomeini, and other Shia ideologues took the same facts of Husayn's death but reinterpreted their meaning into an argument in favor of activism and fighting for justice. Their interpretation: Imam Husayn knew his life was in danger but did not do the easy thing of pledging allegiance, or *ba'ya*, to Yazid. He stood up for justice and answered the calls from the people of Kufa to lead them, knowing it might cost him his life, which it did. The lesson for today: stand and fight for justice, even at great personal risk. Husayn's martyrdom was thus a lesson in activism, in fighting for justice in this world, not a lesson of quiescence and waiting for the next life.[29]

Khomeini's most famous ideological architecture for radical political change came in a series of lectures he gave in 1970 from his exile in Najaf, Iraq. Khomeini laid out an argument for the necessity of regime change in Iran—the removal of the Shah—and its replacement with clerical governance. According to Khomeini's logic, his interpretation of what true Islamic government (*hukumat-i islami*) should look like is both readily apparent through and mandated by a faithful reading of the Shia canon.[30] His key ideological innovation was his radical reinterpretation of the old concept of *velayat-i faqih*, or the obligations of clerics.[31] In orthodox Shia Islam, the concept of *velayat-i faqih* was to lay out certain responsibilities that clerics must accept, mostly with regard to seeing to the proper care of otherwise marginalized members of society, particularly orphans. Islam has a strong egalitarian trend, and seeing orphans or widows cast to the margins to become second- or third-class members of society was to be avoided. It was within the jurisdiction (*velaya* in Farsi, *wilaya* in Arabic) of the clergy to ensure that orphans and similarly marginalized individuals be properly cared for and thus remain within acceptable society. Only a rare and obscure understanding of this concept applied it to the political sphere. Khomeini built on this obscure strand to develop an ideology that mandated clerical rule in a proper Shia society.

Khomeini's understanding of *velayat-i faqih* was similar to Plato's conception of the role of a philosopher-king: a leader (*rahbar*) who stood above day-to-day politics but who through his wisdom, experience, and knowledge could ensure that the ship of state was sailing in the right direction. Such a leader represented legitimate political authority in Khomeini's view, unlike the Shah, who was only on the throne because his father staged a coup against another king a half century before. Since knowledge of Islam and devotion to God were not requirements for a shah, but they were obligations for a top cleric, only such a member of the clergy could exercise proper, legitimate authority. Until the return of the Shia Twelfth Imam (the Hidden Imam, or al-Imam al-Gha'ib) during End Times, it was necessary for Iran to practice clerical rule, not monarchical rule, in Khomeini's thinking.[32] His argument was a radical departure from traditional Shia thought and was not accepted by many leading clerics of the day, including the top cleric in Iran at the time of the revolution, Grand Ayatullah Shariat-Madari, who was kept under house arrest for the rest of his life because of his rejection of Khomeini's politicization of Islam.

In contrast to Qutb, neither Khomeini nor Shariati wrote in detail about the need for armed jihad to achieve the desired political goal. But this message was clear enough in context. Both Khomeini and Shariati called for a revolutionary regime change to bring about the end of twenty-five hundred years of monarchy in Iran, which was highly unlikely to happen peacefully. These were clarion calls for radical political change, in which armed violence was nearly certain. The vocabulary that Shia ideologues like Khomeini and Shariati used was very different from Qutb's vocabulary. Shia ideologues drew on the language of Shi'ism, featuring Husayn, the Hidden Imam, and *velayat-i faqih*—concepts that were absent from Qutb's work. Both Khomeini and Shariati shared a view of the corrupting influences of the West; the Iranians even invented a clever word for it—*gharbzadegi*, or "westoxification," meaning "drunk on the West."[33]

The difference in specific vocabulary and stories should not hide the remarkably common broader world views shared by these ideologues from across a sectarian divide at the same time in history. Both Qutb and Khomeini saw oppressive and unjust regimes (whether in Egypt or Iran) that had imprisoned them and other Muslim critics and, in the case of Khomeini, sent them into exile. They viewed those regimes as embodying injustice born of apostasy, and that apostasy in large measure was a reflection of the power of the sources of global contamination that produce *gharbzadegi*. Both Qutb and Khomeini determined that the injustice and apostasy in the Muslim world was structural, not based on individual personalities such as Nasser or the Shah. The regimes could not simply be reformed and made better; they must be eliminated, root and branch, to allow a truly just and Islamic regime and society to emerge. Both viewed violence as a necessary, if unfortunate, tool on the path to that righteous and just Islamic state and society. Qutb was just a bit more explicit about the need for armed jihad on the path to regime change, which is what got him hanged.

The Shia strand of jihadi thought that emerged in the 1960s paralleled the Sunni strand in fundamental ways, even if the specific vocabulary each used was different. In both cases, the focus on the local, particularly on the necessity for regime change, was the dominant interpretation of jihad into the 1980s. In the Shia world, that local focus remains to this day, because a significant ideological movement of global jihad never emerged out of Shi'ism. For all of the discussions in today's news of the Lebanese Hizbullah or the Quds Force of the Islamic Revolutionary Guards Corps (IRGC) in Iran, or the Popular Mobilization Forces in Iraq, Shia jihadism remains focused on local issues in the Middle East, not on a violent global enterprise. Qassem Soleimani, the Iranian leader of the Quds Force, was revered in militant Shia circles throughout the Middle East not because he preached global jihad but rather because he empowered local Shia militant groups in Iraq, Lebanon, Syria, and Yemen. In a dramatic escalation of the simmering tensions between Iran and the United States, Soleimani was assassinated by the Trump administration while visiting Iraq in January 2020.

JIHADISM AS A "NEAR ENEMY" PHENOMENON

As jihadism grew in the 1970s, its ideology remained rather inchoate. Sayyid Qutb had provided the ideological framework to justify armed violence against the apostate regime in Cairo; in the meantime, Anwar Sadat had replaced Gamal 'Abd al-Nasser when the latter died of a heart attack in 1970. Sadat was considerably friendlier to the Muslim Brotherhood and Islamism in general, viewing such groups as useful ideological and political counterweights to the Arab nationalist movement, which was seen as much more of a political threat to Sadat's new regime. The space for political Islamist (although not violent jihadi) activity opened considerably under Sadat, and the Muslim Brotherhood responded in kind by declaring its peaceful intentions; members of the organization were "preachers, not judges" (al-du'a, la al-quda'), as was famously expressed by the Brotherhood's Guide (murshid) Hassan al-Hudaybi, in a refutation of Sayyid Qutb.

For Islamists, the invitation to participate in the political system, even in the limited way possible under a military and authoritarian regime, was clear under Sadat. But what should a jihadi do? If one believed that violence was still needed to advance one's political agenda under the banner of Islam, against whom should the violence be directed exactly? Was the regime still the primary target? What about influential secular figures in society? Was Israel now to be the primary focus of violence, even as secular and leftist forces within the PLO dominated that effort? Shukri Mustafa, an Egyptian jihadi put to death in 1978 for his role in the kidnapping and killing of a former government minister, famously testified at his trial that he was not interested in helping the infidel Egyptian army defend against a hypothetical invasion by Israel. A pox on both their houses, he argued. While jihad against regional powers was advocated by some, especially against Israel, there was no significant argument to undertake armed jihad against the United States, Europe, or other international powers.

The sharp bias to focus violence on local apostate regimes, as advocated by Qutb, dominated jihadi thinking in the 1970s, but it took the leader of the Islamic Jihad (al-Jihad al-Islami) organization, Muhammad 'Abd al-Salam Faraj, to definitively settle this argument. Before his group's assassination of Anwar Sadat in October 1981, Faraj wrote a fifty-four-page manifesto to members of the Islamic Jihad that laid out the rationale for jihad against the regime, instead of against Israel or anyone else.[34] The "neglected duty" (al-farida al-gha'iba) in Muslim society, argued Faraj, was armed jihad, a central principle that had been largely forgotten. To make his point, he invented the dichotomy of a "near enemy" and a "far enemy"; the near enemy was the local apostate regime, such as Sadat's in Egypt, and the "far enemy" was Israel. Faraj argued that at this moment in history, it would be a waste of resources to target Israel, as Muslim apostate regimes would claim credit for any victory over Israel. Rather, the most important goal was to overthrow the near enemy regimes; after that, everything else would become possible.

The combination of Qutb's manifesto in 1966 and Faraj's follow-on fifteen years later put to rest any serious argument within the Sunni jihadi community over whom the proper target of armed jihad was: it was clearly the local apostate regime, in whichever Muslim country one lived. The issue was settled, at least until the 1980s, when a new strand of jihad at the global level emerged. Although this book is about that new, global strand of jihad, it should be remembered that Qutb's and Faraj's vision about the near enemy remained the dominant form of jihad throughout the prior six decades. Global jihad, while a deadly nuisance that has been responsible for the murder of thousands of innocent civilians, never really supplanted local jihad as the most important and largest form of armed violence under the banner of Islam, and it likely never will.

There is a large literature on why Islamism grew from a fringe movement to a center of political power beginning in the 1970s.[35] Common explanations include the failure of secular postcolonial regimes to deliver the political and economic goods; the rise of conservative, Islam-oriented regimes, especially in Saudi Arabia, with the vast increase of oil wealth in the early 1970s; a reaction against imperialism, particularly given the dispossession of Palestinians at the hands of Israel; and a response to the rise of mass societies in the twentieth century that were at odds with Muslim tradition (modernity with a Western flavor, so to speak). For the purposes of this book, it is enough to understand that both Islamism and local jihadism began to flourish in the 1970s in a way they never had before. Jihadism in particular had gained an ideological architecture from Sayyid Qutb and his successors that it had not enjoyed in prior decades. Global jihad, beginning in the 1980s, was an offshoot of the larger local and regional jihadi movements in the Muslim, primarily Arab, world. Since it began, global jihad has undergone four distinct iterations, or waves, each with a specific crisis that began the wave, and each with distinctive ideologies and agendas to point the way forward.[36] The remainder of this book details and interprets those four waves of global jihad.

THE FOUR WAVES OF GLOBAL JIHAD

Chapter 1 details the first wave of global jihad, triggered by the Soviet Union's invasion of Afghanistan in December 1979. The Afghan tribesmen who initially fought against the Soviets gave rise to the adoption in English of the Arabic word for men fighting in the cause of a righteous jihad: *mujahidin* (singular in Arabic: *mujahid*). The Afghan mujahideen (to use the common English spelling) were eventually joined by thousands of foreign fighters, primarily from the Arab world, chiefly at the urging of the charismatic ideologue Dr. 'Abdullah Yusuf 'Azzam, a Palestinian-Jordanian with a penchant for militancy. The model that developed through serendipity in Afghanistan led 'Azzam to conclude that the same model could be applied anywhere in the world where Muslim lands were occupied by infidel invaders. So was born the idea for the first wave of global jihad just as it was playing out in Afghanistan: the formation of a "solid base" (*al-qa'ida al-sulba*) of pious and strong Muslim warriors from around the world who would assist local Muslim populations in ridding themselves of infidel occupation. To put this notion in better comparative light, I call 'Azzam's idea of *al-qa'ida al-sulba* the Jihadi International, comparable to the old Communist International. 'Azzam hoped that this Jihadi International would next travel to Palestine to liberate his own homeland, and from there to lost Muslim lands around the globe: to Central Asia, Kashmir, the Philippines, and ultimately to al-Andalus (Spain), which had been under Muslim rule for seven centuries before the Moors were forced from power in 1492.

Each wave of global jihad was born of a specific crisis that pointed to a broader general crisis. The first wave of global jihad was launched due to the specific crisis of the Soviet invasion and occupation of Afghanistan, but it pointed to the broader crisis of Muslim lands that had been lost to foreign conquest over the centuries. 'Azzam's vision of a Jihadi International did not have a chance to play out in other lands beyond Afghanistan in his lifetime, as he was assassinated in November 1989, just nine months after the Soviets left Afghanistan, pulling the last of their troops across the Amu Darya (Oxus) river. But 'Azzam's idea did not die with him, as his colleague in the Afghan jihad, Usama Bin Laden, proposed exactly that idea to the Saudi royal family following Iraq's invasion and occupation of Kuwait in August 1990. Bin Laden offered to recruit one hundred thousand mujahideen, many veterans of the Afghan jihad, to defeat the Iraqi forces in Kuwait, just like the Soviet forces had been defeated in Afghanistan. Bin Laden's offer to recreate the Jihadi International was (unsurprisingly) rejected by the Saudis, and the first wave of global jihad effectively ended as a result.

With the Afghan jihad over and its fighters gone back home, a replacement jihad to liberate Kuwait declined by the Saudis, and no charismatic leader to replace 'Azzam, any significant idea or movement of global jihad dissipated in the first half of the 1990s. Simply put, there was no compelling globally focused jihad to fight anymore. That is not to suggest there was a shortage of conflict—far from it. The Palestinians were deep into their first intifada, or uprising, against Israel, but it was an unarmed affair led mostly by secular groups affiliated with the Palestine Liberation Organization, and they had no desire to recruit a fanciful Jihadi International to come muck things up.[37] There were many other often-armed rebellions, some identified as jihads, in the early 1990s—from Bosnia to Kashmir to Chechnya—but they were all local struggles that did not have a compelling global ideological component or agenda. Some Muslims from elsewhere in the world went to fight in the Balkans, Kashmir, and Chechnya to be sure, but they did not do so under an organized banner and explicit ideology of global jihad. Bin Laden himself was mostly holed up in the Sudan, fighting his own local jihad against the Saudi regime, which he now viewed as a "near enemy" that needed to be overthrown. In the early 1990s Bin Laden was also focused on Yemen, which he viewed as another country ripe for armed jihad, but again, not at that point as part of an explicitly global concept of jihad. That would wait a few years.

The second wave of global jihad, the subject of chapter 2, was launched in the mid-1990s. I date it from 1996, when Bin Laden gave a long speech in his new home of Afghanistan, by then under Taliban rule. The speech, which would be transcribed and distributed widely, declared war on the United States and on the Saudi regime. Bin Laden posited for the first time that the "far enemy" was the United States, arguing that it needed to be targeted to drive it out of the Muslim world. This far enemy, or America First, strategy was made even more explicit in 1998 when Bin Laden, Ayman al-Zawahiri, and three other militants declared that it was a personal duty for all able-bodied Muslims to kill Americans and Jews anywhere in the world without regard to military or civilian status.[38] It was a call for mass murder.

For the second wave of global jihad, the specific crisis was the looming defeat of what had been promising local jihads, particularly in Egypt and Algeria. The broader crisis that these imminent defeats pointed to was, in Bin Laden's view, the ability of apostate regimes to survive and defeat jihadi and Islamist challenges. After the enormous expansion of Islamist and jihadi influence in the 1970s and 1980s, the 1990s proved much more difficult. Regimes that should fall did not, and the only way for Bin Laden to understand the durability of apostate regimes was to look at the American superpower that supported them and kept them afloat. The significant expansion of the US military footprint in the Middle East in the 1990s as a result of its first Gulf War with Iraq was further evidence for Bin Laden that the United States had malign intentions in the region and was using local apostate regimes as pawns, preventing them from falling to righteous Muslim forces. America thus needed to be targeted and driven from the region, so that Muslims could overthrow their apostate regimes, reclaim their own countries, and build Islamic states.

The second wave of global jihad was relatively brief if highly traumatic for most Americans, given the terror attacks of September 11, 2001. Its apex lasted just a few years, beginning in 1998 with the bombings of the US embassies in Kenya and Tanzania that killed more than two hundred people, mostly Africans. By 2003, what became known as "al-Qa'ida central" had been essentially defeated, with the overthrow of their host regime in Afghanistan, the Taliban, and the killing or capturing of most of its upper echelons of commanders and leaders. Although Bin Laden had escaped to Pakistan, until his death at the hands of US Navy SEALs in 2011, the main thrust of the second wave of global jihad was over by about 2003. There is no specific battle or event to date the essential defeat of the second wave. Various local groups, or franchises, declared allegiance to al-Qa'ida from time to time, but the only one that seriously shared the global America First agenda of al-Qa'ida was found in Yemen, in a coalition of Saudi and Yemeni jihadis known as AQAP (al-Qa'ida in the Arabian Peninsula). By the time the so-called Arab Spring came to Yemen in 2011, with a subsequent breakdown of the Yemeni state and, later, civil war, AQAP did what all the other al-Qa'ida franchises did: focus on a local jihad with local goals, devoid of any compelling global vision. The second wave of global jihad had truly ended, even if a few true believers remained.

The third and fourth waves of global jihad, described in chapters 3 and 4, respectively, began at nearly the same time but for different reasons and with different goals and agendas. What I call the "Caliphate Now!" third wave, closely associated with the Islamic State in Iraq and Syria (ISIS), began in 2003 with the US invasion of Iraq and was reinvigorated (after a rough start) in 2011 with the civil war in next-door Syria. The Syrian civil war essentially created a large territory of ungoverned space along the Euphrates River valley in eastern Syria, continuing into the rural areas of the Aleppo and Idlib provinces in north-central Syria. These areas were almost entirely populated by Sunni Arabs, a community that was the backbone of opposition to the regime in Syria's civil war and that was more naturally welcoming of a staunchly pro-Sunni group like ISIS. ISIS defeated other groups to claim this territory as its own and then used its Syrian stronghold to grab a large slice of the Sunni Arab areas of northwestern Iraq in 2014. ISIS declared the reestablishment of the Islamic Caliphate in Mosul, Iraq, in June 2014, although without the support of any leading Muslim clerics anywhere in the world.

While the third wave of global jihad was launched through the specific crises of the US invasion of Iraq and the civil war in Syria, the broader crisis was apostasy—a crisis of long-standing for many among the pious. Not apostate *regimes*, such as those that other jihadis objected to, but *apostasy* itself. Shari'a (Islamic law) was not being implemented; Muslims were effectively turning their backs on Islam; corruption—particularly from the West—was evident everywhere. They thought the only way to confront apostasy was to create a territorial Islamic state (*al-dawla al-islamiyya*) that would uncompromisingly implement *shari'a*, eradicate apostasy, and create an Islamic utopia on earth. But it wasn't just the durability of apostasy that was the problem for ISIS and its followers. To make matters worse, both Iraq and Syria (modern conceptualizations that were famously rejected by ISIS) were governed by Shia, who were assigned various negative and well-worn terms, such as rejectionists (*rafidun*), apostates (*kuffar*), or pejorative terms for 'Alawi (*nusayri*), or Shia (*safawi*).[39] Thus the ISIS wave of global jihad ended up having a far more old-fashioned sectarian flavor to it than the other waves of global jihad. This was one of the reasons ISIS was better able to recruit followers and fighters to its cause, as it was in many ways a traditional sectarian fight.

In order both to capture territory by driving out the forces of apostasy and to hold that territory before a full state could be formed, the leaders of ISIS decided that it would be necessary to practice extreme violence, to make a territory ungovernable by enemy forces. This policy of gore by ISIS, put out on slick videos on the Internet, was not a coincidence or something that occurred in the fog of war; it was the purposeful implementation of the "management of savagery" (*idarat al-tawahhush*). For ISIS, grotesque violence was a means to both capture and hold territory. While ISIS's tactics were often obscene, did they constitute a wave of global jihad, or were they just a more extreme local jihad? ISIS supporters will tell you, accurately, that ISIS did not start attacking targets in the West until Western powers began to bomb the so-called Islamic state in Iraq in 2014 in support of the regime in Baghdad. But the answer is yes, ISIS did represent a wave of global jihad for three reasons. First, it was able to recruit fighters and resources from all over the world. Second, ISIS had a global vision: to bring all of the world's 1.7 billion Muslims under its authority and sovereignty. This is the meaning of declaring a "caliphate" as opposed to an "emirate": the latter only claims authority over a specific territory, not all Muslims everywhere. Third, ISIS showed it had a global violent reach, able to undertake terror attacks from Baghdad to Paris, and many places in between.

The third wave of global jihad was quite distinct from the first two waves, which aimed to either liberate occupied territory or to drive the United States from the Muslim world to make local regimes more vulnerable. The ISIS wave, by contrast, focused on state-building, on creating a puritanical state in the heart of the Middle East as a first step toward a global caliphate that would cure the plague of apostasy throughout the Muslim world. As chapter 3 shows, unlike the Jihadi International or the America First waves, the ISIS wave of global jihad focused intently on administrative matters, including taxation, courts, and schools, to name a few. Building a functional state free from contamination by *kufr* (un-Islamic) influences was hard work. Ultimately, ISIS failed to do so for very long, as the territorial state was defeated in 2017 by a coalition of American, Arab, European, Iranian, Iraqi, and Kurdish forces. In a fairly amazing feat, ISIS had succeeded in uniting virtually the entire world against its barbaric practices. In 2017, with its loss of key cities Mosul and

Raqqa, ISIS reverted from a territorial polity to a guerilla group. Although it was still a potent idea with thousands of fighters, ISIS was no longer an Islamic state that held and controlled territory under the banner of a caliphate. Its self-declared caliph, Abu Bakr al-Baghdadi, was killed by a US strike in northern Syria in 2019.

The fourth wave of global jihad began with the destruction of the so-called Islamic Emirate of Afghanistan, the Taliban-controlled Islamist state. The fourth wave of global jihad continues to this day. It is the most durable and longest-lasting wave of global jihad, although it has been the least deadly. While the specific crisis that launched the fourth wave of personal jihad was the loss of Afghanistan in 2001, the broader crisis was the looming defeat of the idea of global jihad itself. The fourth wave was quintessentially about saving the idea of global jihad for a future when its prospects were more advantageous. Thus the fourth wave was defensive in nature, launched out of desperation when the Taliban host had been demolished, and many of the commanders and leaders of al-Qa'ida and associated jihadis were being killed, captured, or hunted down.

The man who took it upon himself to lay out both a vision and a strategy for the survival of global jihad, which became the fourth wave, was Abu Musab al-Suri, the nom de guerre of a Syrian from Aleppo named Mustafa bin 'Abd al-Qadir Sitmiriam Nassar. Abu Musab al-Suri was a veteran of Syria's first round of civil war in the early 1980s, ultimately escaping to Spain and England, before returning to Afghanistan after the Taliban took over. He was a brilliant but ruthless man, thought to have been involved in both the 2004 Madrid train bombings and the 2005 London bombings.[40] Suri saw that the global jihad movement was on the run, being hunted by the United States and other powers in the aftermath of the 9/11 terror attacks. He devised a strategy that would allow global jihad to survive, to live to fight another day. The key to Suri's strategy, published online in a mammoth sixteen-hundred-page book prior to his capture in Pakistan in 2005, was "personal jihad" (*jihad fardi*), which has come into English as "leaderless jihad." Personal jihad is the fourth wave of global jihad's contribution to the phenomenon of *stochastic* terrorism: violence that is inspired and encouraged by others but logistically undertaken autonomously by lone wolves and small cells. The violence is stochastic—a term of probability—in that variations in the number of acts of violence is predictable in occurrence but random in specific implementation. For example, if ISIS puts out a call for its followers to undertake violence, it is predictable that there will be an increase in acts of violence for a period of time, but it is unknown who exactly will actually undertake those acts of violence.

Suri's was a vision of small-scale violence that was networked, decentralized, Internet-connected, and media-savvy. His vision was for a "system, not an organization" (*nizam, la tanzim*) that could survive and fight in a way that a traditional hierarchical organization could not. It was a vision for twenty-first-century jihad that might not represent an existential threat to the United States or any other country but was also nearly impossible to eradicate. Individuals and small groups would learn from each other and carry out violence, preferably against soft targets to inflict maximum fear among civilians, and would engage and shape the media to let it be known that the attack had been carried out in the name of Islam and jihad. Suri focused on the importance of the public narrative of global jihad that could stitch together a logic and a coherent story of otherwise random and disparate attacks.

I refer to this leaderless and always evolving narrative of global jihad as a *wiki-narrative*. Most global jihadi terror attacks since 2017 have been exactly these uncoordinated personal jihads that were not centrally planned or paid for but rather emanated from radicalized individuals and small groups of alienated Muslim extremists. This is a durable form of violence, not particularly threatening in the bigger scheme of things but not easily suppressed either, and potentially very deadly for innocent passersby. While the first three waves of global jihad have mostly run their course, defeated from both within the Muslim world and without, the fourth wave of global jihad is especially durable and not likely to end soon. Because of its inchoate ideology (that is, the wiki-narrative constantly evolves and is never particularly sophisticated ideologically), it will likely slowly fade over time. But it will take a lot of good old-fashioned police and intelligence work—and cooperation—to help prevent the worst of what the fourth wave of global jihad can bring.

The conclusion of the book summarizes my arguments about the four waves of global jihad and, more important, represents a first step in trying to understand global jihad in a broad comparative framework. I have drawn on the insightful but undertheorized concept of "movements of rage" as my entrée into a broader comparative understanding. This concept comes out of the Weberian tradition of social science and is the brainchild of retired Berkeley scholar Ken Jowitt. The word "rage" was an unfortunate choice by Jowitt as it implies blind, irrational violence. "Resentment" or "bitterness" better captures the flavor of the ideologies analyzed but perhaps do not make for such a pithy title. Still, to be true to the origins of the idea, I have stuck with Jowitt's phrasing.

For Jowitt, movements of rage are characterized by a neomillenarian amalgam of a charismatic leader, an apocalyptic ideology, and a strategy of nihilistic violence. Unfortunately, Jowitt never fully detailed his theory, but there is enough in what he did publish and what he lectured on to build a useful comparative framework.[41] If one imagines the entire spectrum of Muslim responses to Western domination in the nineteenth and twentieth centuries, then most of that spectrum would be taken up either by various forms of admiration for Western science, industry, and democracy (but rejection of the imperialism that invariably came with it) or by broader rejection of the West through various forms of Islamic modernism or revival (*sahwa*). The Muslim Brotherhood, discussed earlier in this introduction, represents one form of Islamic revivalism that accepted much of the nature of modernity but rejected the corrupting influences of much of Western culture as un-Islamic (as Sayyid Qutb's reflections on his stay in America demonstrated). At the far fringe of that spectrum lie people who reject all forms of Western culture and its modernity as fundamentally corrupting, an infection that needs to be eradicated.

This extremist response to many elements of Western culture (but typically not a rejection of modern weapons and technologies) can be found in fringe elements around the world, whether Muslim or not, most of which never come to power. But every once in a while, such a movement of rage can have an outsized and usually horrific impact. The Khmer Rouge in Cambodia in the 1970s executed most anyone who spoke a European language, dressed in Western clothes, or even lived in Phnom Penh—capital cities being the epicenter of cultural corruption. I coin the term *gnosicide* to capture the phenomenon of purposefully murdering or violently marginalizing the educated strata of society. Even before it found its jihadi niche, Boko Haram in Nigeria—its very name means to reject Western education—practiced many of the same nihilistic habits that the Khmer Rouge did, albeit without the benefit of coming to power. Even elements of the Nazi coalition in Germany, primarily the Brownshirts, were fundamentally antimodern and nihilistic in their ideological orientation: a movement of rage that came to power with deadly, genocidal results.

While I explore how the movements-of-rage theory can insightfully shed light on important elements of global jihadism, two words of caution are in order. First, one must draw careful distinctions, particularly between political and cultural issues for the ideologues of global jihad. For example, all such ideologues examined in this book view the West (and its fifth columnists within the Muslim world) as the major source of cultural corruption of Muslim society, and in doing so, they follow a rich school of thought that goes back more than a century. These ideologues clearly make cultural and social arguments, but they also make explicitly political arguments. For example, Usama Bin Laden's views of the West are consistent with a cultural pollution argument, but he also asserted extensive political arguments about US policy toward the Middle East that are separate from cultural pollution arguments and should be studied and understood on their own merits. Although he highly valued asceticism, a mark of rejecting the fruits of modernity, he was not averse to employing modern technologies in the service of his cause. These strands must be parsed out and understood, not conflated into one archetype.[42] Second, the movements-of-rage theory can be easily misapplied to and conflated with all Islamists, or even all Muslims, which would be analytically wrong (not to mention morally bankrupt). So Jowitt's theory can be enlightening in understanding key elements of global jihadism, but one must tread lightly in its broader application to the Muslim world.

A final point is necessary about Islam and global ideas to prevent unnecessary confusion. The most pious followers of Islam, like those of Christianity, believe that their truth applies to the whole of humanity. According to this way of thinking, on the Day of Judgment, people will either be Muslim/Christian, or they will be condemned to Hell for all eternity. In that simplistic sense, all pious Muslims, like all pious Christians, have a global vision of their religion. It logically follows that both faiths put an emphasis on proselytizing, to save the souls of all who can be saved from the fires of Hell. In Islam, proselytizing is known as *da'wa*. In the many years that I have lived in the Muslim world, I am not sure if I have met more Muslims who wanted to convert me to Islam, or more Western Christians out to convert Muslims to their "true faith." But the notion of a universal faith, applicable to all humanity, is not what this book is about, nor is it what global jihad over the past four decades has been about. There are many pundits in the West that confuse and conflate the normal and nonviolent proselytizing that goes on in Islam with some type of global jihadi conspiracy. This is nonsense and needs to be rejected as simple-minded propaganda by any clear-thinking analyst.

Chapter 1

THE JIHADI INTERNATIONAL
1979–1990

PRIOR TO 1979, THE CONCEPT OF ARMED JIHAD DID NOT HAVE A significant global component.[1] To be sure, orthodox Islam, like Christianity (and unlike other religions), makes a universal claim that it has sole possession of the Truth, that all humans are subject to God's sovereignty as defined by that Truth, and that those who do not submit to God's will on those terms will face eternal damnation. In that broad, timeless, theological sense, Muslims of all stripes, like their Christian brethren, make an international claim on fellow humans. But when it came to organized violence under the banner of Islam by radical jihadi groups, a global component was absent before 1979. Instead, the violent jihadi groups that began to spring up in the 1970s, beginning in Egypt, focused their attention on local matters. These local concerns were largely about resisting what was viewed as an apostate regime and a corrupt society, very much as Sayyid Qutb had laid out a decade earlier. In pursuit of their mission, such groups attacked the Egyptian Military Technical College in 1974, kidnapped and killed a former government minister in 1977, and often set up new communities on the margins of Egyptian society in which to live untouched by corrupt society.

The actions by local jihadi groups in Egypt hit their apex in 1981 with the assassination of Egyptian president Anwar Sadat.[2] None of these groups in Egypt, or elsewhere in the Muslim world, had a primary or even important ideological or practical focus on conducting violence around the world. This absence of a significant global component in jihadi thought began to change in the 1970s.[3] Indeed, 1979 was a momentous year more broadly in Islamist and jihadi history. In Iran, 1979 saw the overthrow of the Shah and his replacement as leader by Ayatullah Khomeini, a cleric who had spent the previous fifteen years living in exile, mostly in Iraq. Although Iran is a predominately Shia country, the power of the Iranian revolution in Sunni circles around the globe should not be underestimated. Largely under the banner of Islam, a popular revolution had successfully overthrown a ruler widely seen to be among the most powerful in the developing world, both because of Iran's oil reserves and because of its strong backing by the United States. Indeed, US policy toward the whole of the Persian Gulf region, then known as the "twin pillars policy," revolved around strengthening the military capabilities of the Shah's Iran and Saudi Arabia. Khomeini's revolution excited other would-be revolutionaries around the Muslim world, who envisioned a similar political earthquake happening in their own countries.

Months later, a second shock occurred across the Persian Gulf from Iran, when anti-Saudi jihadi militants seized the Grand Mosque in Mecca and held it for two weeks. Led by Juhayman al-'Utaybi, who hailed from a prominent family in the Najd province of Saudi Arabia, the militants declared the arrival of the *mahdi* (who, according to popular Muslim belief, is supposed to set in motion the process leading to Judgment Day), Muhammad 'Abdullah al-Qahtani, who happened to be 'Utaybi's brother-in-law. As in Egypt and Iran, the militants focused on the alleged apostasy of the local rulers, not on global grievances. After Saudi military attempts to regain the mosque were repelled, King Khalid of Saudi Arabia brought in French commando units to do the job, which they successfully completed on December 4, 1979. The seizure of Islam's most important mosque by Sunni militants under the banner of Islam generated even more excitement in Sunni jihadi circles than did the revolution in Iran.

But it was the third shock of 1979 that set in motion the birth of global jihad: the Soviet invasion of Afghanistan on December 24, 1979. After a coup in 1973 that overthrew the Afghan monarchy and established a republic, relations between Kabul and Moscow grew closer. In April 1978 a second coup pushed Afghanistan further into the USSR's political orbit by bringing Nur Mohammad

Taraki to power. Taraki, a founder and leader of the Marxist People's Democratic Party of Afghanistan (PDPA), pushed Afghanistan closer to the Soviet
Union for his own political purposes. Indeed, Taraki wanted more direct Soviet
support of his rule than Soviet leader Leonid Brezhnev was willing to provide.
Taraki's repressive rule and his Soviet-style policies generated considerable
opposition in Afghanistan, particularly outside of Kabul, and the beginnings
of an armed rebellion led by Afghan tribesmen took root. By the spring of
1979, self-styled Afghan mujahideen warriors controlled large parts of rural
Afghanistan. The growing instability inside Afghanistan also impacted elite
politics within the PDPA, such that in September 1979, Afghanistan's foreign
minister, Hafizullah Amin, had Taraki murdered and took power for himself.
The resulting chaos in Kabul only strengthened the hand of the nascent mujahideen forces in the countryside.

Moscow calculated that its allies in Kabul might fall to forces openly hostile
to communist power. The Brezhnev doctrine, formulated in 1968 to justify
the Soviet military intervention in Czechoslovakia that had just crushed the
Prague Spring, was designed to protect fellow socialist countries facing insurrection and potential overthrow. It was even used long after the fact to
justify the 1956 invasion of Hungry to reinstate a pro-Moscow puppet regime in
Budapest. Citing the Brezhnev doctrine, the Soviet army invaded Afghanistan
in December 1979 to prevent the collapse of its allied regime. Soviet forces
immediately engineered a palace coup, killing Amin and installing his colleague Babrak Karmal as Afghan president. The Soviet invasion of Afghanistan
became an immediate international crisis, leading to broad condemnation of
Moscow, including by the United Nations General Assembly and the Organization of Islamic Cooperation (the main multilateral organization of Muslim
states, with a membership of fifty-seven countries). The Carter administration
also condemned the invasion and led a boycott by most countries of the 1980
summer Olympics in Moscow. The small amounts of nonlethal American
assistance to the mujahideen that had been in place since the spring of 1979
were quickly ramped up in coordination with Saudi Arabia and Pakistan.
Significant American military assistance to the Afghan mujahideen would
become a mainstay of the war in Afghanistan, to include the provision of
deadly Stinger missiles in large numbers by 1986, which effectively grounded
Soviet air capabilities against the mujahideen.

The Soviet occupation of Afghanistan also generated enormous opposition among ordinary Afghans, adding significant fuel to the rural rebellion already under way. Initial Soviet plans for a quick exit from Afghanistan were shelved in the face of fierce tribal opposition to their presence that threatened regime survival in Kabul. As international assistance to the mujahideen ramped up, and Pakistani coordination efforts, primarily through military intelligence (ISI), also intensified, the Soviets found themselves in a war they could not win but could not leave without significant strategic costs. The Soviet invasion and occupation of Afghanistan ultimately launched the first wave of global jihad, which was primarily conceptualized by a Palestinian jihadi ideologue named 'Abdullah 'Azzam.

THE LIFE OF 'ABDULLAH YUSUF 'AZZAM

An unusual feature of the Afghan resistance to Soviet occupation, now referred to as the Afghan jihad, was the open call for Muslim volunteers from around the world to join the fight. The most important voice in this call to arms was also the father of global jihad, including its first wave: 'Abdullah Yusuf 'Azzam, a Palestinian cleric born in 1941 in a village near Jenin in what was then Palestine (and is located inside what is known today as the West Bank). 'Azzam was politically active from a young age, joining the Muslim Brotherhood as a teenager and meeting several times with the leader of the Brotherhood in Jordan (a man he would later rival), Muhammad 'Abd al-Rahman Khalifa. 'Azzam spent four years with the University of Damascus (as a distance learner), studying Islamic jurisprudence and graduating with highest honors in 1966. The 1967 Arab-Israeli war made 'Azzam and his family into refugees (technically "displaced persons," not to be confused with Palestinian refugees from the 1948 war), and they settled in the dusty Jordanian town of Zarqa, near Amman, a place largely populated by the earlier wave of Palestinian refugees. After the 1967 war and Jordan's loss of the West Bank to Israel, 'Azzam briefly joined thousands of other Palestinians in an ill-fated guerrilla war campaign against Israel, before heading to Baha, Saudi Arabia, where he taught in a religious high school during the 1967–68 school year.[4] 'Azzam returned to Jordan in 1968.

What set 'Azzam apart from most jihadis, and leavened his radicalism with tradition, were his clerical credentials. Although properly credentialed clerics are not unheard of among jihadis, they are rare. Such clerics typically view jihadi ideologues as uneducated know-nothings, and jihadi ideologues often view high-ranking clerics as lackeys of state power. 'Azzam spent nearly three years in Cairo, graduating in 1973 from the prestigious al-Azhar University with a doctorate in Islamic law. During that period he was active with the Egyptian Islamist community, became close with Sayyid Qutb's family, and may have met 'Umar 'Abd al-Rahman, with whom 'Azzam later became close friends.[5] Rahman, known in the West as the "blind shaykh," was the spiritual leader of many of Egypt's militants and was later arrested while living in New Jersey for participation in the first attack on the World Trade Center in 1993. Rahman was convicted of conspiracy and died in a North Carolina prison in 2017 at the age of seventy-eight.

'Azzam parlayed his Azhar doctorate into a professorship at the University of Jordan, where he taught Islamic law. His charismatic style made his courses quite popular, and his intelligence allowed him to rise to a leadership position in the Muslim Brotherhood. 'Azzam's growing popularity in Jordan and his overtly political lectures caught the attention of Jordan's security services. Of particular concern to Jordanian authorities was that 'Azzam—given his large following, especially among young Jordanian Muslims—was seen as a possible early successor to Shaykh Khalifa, the spiritual guide of the Muslim Brotherhood in Jordan whom 'Azzam had met as a young student two decades earlier.[6] 'Azzam's charismatic popularity, combined with his strident Islamist politics, created too great a political risk for Jordanian authorities, who manufactured an excuse to dismiss him from his university position in 1980. Khalifa had likewise worked to marginalize 'Azzam inside the Brotherhood. In this conflict between the charismatic rabble-rouser and the security and Brotherhood establishments, the latter prevailed and the former went into self-imposed exile.

In many ways, 'Azzam's experience paralleled that of Ali Shariati in Iran at the same time in the 1970s: both were well-educated and highly political; both were charismatic speakers with large followings, particularly among university students; both were independent outsiders without an obvious and powerful social base; both constructed populist ideologies that tightly mixed Islam and politics; both caught the attention of the local security services; and both were compelled into exile by the political establishment that distrusted their politics and their popularity. 'Azzam was driven out of Jordan, while

Shariati was arrested and induced to go abroad, where he died several weeks later under mysterious circumstances as a forty-three-year-old man in 1977.

'Azzam found a job teaching in Mecca during 1980–81 at the shari'a faculty of the King Abdulaziz University in Saudi Arabia, likely with the help of his extensive network of contacts, including Sayyid Qutb's brother, Muhammad Qutb. Usama Bin Laden first met 'Abdullah 'Azzam during 'Azzam's stay in Saudi Arabia, likely introduced by Muhammad Qutb, with whom Bin Laden was close.[7] Energized by the Soviet invasion and occupation of Afghanistan, 'Azzam made arrangements to transfer his appointment to the Saudi-funded International Islamic University in Islamabad, Pakistan, in 1981. Living near the Afghan conflict (mostly in Islamabad until 1986, and then in Peshawar), participating in it, and raising awareness of it would consume the last eight years of 'Azzam's life, until his assassination in 1989.

'AZZAM AND THE AFGHAN JIHAD

In the early years after the Soviet invasion of Afghanistan, few international volunteers came to fight alongside the Afghan mujahideen. The thrust of assistance from the greater Muslim world centered on humanitarian aid, not supplying foreign fighters. More than any other individual, 'Abdullah 'Azzam transformed the Afghan resistance into a cause célèbre around the Muslim world and, in particular, the Arab world. He did this in four main ways. First, 'Azzam raised awareness of the Afghan jihad through persistent talks and short writings that were translated into many languages. He made regular trips to the United States, Europe, and the Arab world, where he lectured his audiences about the events unfolding in Afghanistan and the importance of the cause. Second, and related to his efforts to popularize the Afghan jihad, 'Azzam was responsible for recruiting both men and money to the cause. He considered it an individual obligation (*fard 'ayn*) for all Muslim men to join the battle, and his active encouragement had an impact.

Indeed, this effort further strained 'Azzam's relationship with the Muslim Brotherhood in Jordan (even as he lived outside of Jordan in the 1980s), as Shaykh Khalifa rejected 'Azzam's call for all healthy Jordanian Muslim men to take up arms in Afghanistan, preferring instead to provide humanitarian aid. Inside Jordan, Khalifa's views were widely seen as reflecting those of the Hashemite monarchy, which did not want the security problem of thousands of trained fighters returning to Jordan after doing their jihadi military service in Afghanistan. The precise number of foreign fighters who went to Afghanistan in the 1980s cannot be known but was likely about ten thousand men.[8] A majority of these foreign fighters came from the Arab world. How many of these thousands came because of the urging of 'Azzam is less known, but it is fair to say that no other individual played a greater role in the recruitment of foreign fighters to Afghanistan than did 'Azzam.

A third role that 'Azzam played was to establish and run the Services Bureau (Maktab al-Khadamat) in Peshawar, an organization that helped integrate foreign fighters into the jihad. Usama Bin Laden was 'Azzam's partner in establishing the Services Bureau, which was where Arab volunteers first went to register for the war and to receive their training assignments. The Services Bureau constituted the very first organizational expression of what would become al-Qa'ida. The word "al-Qa'ida" was used at the time as nickname for the al-Ma'sada military camp that Bin Laden set up in Jaji, Afghanistan, in 1986.[9] Years later, Bin Laden revived the word into the romantic, revolutionary *qa'idat al-jihad*: the base or cornerstone of jihad.[10]

By most accounts, Bin Laden and 'Azzam remained on good personal terms throughout the Afghan jihad, despite Bin Laden's efforts to escape the enormous shadow cast by 'Azzam, who was much more famous at that time than was Bin Laden. But Bin Laden and 'Azzam did have one significant disagreement, the same one shared by Abu Musab al-Suri (see chapter 4): To what degree should the Arabs be kept apart in issues of command and control from the Afghan mujahideen and their leaders? 'Azzam, like Suri, thought that Arabs, like all foreign fighters, were there to assist the Afghans and should be integrated into their structures and under the control of Afghan commanders. Bin Laden, by contrast, wanted some or all Arabs kept apart, with separate living quarters, separate units, and separate command-and-control structures. Unlike 'Azzam and Suri, however, Bin Laden was not yet thinking as a global jihadi but rather as a more parochial, traditional jihadi who stuck to his comfortable ethnic Arab roots.

Fourth, and most important, 'Azzam was the chief ideologue for the Afghan jihad in the Muslim world. In his book *The Defense of Muslim Lands (al-Difa' 'an Aradi al-Muslimin)*, 'Azzam laid out why this war was a struggle for all Muslims, not just for Afghans. The primary argument is that the defense of

Muslim lands occupied by infidel forces is a personal obligation (*fard 'ayn*) for all Muslims who have the physical capability to fight or to assist in the fight. This level of obligation is much greater than the more common communal obligation (*fard kifaya*) found in most religious opinions. Although 'Azzam was not the first modern jihadi to use this higher level of obligation to urge men to take up arms, he was the most prominent and the most credentialed given his Azhari doctorate.

'Azzam initially issued *The Defense of Muslim Lands* as a religious opinion, or *fatwa*, in 1984, likely because he had not enjoyed much success up to that point in recruiting foreign fighters to Afghanistan. He could issue a *fatwa* because he had the religious credentials to do so as a trained cleric. By contrast, other global jihadi ideologues featured in this book—Usama Bin Laden, Abu Musab al-Zarqawi, Abu Musab al-Suri—were not clerics and thus did not have the credentials to issue a *fatwa*. (In 1998, Bin Laden tried to issue a *fatwa* but received such a furious backlash from fellow Muslims that he never tried again.) When 'Azzam reissued *The Defense of Muslim Lands* in 1985 as a book, he claimed in the introduction to have gotten the concurrence of Shaykh Abd al-Aziz Bin Baz, then the leading cleric in Saudi Arabia, that seeking to liberate occupied Muslim lands should be seen as a personal duty (*fard 'ayn*) for all able-bodied Muslims, and in particular those Muslims living in close proximity to the battle. In seeking Bin Baz's approval for his fatwa, 'Azzam showed again, as he did in many other ways, a more traditional bent toward religious issues, reflecting his Azhari doctoral credentialing. While Bin Laden would later disparage Bin Baz, then the Grand Mufti of Saudi Arabia, as a tool of corruption, 'Azzam thought it important to gain the concurrence of Bin Baz, one of the top clerics in the Muslim world at the time.

'Azzam likewise sought to situate his *fatwa* in the modern orthodox understanding of jihad as being legitimate only when it is defensive in nature. Although there is a history of offensive jihad, sometimes known as "missionary jihad," only a caliph has the authority to make such a declaration in the view of most clerics.[11] However, in 1924 the Turkish National Assembly, at the direction of Mustafa Kemal Ataturk, abolished the Caliphate entirely, which has made the declaration of offensive jihad problematic ever since.[12] While 'Azzam did not dismiss the possibility of offensive jihad in the present context as some scholars do, he chose not to situate his argument there. By contrast, defending

Islam against attack is never controversial, which was what 'Azzam believed was at stake in Afghanistan. Indeed, both as subtitle and as the first chapter of *The Defense of Muslim Lands*, 'Azzam stated that the "defense of Muslim lands is the first obligation after faith [*iman*]." This is an important distinction from what most jihadi ideologues hold, which is that jihad itself is the most important pillar of Islam after faith (with faith represented by stating the *shahada*, to wit: "There is but one God, and Muhammad is his primary prophet"). For Azzam, it was not just any jihad that tops the list of obligations after faith itself, but that of liberating Muslim lands from occupation by infidels (*kuffar*). This laser focus on liberating occupied lands—on territoriality above all else—set 'Azzam apart from most jihadi ideologues.

To drive home the importance of the defense of Muslim territory, 'Azzam quotes the fourteenth-century Damascus-based Muslim scholar Taqi al-Din Ahmad bin Taymiyya (better known as Ibn Taymiyya) that "the first obligation after faith is the defense of religion and territory (*al-din w'al-dunya*) from the enemy aggressor (*al-'adu al-sa'il*)."[13] Ibn Taymiyya played an important role in the development of the conservative Hanbali school of Islamic jurisprudence and was central in the later development of the Salafi school of thought, including its Wahhabi branch that began on the Arabian Peninsula in the eighteenth century CE. He also is by far the most admired and quoted of all Muslim theologians by jihadis who practice *takfir*, the excommunication of fellow Muslims. In a sharp break with Islamic thought and practice, Ibn Taymiyya encouraged open rebellion against Mongol rulers in Baghdad, believing that they were not true Muslims because they did not rule by shari'a, or Islamic law. His *fatwa* to that effect has been the principal theological justification for other jihadis to go into open rebellion against their own Muslim rulers, something normally and historically frowned upon by Muslim theologians.

For 'Azzam, the obligation for all Muslims to fight the occupation of Muslim lands does not necessarily begin with the invasion itself, but only if the local Muslims are themselves unable to expel the *kuffar*. At that point, the *fard 'ayn* obligation to fight spreads outward to the next circle of Muslims and ever outward until sufficient Muslim power has been mobilized to expel the occupier. "This process continues until it has become *fard 'ayn* upon all the Muslims of the world," 'Azzam argued. Again, 'Azzam turns toward Ibn Taymiyya for support, whom he quotes as saying: "If an enemy intends an attack upon the

Muslims, then repelling him becomes obligatory upon the Muslims under attack, as well as the Muslims not under attack." By extension, 'Azzam argued, consistent with classical jihad jurisprudence, since the Afghans were not able to expel the Russians on their own, it now fell as an obligation to Muslims more broadly to fight with their fellow Muslims to expel the *kuffar* from Muslim lands, beginning with the inner circles of Arab Muslims close to Afghanistan.

'Azzam's book on the defense of Muslim lands is very much directed in its details to the situation in Afghanistan, even addressing such questions as fighting alongside Afghan Muslims who don't know Islam very well (a common complaint among Salafı Arabs who fought in Afghanistan).[14] But while he made it clear that fighting in Afghanistan was the first obligation, 'Azzam was quick to note (in his second chapter) that fighting to liberate his native Palestine was the next obligation for Muslims, as Palestinians could not succeed in this endeavor alone. According to 'Azzam, Palestine was "the foremost Islamic problem" and "the heart of the Muslim world." Thus, in this first of his most important works, 'Azzam laid out a rationale for a type of global jihad that focused on the liberation of Muslim lands. However, it is fair to say that his thinking was evolving throughout the 1980s, and this was not his last word on understanding global jihad.

JIHAD AS PERMANENT REVOLUTION

In his 1929 book by the same name, Leon Trotsky famously argued for a "permanent revolution" to advance the socialist cause in Russia and in similar underindustrialized countries. Because the industrial bourgeoisie was so weak in such countries, they could not play their assigned historical role that, in Marxist terms, meant periodic revolutions led by the emergent revolutionary class. For Trotsky, therefore, revolution could not be an episodic and historic event but must rather be a constant or permanent struggle by the proletariat and its allies to play multiple historical roles constantly to advance socialism. The main point for our discussion here is Trotsky's dramatic change in the notion of revolution from a distinct and episodic event (for example, the French revolution of 1789) to a permanent feature of struggle, even a way of life.

As I noted in the introduction, Sayyid Qutb adopted Trotsky's idea and applied it to the concept of jihad.[15] In the long history of Muslim thought and debate on the meaning of jihad—in this case, the "jihad of the sword," or *jihad al-sayf*—it was always thought to be an episodic event, much like a periodic revolution. An armed jihad was declared by a proper authority in response to a particular event, such as an invasion by an infidel force into Muslim lands. Battles were fought; there was a victor or some other conclusion to the conflict; the jihad ended, and mujahideen returned home or to their barracks. Each jihad had a distinct beginning and end. By contrast, Qutb argued that proper jihad was a permanent revolution without end, a way of life for pious Muslims. That said, he never fully enunciated the justification for why jihad should be viewed as a permanent revolution as opposed to a discrete event, other than that the challenges that Muslims faced were so great and so vast as to justify nearly endless struggle against *jahiliyya*. But this was an incomplete argument that spoke more to the extent of the problems of the twentieth-century Muslim world than it did to a theoretical justification for a dramatic reinterpretation of a core concept in Islam.

'Azzam was profoundly influenced by Qutb, as nearly every jihadi is, and accepted Qutb's interpretation of jihad as permanent revolution. In *The Defense of Muslim Lands*, 'Azzam compares jihad to the regular obligations of Muslims to fast and to pray in order to make the point that jihad is a daily, perpetual obligation, not an episodic event. Just as prayer is required of Muslims every single day, so too is armed jihad. 'Azzam is clearly not referring to the so-called "greater jihad" (*jihad akbar*) of personal struggle against illicit temptation, which is based on a *hadith* rejected as inauthentic by most Salafis, including 'Azzam.[16] Armed jihad (*jihad asghar*, or lesser jihad, according to that same dichotomy), according to 'Azzam, is a perpetual obligation for all able-bodied Muslims.

But 'Azzam went beyond Qutb in giving a broader theological justification for jihad as permanent revolution than simply relying on the scope of problems Muslim faced. For 'Azzam, jihad was the only way for a Muslim to truly embrace *tawhid*, the all-encompassing essence of God.[17] *Tawhid* is usually translated as "monotheism" but has a much richer meaning than that for pious Muslims, especially those with a Salafi orientation. The word *tawhid* suggests the unity of all creation: a reflection of God's omnipotence, omnipresence, and omniscience. Indeed, for the first century of Islam, Muslims generally did not view themselves as having established a new religion so much as forcefully reasserting monotheism in the face of expansive polytheistic practices in

Mecca.[18] They referred to themselves commonly as "monotheists" (*al-muwah-hidun*) instead of "Muslims"—a practice that continues to this day among some Salafis. But according to 'Azzam, appreciating *tawhid* is not something one can do simply from books; it must come from lived experience, and the only real experience in which to appreciate *tawhid* is to fight in jihad. Furthermore, one needn't worry that such fighting would change one's life expectancy (*'ajl*), as that has been predetermined since the beginning of time. Thus, facing death without fear in the midst of jihadi combat is the only true path by which to fully embrace the fullness and oneness of God and thus to know *tawhid*.

This was 'Azzam's theological explanation for why jihad must be perma-nent and ongoing: in order to allow all Muslims, no matter when they were born, the opportunity to fully know *tawhid*. If jihad were merely episodic, entire generations might miss that opportunity to know the fullness of God. 'Azzam's explanation may be compared loosely to the World War II–era English aphorism that "there are no atheists in foxholes." That is, the intensity of war, the awareness that life could be extinguished at any moment, compels man to believe in a higher calling. For 'Azzam and his highly developed sense of predeterminism, jihad was a liberating experience. There was nothing one could do to expedite death or extend life, so one should fight freely and with-out hesitation. Only God should be feared, not death. 'Azzam, more than any other ideologue, even more than Qutb, made the case as to why jihad should be seen as a permanent revolution, a way of life, almost a state of nature. But 'Azzam's permanent jihad applied to jihad in general, not specifically to global jihad. The realization of God's completeness during battle was not limited to only certain jihads; rather, it was a general phenomenon. 'Azzam turned his attention to this concept of global jihad during the last two years of his life.

'AZZAM, THE JIHADI INTERNATIONAL, AND THE BIRTH OF GLOBAL JIHAD

By 1987, 'Azzam's thinking had evolved beyond just Afghanistan and Palestine into a broader argument for global jihad under the banner of a Jihadi Inter-national. By then, it was clear that the Afghan jihad was won, with the new Soviet leader Mikhail Gorbachev signaling his intent to find a way out of the Afghan morass. Although Palestine was still next on 'Azzam's priority list, he set out a much more ambitious program: to liberate Muslim lands everywhere in the world where they are occupied by non-Muslims (*kuffar*). His emerging theory of liberation was to apply the Afghan model internationally, whereby pious and strong Muslim warriors would assist local Muslim populations in a jihad to liberate Muslim lands from infidel control. After Afghanistan and Palestine had been liberated from their usurpers, there were still a dozen or so places around the world where rightfully Muslim lands had been occupied by infidels—from Central Asia to Mindanao in the Philippines to Kashmir and ultimately to al-Andalus (Spain), which had been under Muslim rule for seven centuries.

The core concept for 'Azzam's vision of global jihad was the Jihadi International, a more contextually precise and redolent understanding of what 'Azzam came to mean by his "solid base" concept (al-qa'ida al-sulba). In English, the phrase "solid base" has no really clear meaning and is better translated as "the solid foundation." But 'Azzam had something much bigger in mind that is not captured by either of those literal translations. In a short essay by the same title, 'Azzam himself defined al-qa'ida al-sulba as a "vanguard" (tali'a) but not in the narrow Leninist sense.[19] Rather, what 'Azzam was getting at was more evocative, more akin to the old Communist International.

The Communist International (or Comintern) was formed in 1919 with the support of Communist parties and affiliated groups from around Europe (and beyond, to a limited degree) in order to create an international organization designed to advance the cause of Communism around the world "by all available means, including armed force." The Communist International provided men and material to a number of revolutions and uprisings that were spawned at the conclusion of the First World War, although never at a level that proved decisive in any conflict. The Comintern ultimately proved better at holding conferences than effecting communist revolution around the world and was finally disbanded by Joseph Stalin in 1943 as a favor to his new Western allies. But the idea that informed the Communist International was powerful: to have an international core of able-bodied warriors who could assist local populations around the world who were trying to liberate their countries from bourgeois repression.

This was the same vision that 'Azzam shared—or was beginning to formulate—but instead of liberating countries oppressed by bourgeois capitalism, he wanted to liberate Muslim countries occupied by infidel or kufr powers. It was to be done by forming a Jihadi International of pious and strong Muslim warriors who could travel the world to support local Muslim communities struggling to liberate their lands from occupation. It was the Afghan model, one that 'Azzam was central in creating, that would be exported globally. The best and the brightest mujahideen from around the world would train, study, and be prepared to assist Muslim communities from Palestine to the Philippines to liberate occupied Muslim territories.

'Azzam began to enunciate his concept of the Jihadi International in two works published within months of each other. The first of these was his 1987 book *Join the Caravan (Ilhaq bi'l-Qafila)*, a clarion call for Muslims around the world to come assist the Afghan mujahideen in their fight against Soviet occupation. Just as an old camel caravan would pass quickly, giving one little time to contemplate joining, or perhaps forever regret not joining, so too was the jihad against the Soviets a chance of a lifetime that one should not let slip by. *Join the Caravan* was translated into numerous languages and was arguably the single most successful piece of propaganda in recruiting foreign Muslims, especially Arabs, to fight in Afghanistan.[20] The number of young Arab men seeking to join the jihad in Afghanistan increased so much after the publication of the book that a second edition was published in December 1988. While *Join the Caravan* remained focused on Afghanistan, 'Azzam had begun to think of this same model being applied to other Muslim territories around the world. The same logic that he had first applied in his *fatwa* about defending Muslim land in Afghanistan, and had further expounded in *Join the Caravan*, could certainly be applied to a dozen other places around the globe.

'Azzam further explored his concept of a Jihadi International in his article "Al-Qa'ida al-Sulba," published in the April 1988 issue of *Al-Jihad*, a publication that would never be mistaken for a slick-and-glossy magazine. While the article was short, it detailed 'Azzam's thoughts on the need for a Jihadi International. No real Islamic society (*al-mujtam'a al-islami*) can arise in the absence of an Islamic movement (*al-haraka al-islamiyya*) anywhere in the world, 'Azzam argued. Only such a movement can spark the entirety of the Muslim nation, the *umma*, for the long jihad ahead—one that must be led by a seasoned and powerful movement. The Jihadi International would face the toughest tests and the fiercest challenges, and so must be properly prepared. The members of this vanguard must be devout and loyal to each other, must not mix freely with others outside the band of brothers, and must be prepared to sacrifice. They should be trained through the fiercest trials, sweat and blood. Abstinence from worldly pleasures and asceticism would stiffen the resolve of such warriors and help in their ultimate victory.

Although 'Azzam was not the only (or even the first) jihadi to use the phrase *al-qa'ida al-sulba*, he took the meaning well beyond how others used it. For other jihadi ideologues, and even for 'Azzam early on, the phrase had a strong territorial connotation, often meaning Afghanistan in particular. That is, such jihadis were arguing for the importance of creating a state that was truly Islamic, a "solid foundation" that could inspire other Muslims and be used for the expansion of an Islamic state. This notion of creating an Islamic state was to differentiate the jihadi movement from the clandestine and underground groups that were the norm in many Muslim countries. As long as the Islamic movement, as understood by various jihadi ideologues, was limited to the margins of society, it was easily defeated by state security forces.[21] By contrast, having an actual territory, an Islamic state, would liberate the movement, allowing it to move out of the shadows and into prime time in the Sunni Muslim world. It was only during the last two years of 'Azzam's life that he began to think of the "solid base" as less of a specific territory and more of a fluid movement, as a Jihadi International, that could help liberate not just Afghanistan but Muslim territory around the world.

But 'Azzam did not have a traditional Leninist vanguard in mind, even though he frequently used the Arabic word for vanguard, *tali'a*, which is closely associated with leftist discourse. A vanguard for Lenin was a small elite group that could not stand up to the power of the state directly, so it would militarily provoke the state, hoping for an overreaction by police and security forces. In this state overreaction opportunities arose for the revolutionaries to gain greater public support and turn the balance of power around—a process led throughout by an elite and professional vanguard. When Sayyid Qutb wrote his jihadi call to arms in 1964, he very much had in mind a jihadi version of Lenin's vanguard, another of the many Leninist notions he borrowed and put into an Islamic context. Qutb himself periodically used the word *tali'a* for vanguard, although he seemed bothered that this word was primarily used by leftists and was understood in broader Egyptian society as a word that was politically associated with secular groups. As a result, Qutb would more often use the word *jama'a* (group) for vanguard.[22] Egypt's most famous early jihadi organization, al-Jama' al-Islamiyya, takes its name from Qutb's usage.

For 'Azzam, the Jihadi International was not a small group, even though it was expected to have elite attributes. Rather, it was a part of a larger movement (*haraka*) that would transform the Muslim world. Indeed, he was often critical of those arguing for a purely small vanguard-type organizational model, believing that such an approach would forever banish jihadis to the margins of society. In 'Azzam's view, all Muslims could and should play their part in this broader movement. His assassination in November 1989 prevented him from elaborating further on his Jihadi International model, and there are plenty of areas that need explication. Although 'Azzam's idea was still in the notional stage when he died, he did have success in the one country to which he had applied it, Afghanistan.

The idea of 'Azzam's model was tested, briefly, months after his death by his colleague in Afghanistan, Usama Bin Laden. When Iraqi forces invaded Kuwait in August 1990, Bin Laden approached the Saudi royal family to encourage them not to bring in the Americans and their allies to liberate Kuwait from the secular Ba'thist Iraqi army. Rather, Bin Laden encouraged Saudi Arabia to adopt 'Azzam's model to liberate Kuwait. Bin Laden proposed bringing in one hundred thousand mujahideen from around the Arab world—just like in Afghanistan—and use this Jihadi International to drive out the Iraqi occupiers. Bin Laden himself offered to take the lead in putting the mujahideen band back together again for a reunion tour of sorts. The Saudi monarchy had no interest in inviting tens of thousands of mujahideen warriors to the neighborhood, including many veterans of the Afghan jihad, and so declined Bin Laden's offer. The Saudi response marked an important step both in the radicalization of Bin Laden and in the ultimate failure of the first wave of global jihad.

The idea of a global jihad to liberate occupied Muslim territory has not entirely disappeared, and one should expect it to periodically become salient. The idea of territorial liberation from infidel forces played a role in the jihadi attack on the city of Marawi on Mindanao Island in the Philippines in 2017. This assault led to a bloody five-month standoff before the allied jihadi groups who undertook the attack were defeated. Although even here the main story was about clan competition, the local drug trade, and political malfeasance by President Duterte.[23] What does seem to have ended with 'Azzam's death in 1989 and the rejection of his ideal in 1990 was the establishment of a Jihadi International to help fight the global jihad wherever Muslim territory was occupied.

'AZZAM'S INVENTION OF THE CULT OF MARTYRDOM

While 'Abdullah 'Azzam's most important ideological innovation as the father of global jihad was that of a Jihadi International, a second important innovation was his invention of a cult of martyrdom that was attached to jihad. An emphasis on seeking death, on welcoming martyrdom through violence, was not part of the early jihad movement that emerged in the 1970s; however, it became an emphasis largely because of the work of 'Azzam.

The Arabic term for "martyr" (shahid, pl. shuhada' from the verb sh-h-d) had a rich history in early Islam, including a number of references in the Qur'an. During the early Islamic period, the word's primary meaning was as a witness to the faith, not as a believer killed for his faith. The very first pillar of Islam, the declaration of faith that there is but one God and Muhammad is his primary prophet, is known as the shahada—that is, one who is bearing witness for God. Perhaps ironically, it was linguistic influence from Syriac Christians that gave the word shahid its second meaning of dying for one's faith. Becoming a martyr by bearing witness for God to such a strong degree that it cost one's life was a strong theme in early Christianity, which then influenced its later development in Islam.[24]

Subsequent to this early Christian influence, and for much of Islamic history, dying for God's glory, particularly during a jihad sanctioned by the caliph, constituted martyrdom. To be clear, the concept of martyrdom was not a major theological concern in Islam, as it was for early Christian theologians, but rather a relatively minor issue within orthodox Sunni Islam. Indeed, the concept of martyrdom was far more central in the writings of Shia jurists than Sunni ones, as the former had a focus on the unjust killing of the blood descendants of Muhammad: the murders of the prophet's son-in-law 'Ali, his grandson Husayn, and many subsequent Shia leaders.[25] Sunni Muslim scholars did praise Muslims who had died struggling in the path of God (fi sabil allah) and suggested their path to heaven and its rewards was clear. My point is that although the issue of martyrdom was a source of some discussion among orthodox Sunni theologians over the course of Islamic history, it was not a centerpiece of debate and commentary.

Nor was martyrdom particularly important for early jihadis in the 1970s. As Thomas Hegghammer observantly notes, the seminal text by Egyptian jihadi Muhammad 'Abd al-Salam Faraj, al-Farida al-Gha'iba, hardly mentions martyrdom as he lays out the case for assassinating Anwar Sadat and other "near enemy" Muslim leaders.[26] It was not the rewards of heaven that should prompt jihadi action, according to Faraj, but the temporal needs of the Muslim community abiding by the commands of God.

In contrast, 'Azzam held that all jihadis, and indeed all Muslims, should actively seek martyrdom. It was 'Azzam—with his religious credentials from al-Azhar—who dug up old *hadiths* (sayings of the prophet Muhammad) and other justifications for dying as a martyr and thus getting the greatest rewards heaven has to offer. The Qur'an itself was not much use in this matter: although there are a number of verses venerating those who witness for God, very few verses seem to equate witnessing for God with death in combat, most clearly stated in chapter 9, verse 111: "Indeed, God has purchased from the believers their lives and their properties in exchange for which they will have Paradise. They fight in the cause of God, and so they kill and are killed. This promise of Paradise is a binding commitment from God, found in the Torah and the Gospel and the Qur'an. And who is truer to his covenant than God?"[27]

In *Join the Caravan*, 'Azzam quotes a *hadith* that outlines the rewards of heaven. The sayings of Muhammad and his close associates have been debated by Muslim theologians for centuries, centering on issues of authenticity. The more trusted the chain (*isnad*) of communication, the more reliable the *hadith*. One of the six major compilations of *hadiths* viewed as authentic was done by Muhammad bin 'Issa al-Turmidhi, a ninth-century Persian Sunni scholar who recorded the prophet Muhammad telling his companion, Miqdim bin Ma'd, that:

> The martyr has seven gifts from God. First, his sins are forgiven with the first drop of spilt blood; second, his entry to heaven is assured; third, he will wear the shroud of the believer; fourth, he will have 72 houris in heaven; fifth, he is spared the Judgment Day (qiyama); sixth, on his head will be a crown of dignity, where one jewel is worth more than all worldly possessions; and seventh, he will be granted 70 servants in his heavenly household.[28]

Another major compilation of authentic *hadiths* by Muhammad al-Bukhari, also in the ninth-century CE, records a saying by the prophet Muhammad that emphasizes the heavenly glories of those who fight in the path of God: "In heaven, there are 100 different levels that God has prepared for mujahideen, and the difference between each level is like the difference between heaven and earth." 'Azzam quotes this hadith in *Join the Caravan*, in a section titled "Wishing for Martyrdom and the Best of Heaven's Rewards." In his writings and speeches, 'Azzam emphasized these tangible rewards that martyrs fighting for God will receive. Heaven, or paradise, is not treated as an abstract concept by 'Azzam, but rather viewed in an almost infantile manner, with the tangible benefits of heaven unmistakable to even the most illiterate person.

It is not clear how many people joined in jihad simply based on 'Azzam's promises of heavenly reward. The number is probably not exceptionally high. Certainly when it comes to suicide bombings, as the scholar Robert Pape has shown, the best predictor of such action is the occupation of territory by liberal democracies, not heavenly rewards.[29] There is little evidence that such heavenly rewards outlined by 'Azzam have motivated a significant number of men with no earthly grievances to undertake a suicide bombing in order to reach paradise. Still, 'Azzam changed the discourse in jihadi circles and, to some degree, in the societies in which they operate. The open references to the glories of martyrdom and the benefits of seeking death in battle are far more prominent today than they were in the Muslim world in, say, the 1970s, when such discourse was virtually absent.[30] The cult of martyrdom and the discourse that went with it for Sunni jihadis was the handiwork of 'Abdullah 'Azzam.[31]

While 'Azzam himself never advocated for suicide bombings, or "martyrdom operations" (*'amaliyat ishtishhadiyya*) as jihadis call them, there is an obvious logical link between his advocacy for seeking death in the path of a righteous jihad and becoming a suicide bomber. Such "smart bombs" can be very effective in delivering a weapon to precisely where one desires, inflicting maximum casualties for the amount of payload used. But in order to justify such martyrdom operations, jihadi ideologues must be able to get around Islam's clear prohibition against suicide. Both the Qur'an (verses 4:29 and 2:195) and, even more so, the *hadiths* forbid suicide, saying it will result in the eternal damnation of hellfire.[32] But this is where 'Azzam's argument linking jihad and *tawhid* came into play. He argued that, while armed jihad is the only path for the full realization of God, it does not have any impact on life expectancy (*'ajl*). Therefore, no action can bring death any sooner or stave it off any longer than the date that God ordained at the beginning of time. If God does not want a warrior to die in battle, according to 'Azzam, he will produce miracles that ensure continued life.

Stretching 'Azzam's logic to suicide bombings (which he himself never discussed), then, would suggest that death will only occur if God had already determined it should happen, and thus it would not be suicide at all. Only God will determine when the moment of death occurs. By this logic, a suicide bomber will survive his attack if God has willed it, so the operation by itself cannot be seen as attempted suicide. Indeed, 'Azzam's logic, if pressed to the extreme, means that there is no such thing as suicide at all, as only God chooses the moment of death. This fatalism, combined with arguments of the greater good, allows jihadis to circumvent the prohibition on suicide, and 'Azzam provided all the intellectual tools needed to do so.

Consistent with the recentness of the intellectual framework used to justify suicide bombings, the actual fact of widespread suicide bombings is quite new to the Middle East, beginning only in the 1980s. In fact, while Hizbullah was the first group to use a suicide truck bomb (in 1983), it was the secular nationalist Tamil Tigers in Sri Lanka that invented the suicide vest and generally perfected suicide bombings as a tactic of war in the 1980s. That knowledge was largely imported into the Middle East from South Asia, with Hizbullah adopting the use of the suicide vest as part of its repertoire. Hizbullah members then passed on their knowledge to deported Palestinians from Hamas and Islamic Jihad in the early 1990s, who began to use suicide vest bombings against Israeli targets in the mid-1990s. From there, the tactic gained widespread approval by jihadis and some other violent extremist groups throughout the region. I want to stress that 'Azzam himself did not advocate for such suicide bombings, but he did lay the intellectual foundations for this type of violence and encouraged an emphasis on martyrdom. The cult of martyrdom in Islam is a new phenomenon and, of course, still quite limited in the Muslim world, but it is more prevalent today because of the work of 'Abdullah 'Azzam.

TAKFIR, FITNA, AND THE ASSASSINATION OF THE IMAM AL-JIHAD

One of the great debates among jihadis everywhere is over the concept of *takfir*, or excommunication of fellow Muslims. *Takfir* has been an institution in Islam from its early days, in a similar way to the same practice in the

Catholic Church. Much like excommunication in Catholicism, *takfir* historically was a rarely used penalty for apostasy that had to be implemented by a proper religious authority based on evidence. The most common charge that could lead to a consideration of apostasy, or leaving the faith, would be when a Muslim had converted to another religion. In the *hudud*, or criminal penalties within Islamic law, a finding of apostasy is punishable by death.[33] *Takfir* refers to the entire *process* of finding one has abandoned Islam based on evidence presented to a qualified jurist. A typical process for *takfir* is for a *qadi* (shari'a court judge) to be presented with evidence of apostasy, hear both sides, and make a determination of guilt or innocence. Just as a finding of apostasy carries significant penalty, the finding of bearing false witness is also a crime. Thus, as one can imagine, bringing formal charges of apostasy and initiating a process of possible excommunication was seldom used in practice, even though it had legitimacy in Islam. Apostasy was not a charge to be brought lightly.[34]

Historically the process of *takfir* has been undertaken at the individual level. There is not an orthodox Islamic practice of formally excommunicating whole categories of people.[35] As was briefly noted earlier, the first major use of *takfir* as an attempt to delegitimize political rulers was done at the beginning of the fourteenth century by Muslim theologian Ibn Taymiyya. The Ilkhanate Mongols, descendants of Genghis Khan, had infamously sacked Baghdad in 1258 and had on multiple occasions thereafter sought to extend their rule to the lands of Syria (*bilad al-sham*). Ibn Taymiyya wrote three *fatwas* (religious opinions) on the Ilkhanate Mongol rulers of Baghdad, the second of which famously excommunicated them as a group. His reasoning was that even though the Mongols had converted to Islam, they still implemented *Yasa*, or tribal laws emanating from Central Asia, instead of the shari'a. Thus, Ibn Taymiyya reasoned, their conversion to Islam was abrogated by their failure to implement Islamic law in the areas they ruled, even though they had been warned about this issue many times. True Muslims were thus encouraged, indeed obliged, to seek the overthrow of the infidel Mongols and their replacement with true Muslims.

The immediate goal of Ibn Taymiyya's *fatwas* was accomplished, which was to prevent the expansion of Mongol rule into Syria. Buoyed by his *fatwa*, a Mameluke army (helped by Christian Crusader forces) decisively defeated the Ilkhanate army outside Damascus in 1303. But Ibn Taymiyya set a dangerous precedent that many contemporary jihadis have sought to emulate: to declare a ruler or a broader regime as apostates (through *takfir*) that effectively calls for their deaths. The tool of *takfir* has become the most important vehicle by which jihadis justify attacks on political leaders (and others). Toward the end of his life, Ibn Taymiyya himself seemed to regret the Pandora's Box he had opened for Muslims seeking to delegitimize fellow Muslims, when he said that any Muslim who prays cannot be declared a non-Muslim.[36]

'Abdullah 'Azzam strenuously argued against the modern misuse of *takfir* by fellow jihadis.[37] He viewed that the vigorous use of excommunicating fellow Muslims, which was being espoused by Ayman al-Zawahiri and others, constituted a slippery slope toward Muslim weakness. In particular, the misuse of *takfir* was a recipe for *fitna*: Muslim-on-Muslim discord and violence that would only weaken Muslims in the face of their real enemies. There is a historical consensus by Muslim scholars that *fitna* is synonymous with schism within Islam and has a strongly negative connotation. Internal Muslim discord and strife were to be avoided at all costs. For 'Azzam, it would only bring schism and weakness for jihadis to declare fellow Muslims as their first and most important enemy, even if those Muslim leaders were following a wrong path. Recall that 'Azzam had a positive relationship with Shaykh Bin Baz and the Saudi monarchy in general, and he was not inclined to wage jihad against such rulers, even in spite of their shortcomings. This is not to suggest that 'Azzam rejected the established principle of *takfir*, but rather to argue that he believed it to be a tactical mistake for jihadis to go down the path of *takfir*, which would lead only to Muslim fratricide and weakness.

The debate over *takfir* among jihadis came to a head with the final Soviet withdrawal from Afghanistan in February 1989, as it fundamentally raised the question of who the next enemy would be. If jihad is a way of life, not an occasional duty, then there must be a next enemy; it is not enough to tell the fighters of the Jihadi International to simply go home and get back to their lives (as most actually did). The battle line was drawn between *takfiris* and anti-*takfiris*. The former, led by Zawahiri, argued for the use of *takfir* as the religious justification for targeting apostate Muslim regimes, beginning with Egypt. Thus the Mubarak regime in Cairo was the legitimate next enemy for

Zawahiri and his followers. Those arguing for a "near enemy" approach to jihad should not be categorized as global jihadis, as they viewed the mission as an internal one that aimed to rid the Muslim world of apostate regimes. The *takfiris* were countered by ideologues very much opposed to this use of *takfir*, led by 'Azzam. He argued for the application of the Afghan model—the Jihadi International—to liberate other occupied lands, beginning with Palestine. Israel was therefore the most appropriate next enemy. 'Azzam forcefully argued against the use of *takfir* as the defining criterion of global jihad.

The issue of *takfir* is controversial even within the jihadi community, and much more so within the general Muslim population. If just anyone can excommunicate any other Muslim, there would be no end to the slippery slope of division and violence. A sort of hubris is involved: Who are these jihadis who think they can sit in judgment over someone else's Muslim faith? Regimes and other critics of the jihadi movement have often given jihadis the pejorative label of "those who practice *takfir*," emphasizing how unpopular such a practice is. Even Sayyid Qutb avoided taking this step and openly rejected the notion that he was leveling the charge of apostasy in his arguments of *jahiliyya*. *Takfir*, he maintained, was to be applied to an individual who stood accused of apostasy; *jahiliyya*, by contrast, was a characteristic of larger groups, such as regimes or societies. *Jahiliyya* is not a specific crime in Islamic law and thus does not carry a specific *hadd* (penalty), such as death for apostasy. For Qutb, *jahiliyya* was not the same thing as apostasy. Qutb did not want to be painted with the brush of *takfir*.[38]

'Azzam's rejection of Zawahiri's *takfir* model, where the Egyptian regime was the logical next target, may have gotten him killed in November 1989. No one has claimed credit for the powerful blast that killed 'Azzam and two of his sons as they drove to a mosque in Peshawar, Pakistan, where 'Azzam was scheduled to deliver the sermon that day. There is a long list of potential suspects in the assassination, but a persistent rumor is the killing was done by the hand of Zawahiri and his allies to eliminate his main antagonist in the *takfir* argument over where to take armed jihad next. However, such a precise and powerful blast was unlikely to have been the work of amateurs, which Zawahiri and his gang very much were. It is more likely to have been the work of seasoned professionals within Pakistani military intelligence for whom the charismatic and popular 'Azzam had already served his purpose with the

Soviet departure and now represented a dangerous and independent actor not under Pakistan's control (as many other mujahideen leaders were). But, as of this writing, the murder mystery has not yet been solved, and 'Azzam retains the aura of heroic martyr for much of the jihadi community.

EVALUATING THE FIRST WAVE OF GLOBAL JIHAD

The first wave of global jihad never really left its home base of Afghanistan, and its success there was part deliberate action by 'Abdullah 'Azzam and part historical serendipity. There is no doubt that 'Azzam played the key role, more than anyone else, in recruiting foreign fighters (primarily Arabs) to help the Afghan mujahideen fight the Soviets in the 1980s. At least before 1987, his recruitment of Arabs to fight in Afghanistan was done primarily to win that war, and not in the cause of a larger, global struggle. Even then, the Arab volunteers did little to alter the course of the Afghan jihad, despite their self-created mythologies.[39] But the success of this Afghan model led 'Azzam in the last two years of his life to think and write more broadly about how the Afghan model could work elsewhere in the Muslim world, and in particular anywhere Muslim lands were seen to be occupied. Thus was born 'Azzam's new interpretation of the idea of *al-qa'ida al-sulba*, the solid base, or less literally and prosaically, the Jihadi International.

About ten thousand foreign fighters were recruited to fight in Afghanistan during the course of the war (there were never that many in Afghanistan at the same time). Some stayed for years, while others came and left quickly. As noted, many came beginning in 1987 with 'Azzam's call to "join the caravan." In any case, there were far more foreign fighters in the Afghan jihad than al-Qa'ida ever had on its membership rolls, before or after the 9/11 terror attacks in 2001. ISIS far out-recruited either of the earlier waves of global jihad. Although we do not have any exact figures, it is clear that the vast majority of those foreign fighters in Afghanistan did not consider themselves permanent or global jihadis, just fighters in a specific righteous cause. Most went home and lived uneventful lives after the Afghan jihad ended. The number of those jihadis prepared to sign up for such a Jihadi International to fight in Palestine or elsewhere would certainly have been small.

'Azzam's influence within the broader jihadi community went beyond the Jihadi International concept. His construction of the idea of a cult of martyrdom had far-ranging impacts throughout the Sunni Muslim world in the years that followed. Also, 'Azzam's insistence that young men ignore local clerical authority (and their parents) to go fight in a distant jihad continues to have reverberations undermining clerical authority. Once you have instructed young Muslims to ignore local clerical and familial authority, how do you convince them to respect that authority in the future?[40]

'Azzam's death and Bin Laden's failure to sell the Jihadi International idea to the Saudi leadership as a better means to liberate Kuwait in 1990 effectively ended the first wave of global jihad before it had much of a chance to work globally outside of Afghanistan. Most of the foreign fighters from Afghanistan either went home or went to fight in other jihads in the Balkans, Chechnya, and elsewhere, although not under any specific banner of global jihad. The idea of territorial liberation still holds some appeal among jihadis, as the events of 2017 in Marawi, the Philippines, suggest. But the failure of the idea of a Jihadi International designed to liberate occupied territory to catch on is apparent. Indeed, the idea of global jihad was to move in a starkly different direction as the 1990s wore on.

It is important to note that the movement of *global* jihad itself went into relative hibernation in the early 1990s, as there was no clear program and idea to attach to. There were plenty of local jihads in the early 1990s, from Egypt to the former Yugoslavia to a nasty civil war with a strong jihadi component in Algeria, and plenty of others in between. In the Balkans and elsewhere, fighters from other lands would sometimes join the jihad. However, none of these jihads was specifically global in its orientation, and the foreign fighters that joined did not do so under some organized banner of global jihad. Rather, these jihads represented old-fashioned jihadi goals of regime change or local territorial conquest and/or defense. The preeminent global jihadi ideologue, 'Abdullah 'Azzam was dead; Ayman al-Zawahiri remained focused on regime change in Cairo; and the next major theoretician of global jihad, Usama Bin Laden, was still in his "near enemy" phase. Alienated from the Saudi regime since 1990 and stripped of his Saudi citizenship, Bin Laden spent the early 1990s holed up in the Sudan. He claimed to have played a hand in the Black Hawk Down incident in Somalia as well as some activity in Yemen during the early 1990s, but the evidence is spotty.[41] It wasn't until the mid-1990s that Bin Laden would decisively move into the global jihad camp.

The first wave of global jihad at best enjoyed limited success. The Afghan jihad was won, but that had little to do with foreign fighters and the emerging notion of a Jihadi International. While 'Azzam was a charismatic and persuasive man, his idea of a Jihadi International did not outlive him, at least not in any significant way. The second wave of global jihad would take a markedly different turn from where 'Azzam left it.

Chapter 2

AMERICA FIRST!
1996–2011

THE MUJAHIDEEN VICTORY OVER THE SOVIETS IN AFGHANISTAN in 1989, the death of 'Abdullah 'Azzam a few months later, and the Saudi rejection of a Jihadi International force in Kuwait in 1990 essentially left global jihadis without a champion or a unified cause. The *takfiris* had won the day by default, and their argument to focus on overthrowing local regimes prevailed. Indeed, it is fair to say that global jihad as an idea and a movement went into virtual hibernation in the first half of the 1990s.

That is not to say there was an absence of self-declared jihad movements during the early 1990s; in fact, there were many. The end of the Cold War and collapse of the Soviet Union in 1991 created a more unconstrained international environment in which all sorts of local violent groups—ethnic, nationalist, and ideological—took up arms against their neighbors or against their states. The end of the Cold War and the international disorder that ensued unleashed nasty ethno-national conflicts in many regions, including the genocide of Tutsis in Rwanda by the Hutu majority, the sequential wars in the former Yugoslavia, most especially in Bosnia, and Chechnya's bloody secessionist campaigns and their suppression by Russia. Smaller but important conflicts raged in many other places during this period as well, including in Kashmir, Palestine, and Somalia. Afghans took up arms against each other again beginning in 1992, primarily along ethnic and tribal lines. In Afghanistan, as elsewhere, the civil war also included an element of local jihadism, with the rise of the Taliban in 1994 (and its coming to power in much of the country by 1996). Hamas, in Palestine, was formed in 1988 during the first intifada, or uprising, against Israel, although that uprising was primarily unarmed.[1] The Shia jihadi group Hizbullah, formed a few years earlier, transformed itself in the 1990s into a powerful political actor to go along with its violent activities. However, none of these groups, including the jihadi ones, could accurately be described as *global* in its primary orientation; rather, these groups were interested in fighting local battles and local causes.

The one potential exceptional act to this pattern of localized jihads in the early 1990s was the World Trade Center truck bombing in New York City in 1993 that killed six people and injured hundreds more. The bombing was financed by Khalid Sheikh Muhammad and led by his nephew Ramzi Yousef. But even here, the perpetrators noted in a letter to the *New York Times* that they undertook this action primarily as retaliation against America for its support of Israel and its crimes against the Palestinians (while Yousef is ethnically Baluchi on his father's side, he has Palestinian roots on his maternal side).[2] It appears that there was no global jihadi ideology or organization at work in this attack; instead, it was an angry and murderous reaction to US policies in the Middle East. Khalid Sheikh Muhammad would go on to be a top lieutenant for Usama Bin Laden, including taking a lead role in a second attack on the World Trade Center eight years later. Unlike the 1993 bombing, the 2001 attack on the World Trade Center was definitely done under the banner of global jihad, with a broader global strategy informing it.

Two of the most important local jihadi causes during the early 1990s occurred in Egypt and Algeria. Egypt fancies itself as the center of the Arab world, and rightly so. It is by far the largest of all Arab countries, with a population today nearing one hundred million. It has been the center of Arabic culture for the past century, being the major producer of films, television shows, and music that are seen and heard around the Arab world. It is a truism that even today nearly all Arabs can understand Egyptian Arabic because of this cultural production. Egypt was also the first Arab country to create a significant industrial economic base, to nationalize a major strategic resource (the Suez Canal in 1956), and to establish liberal constitutional institutions of government. In addition, the country was an early leader in the Arab world in building universities. Many of the broad political and cultural trends that ultimately swept through the Arab world began in Egypt, and that includes Islamism and jihadism. What happens in Egypt often influences the broader Arab world.

Egypt experienced a serious low-intensity conflict from jihadi extremists in the 1990s. The violence was perpetrated by two jihadi groups in particular. The first, the Islamic Group (al-Jama'a al-Islamiyya), began life as a regional protest movement in southern Egypt against domination by Cairo but ultimately evolved into a deadly jihadi group.[3] The second, al-Jihad al-Islami, or simply al-Jihad, which was most infamous for its assassination of Egyptian president Anwar Sadat in 1981, had come to be led by Ayman al-Zawahiri beginning in 1991. The low-intensity conflict in Egypt was bloody but did not devolve into an all-out civil war (as was happening concurrently in Algeria). The most violent years in Egypt were 1993 through 1995, when well over one thousand individuals (police, civilians, and jihadis) were killed in the violence. Assassination attempts against top officials became one of the Egyptian jihadis' favorite forms of violence, with attempts made on the lives of Egypt's prime minister, interior minister (three times), and President Mubarak himself in 1995 while he was visiting Ethiopia. Leading public intellectuals, such as professor and activist Farag Foda, were also assassinated.

In the early 1990s, Egyptian security officials were on the defensive and were widely seen as losing a long war. Parts of the country were dangerous places for police and security personnel, including a large neighborhood in Cairo jokingly nicknamed "the Islamic Republic of Imbaba." Indeed, numerous observers concluded it was only a matter of time before the Mubarak regime would be overthrown, likely by some coalition of jihadi and Islamist militants. Writing in 1994, one leading expert on Egypt famously published an anonymous analysis arguing that it was not too late yet to prevent the overthrow of the regime, but that time was drawing short.[4]

Egypt's jihadi rebellion would last two more years, but by 1995 it was becoming clear that the state would prevail and put down the revolt. This change occurred due in large part to the jihadis' indiscriminate use of violence. The Egyptian public, appalled by the murder of innocents at the hands of the jihadis, gradually turned against them, thereby allowing the government to use increasingly harsh measures to end the revolt. By 1997 most of Egypt's jihadis were either dead or in prison, and those in prison began a remarkable transformation process of renouncing their use of violence, calling it a mistake.[5] Even Ayman al-Zawahiri's co-leader of the Jihad organization, Sayyid Imam al-Sharif ("Dr. Fadl"), renounced the violence that had been used in Egypt, making him a traitor in other jihadi circles.[6] The 1997 terror attack on the grounds of Queen Hatshepsut's temple in Luxor that left sixty-two people dead, mostly foreign tourists, was the last gory act of a defeated jihadi movement.

Algeria's civil war paralleled Egypt's conflict in time but was much costlier in human lives. A hot war as opposed to a low-intensity conflict, Algeria's civil war left tens of thousands of civilians dead and displaced another 1.5 million people.[7] The events leading to the civil war began in the late 1980s, when the usual combination of severe economic problems, especially high unemployment, and few avenues for political redress under a one-party state, caused significant discontent. In October 1988, Algeria saw its largest protests since its 1954–62 struggle for independence from France. Shaken by these protests, the regime agreed to open up the political system, legalizing new political parties and holding elections. In June 1990 municipal elections were held across the country; these were dominated by the Islamic Salvation Front, the new Islamist party more commonly known by its French acronym, FIS. The FIS was an umbrella Islamist party, somewhat akin to the Muslim Brotherhood in Egypt, although it was not an official branch and did not share the intense organizational discipline of the Brotherhood.[8] Like the Brotherhood, the FIS drew most of its support from the urban middle and lower classes, and adopted many typical Islamist political positions.

The FIS won an absolute majority of all votes cast in the 1990 local elections, nearly doubling the total of the governing party, the National Liberation Front, or FLN in its French acronym. The FIS took control of city and town councils throughout Algeria. Two rounds of national elections for parliament were scheduled for December 1991 and January 1992. The FIS again dominated the first round of voting and would have likely won an outright majority in parliament had the second round taken place. Instead, the Algerian military, with Western support, canceled the vote, arrested thousands of FIS members, and took direct control of the state. The military coup launched a bloody civil war in Algeria, with armed opposition to the military organizing itself primarily into jihadi groups, most notably the Armed Islamic Group, known by its French acronym, GIA. Like in Egypt, the violence in Algeria was most intense from 1993 to 1995. Unlike in Egypt, the intentional targeting of civilians by all sides in Algeria was so blatant and so extensive that the conflict earned the moniker of "the dirty war" (*la sale guerre*). Also as with Egypt, by the close of 1995, it was clear that the government forces would prevail over their jihadi opponents, although in both cases it took until 1997 for a ceasefire to be declared. In the case of Algeria, the opposition was further weakened by internecine violence that erupted in 1994, when the GIA declared war on the FIS over its negotiations with the military government.[9]

While the defeats of the jihadi rebellions in Egypt and Algeria were the most consequential and important of such state victories in the Arab world during the 1990s, those defeats were part of a broader movement of jihadi decline during that time. As the French scholar Gilles Kepel has shown, after a significant expansion of jihadism and Islamism in the 1970s and 1980s, when the movements went from a fairly small fringe to important actors in many Muslim-majority countries, there was a noticeable decline in their fortunes in the 1990s.[10] The decline occurred for a number of reasons, including the ability of states to adapt their tactics to defeat jihadi challengers and, most important, the often gratuitous use of violence by jihadis against civilians that spoiled any chance of winning over the general population to their cause, even in the presence of unpopular and authoritarian regimes. The message was unmistakable: in the early 1990s, jihadis and Islamists were on the cusp of taking power in two of the most important and powerful countries in the Arab world, but by 1995 it had become clear that the secular regimes would prevail and endure. This was a shocking development for jihadis who surveyed the Muslim world of the 1970s and 1980s and saw only empowerment and victory. Now these groups who had believed that their path to power had been ordained by God had to make sense of defeat, particularly in the centrally important countries of Egypt and Algeria.

Usama Bin Laden sought to decipher the growing precariousness of the jihadi movement. Apostate regimes—including, as he had come to believe, the one in Riyadh—should not be able to defeat the forces of true Islam, of brave mujahideen who had recently been unmistakably on the offensive. This was the same powerful force, according to the popular jihadi narrative, that had defeated a superpower in Afghanistan and, by extension, brought on the collapse of Communism. Yet the apostate regimes were no longer on the defensive; instead, they were playing offense against the jihadis. Bin Laden concluded that these apostate regimes—the so-called "near enemy"—were not inherently strong themselves but rather were made strong by a "far enemy": the United States. As if to underline the point of American omnipotence in the Middle East in the victorious aftermath of the Cold War, US military forces continued to expand their regional footprint in the years after 1990, serving as a praetorian guard for apostate regimes, in Bin Laden's view. If jihadis focused their attention on driving the United States from the Middle East and the broader Muslim world, he argued, the apostate regimes would lose the source of their strength and be much easier to defeat in the future. Thus was born the second wave of global jihad.

THE LIFE OF USAMA BIN LADEN

Usama Bin Muhammad Bin Laden was born in Riyadh in 1957 to the most important construction magnate in Saudi Arabia.[11] His father, Muhammad Bin Laden, was a Yemeni raised in the Hadramawt region of southeastern Yemen, who had sought his fortune as a young man by moving to Saudi Arabia. In 1930, the elder Bin Laden started his own construction company—today known as the Saudi Binladin Group, a multi-billion-dollar firm—and through serendipity caught the attention of the founder of Saudi Arabia, King Abdulaziz Ibn Saud. As an outsider in the Kingdom, Bin Laden was quite vulnerable, so he built a reputation for extreme loyalty to the House of Saud. He was rewarded with monopoly contracts that eventually encompassed much of what became modern Saudi Arabia, particularly in Mecca and Jedda. The Bin Laden family grew to be among the richest families in Saudi Arabia outside of the ruling monarchy.

Usama Bin Laden's mother, Alia Ghanem, was equally unusual for Saudi society: she was an 'Alawi Muslim who grew up in Latakia, on Syria's Mediterranean coast. Pious Sunni Muslims—which, by all accounts, described Muhammad Bin Laden—typically view the Shia offshoot 'Alawi sect as heretical, in particular for their veneration of 'Ali, the son-in-law of the prophet Muhammad and the fourth caliph of the Sunni Muslim community. 'Alawis spent centuries holed up in the mountains west of Aleppo avoiding persecution by the dominant Sunnis within the Ottoman Empire and developing their own folk religious traditions along the way. For a pious Sunni to marry an 'Alawi was extremely uncommon, as it remains rare even today.[12]

Usama Bin Laden's 'Alawi connection strengthened further with his marriage at the age of seventeen to his mother's niece, Najwa Ghanem. There was nothing uncommon about him marrying his first cousin, which is the most widespread form of marriage in the Arab world. But again, as was the case for his father, it was unusual for a relatively pious young man like Usama Bin Laden to marry an 'Alawi. At the risk of getting ahead of our story, it is worth mentioning that, unlike most of his Salafi jihadi peers, Usama Bin Laden did not share an open, visceral hatred of the Shia. It is common for Salafi jihadis, especially those from the greater Arabian Peninsula area, to demonize the Shia. For example, ISIS ideologues openly targeted the Shia in terror attacks in an attempt to launch a sectarian war in Iraq (see chapter 3 for more on the anti-Shia views of ISIS ideologues, including Abu Musab al-Zarqawi). Bin Laden, by contrast, did not demonize the Shia, although neither did he defend them. Part of Bin Laden's stance can be understood through his "America First" ideology, in which a sectarian war between Sunnis and Shia would undermine the goal of driving the United States out of the region and indeed could provide an excuse for the Americans to stay longer.

But part of Bin Laden's hesitancy to join the virulent anti-Shia diatribes issued by numerous Salafi jihadis must be understood through his family history, and the Shia roots of both his mother and his first wife. Bin Laden's parents divorced when Usama was only three years old; afterward, his father did not play a significant role in Usama's life (he died in a plane crash in 1967 when Usama was ten). Muhammad Bin Laden had fifty-four children with multiple wives, making it difficult for him to be too involved in one child's life. Rather, Usama was raised much more by his stepfather, Muhammad al-'Attas, who had worked with Muhammad Bin Laden and had been encouraged by him to marry Bin Laden's ex-wife.[13]

There is nothing in Usama Bin Laden's young life that would indicate a future of extreme violence. He was relatively studious and pious but not radical, and even after the divorce of his parents, he was raised in privilege as a member of the Bin Laden family. That began to change in the late 1970s when he went off to college at King Abdulaziz University in Jedda, in part because of what was happening in the region and inside Saudi Arabia at the time. As noted in chapter 1, the year 1979 was momentous in the Middle East, with the revolution in Iran, the armed seizure of the Grand Mosque in Mecca by Sunni jihadis, and the December invasion of Afghanistan by the Soviet Union. Also percolating in the region was the first round of the long Syrian civil war, which was of interest to Bin Laden given his mother's heritage.[14] The intellectual fervor in political circles at universities and salons in Saudi Arabia was intense, particularly given the seizure of the Grand Mosque, and was made even more so by the arrival of Abdullah 'Azzam from Jordan. Bin Laden and 'Azzam were reacquainted in Saudi Arabia in 1980, after having first met two years earlier in Indianapolis, Indiana.[15] The charismatic 'Azzam had a clear impact in the gradual radicalization of Usama Bin Laden, including Bin Laden's decision to quit university before he completed his degree to join the jihad in Afghanistan.

Bin Laden spent most of the 1980s shuttling between Saudi Arabia, Pakistan, and Afghanistan in furtherance of the Afghan jihad. He played two primary roles for the Afghan jihad: as fundraiser and as organizer. Because of his family name, Bin Laden knew most of the wealthy families in Saudi Arabia and many princes and others tied to the government, and he had a knack for raising monies for what was widely seen as a righteous cause. While 'Azzam was the great popularizer and ideologue of the Afghan jihad, Bin Laden was its most successful private fundraiser, helping to arrange for tens of millions of dollars to flow from the Arabian Peninsula in support of the Afghan jihad. Bin Laden was also an organizer for the Arab fighters who came to Afghanistan, helping to establish the Services Bureau (Maktab al-Khadamat), which assisted Arab fighters when they first arrived in Afghanistan in need of housing and assignments.

Bin Laden was apparently not much of a fighter himself. While there is some mystery surrounding his service in battle, given both the hagiographies of his supporters and the attacks against him by his detractors, it appears that Bin Laden only ever participated in one significant battle against Soviet forces in Afghanistan, which occurred in Jaji in 1986. His followers tell of Bin Laden fighting heroically to the point of near death, while his detractors say that Bin Laden admitted to having fainted early in the battle and not coming to his senses until after the Soviets had been driven back.[16] Usama Bin Laden came out of the victorious Afghan jihad a much-respected man in Saudi Arabia. Along with 'Azzam, he was widely viewed as one of the leading Arabs who had helped the Afghan mujahideen defeat the Soviet army in Afghanistan. For a year and a half, from the withdrawal of the Soviets from Afghanistan in February 1989 to Iraq's invasion of Kuwait in August 1990, Bin Laden's star shone brightly. He still showed no serious signs of political radicalism. The jihad in Afghanistan was an old-fashioned jihad that all Muslims could support: driving out a foreign invader from a Muslim country. Activism in support of the Afghan jihad very much fell within the bounds of orthodox Islam, where the Afghan jihad was greatly encouraged and supported, especially after it succeeded.

Bin Laden's evolution toward radicalism took a big step forward when Iraq invaded Kuwait on August 2, 1990. To be more precise, that step occurred when the Saudi government rejected his plea to bring in one hundred thousand jihadis from around the Arab world to drive Iraq out of Kuwait, instead choosing to bring in American and coalition forces to do the job. That rejection of 'Azzam's Jihadi International model was a breaking point for Bin Laden. He had spent the past several years hearing Ayman al-Zawahiri's argument about how the real enemy for Muslims was local apostate regimes who did the work of foreign powers and prevented the implementation of God's laws in the Muslim world. The path to building a true Islamic state lay in ridding the Muslim world of these "near enemies," these apostate regimes in Cairo, Riyadh, and elsewhere. Bin Laden had been on good terms with the Saudi regime throughout the Afghan jihad, which had made possible his fundraising prowess. But now he was seeing in person what Zawahiri had argued: the Saudi state preferred to invite the infidel Americans to protect it, rather than to rely on the righteous mujahideen.

Such a position was unfathomable to Bin Laden, and he quickly joined other Saudi Islamists in denouncing Riyadh's decision to rely on American forces. The early 1990s in Saudi Arabia became known as the *sahwa* (awakening), a time rife with Islamist demands on the Saudi royal family, most of which stemmed from the contentious decision to bring American forces into the heartland of Islam. The ruling family took a dim view of these demands, and many prominent Islamists, such as *shaykhs* Safar al-Hawali and Salman al-'Awda, were sent to prison for their criticism of Saudi policies. While Hawali and 'Awda did not explicitly call for the overthrow of the Saudi regime, others did. Bin Laden was close to two such organizations, both of which reemerged in London in 1994 after being expelled from Saudi Arabia: the Committee for Advice and Reform (Hayat al-Nasiha w'al-Islah), which Bin Laden helped form along with Khalid al-Fawwaz, and the Committee for the Defense of Legitimate Rights (CDLR, or Lajnat al-Difa' 'an al-Huquq al-Shar'iyya), led by Muhammad al-Mas'ari.[17] Both groups were active in faxing letters of opposition to Saudi Arabia and in popularizing Islamist dissent in Saudi Arabia to the English-speaking world.

From 1990 to 1993, Bin Laden took care with his words when giving public speeches in Saudi Arabia and Yemen (a favorite cause), but by 1994 this diplomatic restraint was replaced by open dissent against the Saudi regime.[18] A major development in breaking Bin Laden's relative restraint toward the Saudi regime was the civil war in Yemen in 1994 and the subsequent Saudi support for the (southern) Yemeni Socialist Party, one of the last Communist parties left in the Middle East. The Yemen civil war and perceived Saudi duplicity against Muslims featured prominently in the critical messages being faxed frequently by the Bin Laden–backed CDLR in 1994.[19] Bin Laden's criticism of the Saudis was fierce enough that Saudi Arabia took the unusual step of stripping him of his citizenship in 1994; this also stripped Bin Laden of much of his wealth, which was still tied up in Saudi Arabia. What wealth that remained, Bin Laden took with him to Sudan, where he lived full-time from 1994 until his return to Afghanistan in May 1996. While in Sudan, Bin Laden remained vocal in his criticism of the Saudis. He took an interest in jihadi activities in neighboring Somalia and Yemen in the early 1990s, although it seems apparent he later exaggerated his participation in those events.

From 1990 to 1996, it is fair to say that Bin Laden entered into a second stage in his evolution as a jihadi, to a believer in the "near enemy" theory of jihad, which held that the primary problem Muslims faced was the existence of apostate regimes in their own lands. Zawahiri's argument had hit home, finally, and 'Azzam's warning against such a position was forgotten. But it is important to also remember that a "near enemy" understanding of jihad is essentially a rejection of global jihad, since it is a parochial view of jihad as regime change at home and lacks the international component necessary for global jihad. This is why I argue that, from the withdrawal of Soviet forces from Afghanistan in 1989 to Bin Laden's Declaration of War in 1996 (discussed further below), there was no significant movement for global jihad anywhere in the Muslim world. There were plenty of local jihads during this time, but no serious movement or organization with a specific globalist ideology and agenda.

Bending to international pressure, Sudan expelled Usama Bin Laden in 1996, although not before confiscating much of his remaining fortune. Contrary to oft-repeated mythology, Bin Laden went to Afghanistan with little money left to his name. He spent the remainder of his life in Afghanistan and Pakistan. He relaunched al-Qa'ida from Afghanistan, but this time with a clear global jihad mandate. Al-Qa'ida gained notoriety in 1998 with the bombings of American embassies in East Africa and reached the apex of its infamy three years later, with the terror attacks in the United States on September 11, 2001.

In December 2001, Bin Laden barely escaped with his life when he was trapped by attacking American forces in Tora Bora, Afghanistan. But the strategically inexplicable diversion of American resources at that time for the brewing invasion of Iraq likely allowed him to escape both Afghanistan and justice. It appears that Bin Laden spent the next five years primarily in Waziristan, in the Federally Administered Tribal Areas (FATA) of Pakistan. The writ of government is weak in the FATA lands, and during Bin Laden's many years in Afghanistan, he had built a network of tribal Pashtun supporters, which allowed him to escape easy detection. In 2006 he moved with his family to a comfortable compound in Abbottabad, Pakistan, just a few miles from the Pakistan Military Academy. It is implausible that Bin Laden did not have the protection of some powerful actors within the Pakistan military's ISI (Inter-Services Intelligence) during his five-year stay in central Pakistan. On May 2, 2011, he was killed in his Abbottabad compound by commandoes from the US Navy SEALs, bringing to an effective close the second wave of global jihad.

THE NEAR ENEMY–FAR ENEMY DEBATE

In his 1979 manifesto to fellow Egyptian jihadis, Muhammad 'Abd al-Salam Faraj warned against wasting precious resources on fighting Israel. Any attack against Israel would be made much more difficult by the existence of apostate regimes in the Levant who would seek to prevent such actions, he argued, and in any case, if the jihadis somehow succeeded in such endeavors, the apostate regimes would be the ones who would claim credit for any victory. It was far more important to focus the jihadis' limited resources on overthrowing the apostate regimes first; only then would the liberation of Jerusalem be possible. To make his case, Faraj invented the duality of a "far enemy" (*'adu ba'id*) and a "near enemy" (*'adu qarib*). The far enemy was Israel, a Crusader outpost that occupied Jerusalem and must be defeated eventually. But that jihad must wait, Faraj cautioned, until Cairo and the surrounding Arab states were governed according to God's law, by true Muslims, at which point victory over Israel and the liberation of Jerusalem would be assured. Reminiscent of the old Arab nationalist line from the 1960s, Faraj argued that the road to Jerusalem passed through Cairo first.[20]

As the founder and leader of the Egyptian group al-Jihad (of which Zawahiri was also a member), Faraj's argument carried significant weight in jihadi circles.[21] Al-Jihad's assassination of Egyptian president Anwar Sadat in 1981, for which Faraj was tried and executed, further strengthened the appeal of his argument. Indeed, Faraj's invented duality quickly became part of the standard discourse among jihadis, and his admonition to focus on local apostate regimes became their dominant logic. To be sure, Palestinian jihadis did not always agree, insisting that the liberation of Jerusalem should be the top priority, as Dr. Fathi al-Shiqaqi of the Palestinian Islamic Jihad argued.[22] But Faraj's (*takfiri*) argument to attack the near enemy, not the far enemy, prevailed throughout Arab jihadi circles for years—until Usama Bin Laden issued his Declaration of War in 1996. The Afghan jihad did not fall easily into Faraj's duality, as it was neither viewed as an attack on a far enemy nor the overthrow of a local Muslim apostate regime. Rather, Afghanistan was seen as a traditional jihad to expel a foreign invader from a Muslim country, not as an ideological crusade to defeat a new far enemy. After all, the mujahideen fought against Russian forces only in Afghanistan and did not pursue them to Moscow.

When Bin Laden rediscovered Faraj's argument in 1996, he turned it on its head. No longer should the dominant goal be to attack local apostate regimes, he argued; now, it should be to attack the far enemy whose support allowed the local regimes to survive. If the far enemy were removed from the picture, local apostate regimes would surely lose that which kept them in power and thus fall in the face of jihadi actions. No longer should the far enemy be understood to be Israel; now, it should be understood as the United States. Israel was merely a by-product of a far greater American enemy. It was America that had to be confronted first and foremost in Bin Laden's view.

BIN LADEN'S 1996 DECLARATION OF WAR

Bin Laden's shift to a "far enemy" jihad as seen in his 1996 Declaration needs to be understood in the context of events playing out in the Arabian Peninsula between 1990 and 1996. As noted above, Bin Laden was shocked when the Saudi state responded to Iraq's invasion of Kuwait by inviting in American forces. But two other changes of significance occurred. First, the American forces did not leave the region after the war was won in 1991. Prior to 1990, there was no permanent, large American military presence in the Persian Gulf. There had been episodic military cooperation by US forces—for example, with the "reflagging" of Kuwaiti oil tankers in 1987 that had allowed them free passage in the Gulf during the Iran-Iraq war. Iraq's invasion of Kuwait changed that, with five hundred thousand US troops sent to Saudi Arabia to lead the effort to liberate Kuwait. Although most US forces returned home after 1991, thousands stayed behind on the new military bases established in Saudi Arabia and Kuwait. In subsequent years, the United States established its Fifth Fleet headquarters in Manama, Bahrain, and stationed significant and permanent forces at new airbases in Qatar (Udayd) and the United Arab Emirates (Dhafra), among others.

This large expansion of the US military footprint in the Persian Gulf starting in 1990 was seen by Bin Laden (and other Arabs) as a new round of Western imperialism, designed to keep Muslims weak by taking their oil under the guise of security. To Bin Laden's way of thinking, this theft of Muslim resources was made possible by the quisling and apostate regimes in Riyadh and elsewhere. While Bin Laden was a religious man, he was also intensely political. The US military buildup in the Persian Gulf was tightly linked to the end of the Cold War and a historical unipolar moment for American power and muscle-flexing around the world.

The American military presence that remained behind after 1991 (and was built up around the Gulf) had as its primary mission the containment of Saddam Husayn's regime following its defeat in the 1991 war. That containment centered on enforcing a harsh sanctions regime on Iraq that had been adopted just days after Iraq's invasion of Kuwait. The sanctions were not lifted after Iraq's military defeat in 1991, instead being kept in place to gain leverage on Saddam's regime. The sanctions regime was another factor that caused Bin Laden to shift to the strategy of a far-enemy jihad. The sanctions regime, which became part of the Clinton administration's notorious "dual containment" policy, caused a humanitarian disaster in Iraq. For all the talk of "smart sanctions," these sanctions were in fact a blunt instrument that mostly impacted Iraqi society. UNICEF calculates that the sanctions caused an increase in child mortality in Iraq of five hundred thousand from 1991 through 1998.[23] According to some sources, UNICEF's numbers may have actually been too conservative.[24]

Either way, while the humanitarian crisis in Iraq that the sanctions caused received periodic coverage in the United States, it was daily headlines in the Arab world. When the Al-Jazeera satellite television station was established in 1996, the crisis in Iraq regularly led its daily news broadcasts. From many different news sources at the beginning of an information revolution in the Middle East, Arabs were reminded daily of the suffering occurring in Iraq as a result of American-led sanctions. Thus, as Bin Laden surveyed the landscape of his home region from his new abode in Afghanistan in August 1996, he saw a region worse off than it had been a decade earlier. In his view a man-made humanitarian catastrophe in Iraq was being enforced by American military power that had become entrenched in the Persian Gulf region following the 1991 war. This catastrophe was made possible by local apostate regimes more concerned about their own survival than about the welfare of Muslims. In addition, Bin Laden saw friendly jihad movements on the defensive and facing defeat, most especially in Egypt and Algeria. In this context, he issued his 1996 "Declaration of Jihad Against the American Occupiers of the Land of the Two Holy Mosques: Expel the Polytheists from the Arab Peninsula."[25]

It is often said, incorrectly, that Bin Laden's 1996 document was a *fatwa* (religious opinion). It was not. Bin Laden initially presented the document as a speech given in August 1996 in the Hindu Kush region of Afghanistan, after which it was distributed on audiocassettes and ultimately transcribed and translated by various authors, most notably by Bin Laden ally Muhammad al-Mas'ari of the CDLR in London. Nowhere on the audiocassettes or in the various Arabic transcriptions does Bin Laden claim to be issuing a *fatwa*. Given his lack of religious credentials, it would have been an outrageous act for him to have done so. The Mas'ari transcription, upon which I rely, and from which all the quotes in this section are taken, uses the term *'i'lan* (declaration) in the title and then below says it is a *risala* (letter or epistle) from Usama bin Muhammad bin Laden, with no clerical credentialing claimed. The various transcriptions and translations of his declaration have not been consistent in what they include and exclude, with some excising thousands of words.[26]

Bin Laden's 1996 declaration is much longer than most of his other pronouncements over his last fifteen years of life, when he seemed to have learned the benefit of brevity when it comes to marketing and recruitment. But he had not yet learned that lesson in his 1996 speech, in which he attempted to make a complete case, with full Qur'anic justification, for his campaign of guerilla violence. Bin Laden made three broad arguments in this declaration: first, that fighting against the Americans was a necessary defense as they were engaging in a war against Islam; second, that the "near enemy" Saudi regime had lost any legitimacy it ever had and must be replaced by a true Islamic state; and third, this was not a fool's errand, as both the Americans and the Saudis had shown their weakness and could be, in fact, defeated. I'll deal with each of these points in turn.

For Bin Laden, the United States was leading a global war against Islam by plundering Islam's resources and killing Muslims. The "Jewish-Christian alliance and their collaborators" had spilt Muslim blood around the world because Muslim blood had become "cheap," and Muslim wealth and assets had been "looted at the hands of their enemies." The list of Muslim lands where the Americans and their allies were on the rampage is long. He wrote in the declaration:

> [Muslim] blood was spilled in Palestine and Iraq . . . and in Lebanon. Massacres took place in Tajikistan, Burma, Kashmir, Assam, the Philippines, Fattani [southern Thailand], Ogaden [Somali region of Ethiopia], Somalia, Eritrea, and Bosnia-Herzegovina. Massacres of Muslims that sent shivers down the body and shook the conscience. . . . A conspiracy between America and its allies prevented the weak from acquiring arms to defend themselves, using the United Nations as cover. Muslims became aware that they were the main target of the Jewish-Crusader alliance of aggression. The false human rights propaganda vanished under the weight of massacres committed against Muslims everywhere. And now, the most recent aggression is the worst catastrophe inflicted upon Muslims since the death of the Prophet: that is, the occupation by the American Christian army and their allies of the land of the two holy mosques, the cradle of Islam, the place of the Ka'ba.

Bin Laden concluded that "driving back the American occupier enemy is the most essential duty for Muslims after faith itself.... Clearly, after belief, there is no more important duty than pushing the American enemy out of the holy land."

But this was not, strictly speaking, a "far enemy" document. Bin Laden reserved equal disdain for the Saudi monarchy and the quisling Muslim clerics who allow the monarchy to run roughshod over Islam. He pointed to the "corruption, repression and intimidation taking place in the country," and how Saudi princes quarreling over personal interests and profit "have destroyed the country." The declaration said:

> Through its actions, the regime has ripped asunder its legitimacy to rule. It has suspended God's law and replaced it with man-made law, thereby inviting bloody confrontation with devoted scholars and righteous youth. No one is above God. And the regime has failed to protect the country, allowing enemy Crusader-American forces to occupy our land for years, which has been a disaster in every respect.... The regime permitted the crusaders to enter the land of the two holy mosques. The king himself wore the Christian cross. The land was filled with American and allied military bases. The regime was unable to keep control of the country without the help of these bases. The regime betrayed the country and joined the infidels in working against Muslims.

Bin Laden detailed all the efforts by righteous Muslims to warn the regime against its perilous course of action—essentially, the *sahwa*, or awakening of the early 1990s—but to no avail. The Saudi monarchy ignored all such entreaties. Although Bin Laden's wrath was directed at the Saudi royal family in particular, he continued, by implication, his attacks on the top levels of state clergy in Saudi Arabia, including Shaykh Abdalaziz Bin Baz who as the Grand Mufti at the time was Saudi Arabia's top cleric. Bin Laden had previously written two open letters to Bin Baz, in 1994 and 1995, in which he criticized Bin Baz both for specific items in *fatwas* he had issued but more critically on his failure to keep the Saudi regime on an Islamic path. In the 1996 declaration, Bin Laden referenced his earlier criticisms by noting the *fatwa* that Bin Baz had authored allowing American troops inside Saudi Arabia, which had been based on "lies" told him by the king.

While the principal exercise in Bin Laden's 1996 declaration was to attack in equal measure both the United States and the Saudi regime—the far and near enemies, respectively—and call for an armed insurrection to remove both, Bin Laden also tried to assure his followers that this was not an exercise in futility. The Americans cut and run at the slightest defeat, he wrote, recounting the deaths of 241 US Marines in Beirut in 1983 that led to a quick US withdrawal of troops from Lebanon. He further noted a 1992 hotel bombing in Aden, Yemen, that "compelled [the United States] to leave Aden within 24 hours," and the 1993 Black Hawk Down events in Somalia, "when dozens of your troops were killed in minor battles, and one American pilot was dragged through the streets of Mogadishu, you left the area defeated, carrying your dead in disappointment and humiliation." Bin Laden believed that, given the Americans' low tolerance for casualties, a war against them was a winnable endeavor.

Some final comments should be made regarding Bin Laden's perspective on Palestine and Iraq as expressed in his 1996 declaration. Some pamphleteers have tried to make the case that Bin Laden had no concern for the plight of Palestinians until he had to sell the 9/11 terror attacks to a broader Muslim audience. This is simply false. As it does for many Arabs and Muslims, the Palestine issue clearly weighed significantly for Bin Laden from his early days, and the 1996 document contains many references to it, as did earlier statements of Bin Laden. Palestine may not have been as important as the American "occupation" of the holy land of Mecca and Medina, but it was a serious issue for Bin Laden that demonstrated more than most issues the humiliations that the Palestinians—and thus all Muslims—were enduring at the hands of the "Jewish-Christian coalition." As well, a good deal of this long document was devoted to the plight of Iraq at the hands of the Americans during the 1990s, when the American-led sanctions regime caused a grave humanitarian calamity. Bin Laden was preaching to the choir, as it were, as revulsion at Iraqi suffering under American-enforced UN sanctions was widely shared in the Arab world.

Usama Bin Laden's 1996 declaration was a bright signal that global jihad was back on the agenda, with an armed insurrection against America and its allies the primary step needed to weaken the Saudi regime and other apostate governments. But in some ways, it was only half a step toward an "America First" global jihad position, as Bin Laden saved equal venom for the Saudi regime. Logically, both enemies cannot be foundational problems at the same time: one must cause the other, as the disease must cause the symptom. The

1996 declaration conflated the disease with the symptom and was thus not logically consistent. It would be nearly two more years before Bin Laden sorted out the causal chain, and then he unambiguously viewed the Saudi regime as simply a subset of the larger problem of America. But the 1996 declaration marks the beginning of the idea of a second wave of global jihad.

THE 1998 FATWA AND THE LAUNCH OF THE SECOND WAVE OF GLOBAL JIHAD

If the much longer 1996 declaration of war had one foot each in the near enemy and far enemy camps, Bin Laden's 1998 *fatwa* was unequivocally a far-enemy document, and within weeks of its issuance the "America First" campaign of violence of the second wave of global jihad commenced. The *fatwa* is a remarkable document in several ways. First, it is plainly labeled as a *fatwa* and has the stylistic characteristics associated with the issuance of a religious opinion. Its first author (of five) is listed as *shaykh* Usama bin Muhammad bin Laden, which ascribes religious credentials to Bin Laden that he did not have.[27] Not only had Bin Laden never received an advanced degree in Islamic jurisprudence or theology, he had never even finished college. To take on the honorific of a religious *shaykh* was a case of false advertising, and it generated a lot of blowback from Muslims who criticized Bin Laden for pretending to have such credentials.[28] While Bin Laden's followers often referred to him as *shaykh*, Bin Laden himself would never again ascribe those credentials to himself on his public pronouncements.

The substance of the *fatwa* concisely made the case for a far-enemy understanding of the underlying problem facing Muslims. It read:

> For more than seven years the United States has been occupying the lands of Islam in the holiest of places, the Arabian Peninsula, plundering its riches, dictating to its rulers, humiliating its people, terrorizing its neighbors, and turning its bases in the Peninsula into a beachhead through which to fight neighboring Muslim peoples ... America's occupation of the Peninsula allows for its continued aggression against the Iraqi people, even though all the local rulers are against their territories being used for that end, but they are helpless. The Crusader-Zionist alliance has devastated the Iraqi people, killing more than one million, and imposed a protracted blockade after its ferocious war of fragmentation and devastation. This alliance seeks to annihilate what is left of the Iraqi

people and to humiliate their Muslim neighbors. The Americans also aim to serve the Jews' petty state and divert attention from its occupation of Jerusalem and its murder of Muslims there. The best proof of this is America's eagerness to destroy Iraq—the strongest neighboring Arab state—and to fragment all the states of the region such as Iraq, Saudi Arabia, Egypt, and Sudan into paper statelets and through their disunion and weakness to guarantee Israel's survival and the continuation of the brutal crusader occupation of the Peninsula.[29]

In this telling, it is the far enemy—the United States—that is the source of Muslim discontent. No longer is the Saudi regime or any other apostate near-enemy regime equally responsible for these travails. Rather, they are now powerless to stop the American occupation and aggression; they merely get told what to do. In addition, America is simultaneously doing its own bidding and covering for Israel's occupation of Jerusalem. So although Israel, the "petty state of the Jews," is part of the problem, it is not a case of the tail wagging the dog. For Bin Laden, Israel is seen as another symptom of the larger disease, which is the American war against Muslims and Islam itself. Israel is merely a junior partner in this coalition, like other states under US control.

Bin Laden's strategic world view can be compared to the old children's Bobo Doll punching bag toy, consisting of a plastic air-filled clown, about a meter tall, roughly in the shape of a bowling pin that was kept upright by a weighted bottom. When a child punched the Bobo Doll, it would lean way over, but the weight in the bottom would force it upright, again and again. For Bin Laden, jihadis could keep punching the Bobo Doll—the near-enemy apostate regime—and it would wobble and lean, but it would always bounce back up. If the weight were removed from the foot of the doll—if the far enemy's support were removed from the regime—then when jihadis punched the regime, it would fall over and not get up. Without that external support keeping them upright, apostate regimes would be much easier targets for overthrow.

Because all of the "crimes committed by the Americans are a clear declaration of war on God," Bin Laden's *fatwa* called on all Muslims "to kill Americans and their allies, civilian and military, in any country in which it is feasible." Following his call, Muslims would liberate the holy mosques in Jerusalem and Mecca and "will force their armies out from all the lands of Islam, defeated and unable to threaten Muslims again." In addition to starkly laying out Bin

Laden's logic for an America First strategy, this *fatwa* was a clarion call for mass murder, explicitly calling for the killing of American civilians wherever it is feasible, without exception. Thus Bin Laden and his colleagues swept away centuries of Muslim thinking on just-war theory, including what constituted a legitimate target during combat and what did not. By contrast, even 'Abdullah 'Azzam, as a trained cleric, took pains to distinguish legitimate targets from illegitimate ones. For Bin Laden, any American, young or old, male or female, able-bodied or not, was a legitimate target. Not only that, killing Americans was a *fard 'ayn*, or obligatory, for every able-bodied Muslim—at least, if one followed the advice of Usama Bin Laden.

The radicalism of this text is apparent, but it was also shrewdly constructed. By comparison to the 1996 document, the *fatwa* was concise and short, to the point, and with an eye toward broad appeal. It focused on three broadly known issues that resonated in the Arab and Muslim worlds: the "occupation" of the Arabian Peninsula by US military forces, the devastation of Iraq under a sanctions regime, and Israel's occupation of Islam's third holiest mosque. These were all widely known issues in the Arab and Muslim worlds, and most Arabs and Muslims would be generally sympathetic to Bin Laden's critique. That does not mean most Arabs and Muslims were keen to sign up for Bin Laden's cause— very few were—but his marketing of the message was far shrewder than his previous attempts. For example, the details found in the 1996 document about which Saudis had been arrested or criticized were largely unknown outside of fairly narrow Saudi circles; most Muslims did not know those details and did not care about them. But the American military "occupation" (*ihtilal*) of Arabia, the human suffering seen daily in Iraq, and the plight of the Palestinians were issues that were widely known and cared about around the Muslim world. Even if it did not generate lots of new recruits, the 1998 *fatwa* was a giant step up in the marketing of Bin Laden's global jihad message.

The 1998 *fatwa* effectively announced a merger between the remnants of Egypt's al-Jihad al-Islami group under Zawahiri (those who had not been killed or imprisoned by the time of the 1997 ceasefire) and Bin Laden's now reborn al-Qa'ida group. At this point, al-Qa'ida was still more of an idea than a force with operational capabilities, although Bin Laden had recently revamped training camps in Afghanistan to provide some capabilities to his new force.[30] Of the two groups, only Zawahiri's had the ability to carry out significant acts of violence in 1998. However, by deciding to link up with Bin Laden, whose primary focus was on attacking the United States, Zawahiri actually weakened his group's ability to carry out terror attacks, as most Egyptian al-Jihad members thought this new mission was a mistake and wanted to remain focused on Egypt's situation. Only a portion of al-Jihad followed Zawahiri on the global jihad path and those cadres, combined with Bin Laden's recruits to al-Qa'ida, hardly made for much of a fighting force.

It was those members of al-Jihad who had chosen to join Zawahiri in his merger with al-Qa'ida who were principally responsible for carrying out the initial "America First" attack in the second wave of global jihad. On August 7, 1998, truck bombs were set off in front of the US embassies in Nairobi, Kenya, and Dar es Salaam, Tanzania, killing 224 people and seriously injuring many hundreds more. Most of the deaths occurred in Nairobi, and the vast majority of those killed and injured were local Africans and Muslims, not Americans: only 12 of the 224 killed were Americans. In response to these 1998 attacks, the United States launched cruise missiles into Bin Laden's training camps in Afghanistan, although these still-small sites were not target-rich environments at the time, and Bin Laden was put on America's most-wanted list.

The newly revived al-Qa'ida, based in Afghanistan and hosted by the Taliban regime that had gained control of most of the country by 1996, began training hundreds of young men, mostly Arabs, who wanted to join this emerging "America First" global jihad. Planning for new attacks began as well, including a series of attacks to take place on or around January 1, 2000, known as the Millennium attacks. While grandiose in scope, these attacks ended up being duds, as they were all compromised before they could take effect. The planned attacks included a bombing of Los Angeles Airport by Ahmed Ressam, an Algerian living in Montreal, who was discovered and captured with explosives in his possession while trying to cross into Port Angeles, Washington, from Canada; a series of attacks on tourist areas in Jordan that were foiled by Jordanian authorities; and the planned sinking of the USS *The Sullivans* while it was refueling in Aden, Yemen. In that last case the attack boat was overladen with explosives and sank before it could reach its target.

While al-Qa'ida's Millennium attacks did not go as planned, the global jihadi group pressed on with its vision to attack American targets. Months after comically failing to sink the USS *The Sullivans* in the Aden harbor, the same plot exactly was carried out in October 2000 with tragic success against the USS *Cole*, which, like *The Sullivans*, was also making a port visit in Aden. This time the small attack boat, which was not overloaded to the point of sinking, came astride the *Cole* and blew a large hole in its side. Seventeen American sailors were killed in the attack. Most of those involved in the attack on the *Cole* were subsequently killed or arrested, including 'Abd al-Rahim al-Nashiri, the alleged mastermind of the attack, who has been held by US forces since 2002, mostly at Guantanamo Bay, Cuba.

9/11: THE APEX OF THE SECOND WAVE

Al-Qa'ida's four-pronged attack on the United States on September 11, 2001, was the deadliest attack on US soil since Japan bombed Pearl Harbor in 1941.[31] Four commercial airplanes, all chock-full of fuel as they were bound for California, were hijacked shortly after take-off from airports on the East Coast of the United States. Nineteen hijackers in all participated, fifteen of whom came from Saudi Arabia.[32] Two planes rammed into the World Trade Center's Twin Towers; a third hit the Pentagon; the fourth, on its way to hitting the Capitol building in Washington, DC, crashed in Shanksville, Pennsylvania, apparently as passengers tried to storm the cockpit after having heard on their cell phones about the other hijackings. Nearly three thousand people died during the attack, while others succumbed to their injuries in the months that followed. More than three hundred of the dead came from ninety countries around the world.

While Usama Bin Laden was the mastermind of the 9/11 attacks, Khalid Shaykh Muhammad was their principal architect. An ethnic Baluch from Pakistan, Muhammad was raised in Kuwait and went to college in North Carolina, where he earned a degree in mechanical engineering in 1986. The following year, he went to fight in Afghanistan, ending up in a camp run by 'Abdullah 'Azzam. Muhammad's radicalization appears to have occurred slowly over time and, by his own admission, his animus against the United States was driven not so much by his personal experience in the United States as by American policy toward Israel.[33] His nephew, Ramzi Yousef, was a chief conspirator in the 1993 attack on the World Trade Center, and both men were involved in planning the unsuccessful 1995 Bojinka plot designed to hijack and blow up multiple large airliners leaving Asia over the Pacific Ocean. There was a clear fascination in the family with using airplanes as weapons and with attacking the World Trade Center.

Without demeaning the gravity of the 9/11 terror attack, it must be noted just how lucky al-Qa'ida had to have been in order to succeed that day. Many red flags needed to have been missed, ignored, or downplayed at many levels, from everyday police and intelligence officials to President Bush himself, who was given a Presidential Daily Brief on August 6, 2001, titled "Bin Laden determined to attack inside the US" and that described "patterns of suspicious activities in this country consistent with preparations for hijackings." The report went on to detail multiple al-Qa'ida attempts to sneak operatives into the United States intent on carrying out attacks, al-Qa'ida's determination to hijack airplanes inside the United States, and the approximately seventy FBI investigations going on in 2001 regarding possible al-Qa'ida terror operations inside the United States.[34] Had the White House taken this warning seriously, had any of those seventy FBI investigations found smoking gun evidence that was acted upon, had any of the hijackers let slip what they were up to (as criminals often do) in a way that was acted upon by law enforcement—had any of these things happened, the 9/11 terror attacks would likely have been foiled, just as the Millennium attacks had been foiled a year earlier. The terror attacks of 9/11 were an audacious, if evil, sucker punch that found its target due to a wealth of dumb luck.

The attacks that fall morning represented the apex of the second wave of global jihad. Within months, what came to be called "al-Qa'ida Central" had been largely destroyed, al-Qa'ida's sanctuary in Afghanistan overrun by US and coalition forces, its protectors the Taliban ousted from power, and its leadership dead, captured, or in hiding. For Americans, the second wave of global jihad will likely always be the most haunting because of all those lives lost on 9/11 and the horrific video of planes ramming into buildings that then collapsed. But by most measures, the al-Qa'ida wave of global jihad was the shortest and in many ways the weakest of all the four waves, save for that tragic day in September.

THE DEFEAT OF AL-QA'IDA AND THE "AMERICA FIRST" IDEA

While the top two leaders of al-Qa'ida, Usama Bin Laden and Ayman al-Zawahiri, survived the destruction of al-Qa'ida's operation in Afghanistan, many of its other top officials did not, either being killed in American operations or captured (often by Pakistani forces) and handed over to US troops. Top jihadi ideologue Abu Musab al-Suri, who himself was captured in 2005 in Pakistan (see chapter 4 for more on Suri), wrote in his massive 2004 online book, *The Call for Global Islamic Resistance*, about the scope of destruction of al-Qa'ida after 2001, which was, according to Suri, much more extensive than even the Americans appreciated. By 2003 or so, al-Qa'ida central—the physical organization run by Bin Laden first in Afghanistan and then in hiding in Pakistan—had largely ceased to operate beyond occasional letters (often seeking money) ferried about by couriers, or clandestine statements or videos issued through al-Sahab media, al-Qa'ida's in-house brand. For statements in English, al-Qa'ida usually turned to Adam Gadahn, a convert to Islam who hailed from California.[35]

While al-Qa'ida central was largely defeated by 2003 or so, a shell of its organization continued as long as Usama Bin Laden was alive.[36] When Bin Laden was killed by US Navy SEALs in 2011, the organization was left in the hands of Ayman al-Zawahiri, a toxic and polarizing figure even within the jihadi community. But for a number of years, al-Qa'ida *as an idea* had been kept alive by affiliated groups around the region, most notably in Yemen. Given the Bin Laden family's connection to Yemen and, more important, the lack of effective governance in the country that allowed criminal and other nonstate organizations to prosper, the emergence of an al-Qa'ida franchise there was not surprising. What came to be known starting in 2009 as al-Qa'ida in the Arabian Peninsula, or AQAP (Tanzim al-Qa'ida fi Jazirat al-'Arab), was essentially a merger of local, Yemeni jihadis and those from Saudi Arabia who had fled when Riyadh undertook a serious crackdown on its own jihadi problem.[37] Both the Saudi and the Yemeni jihadis shared Bin Laden's antipathy toward the United States and thus adopted his "America First" ideology. Indeed, AQAP attempted several attacks on American targets, most notably the failed airline bombing over Detroit by the so-called "underwear bomber," 'Umar Faruq 'Abd al-Mutallab, on Christmas day in 2009. A year later, two bombs in cargo planes bound for the United States were discovered and dismantled before they could go off.

As the Arab Spring events in Yemen in 2011 devolved into civil war, AQAP largely reverted to a local jihadi group and mostly left the global jihad business. Following the chaos that ensued with the breakdown of the Yemeni state,

AQAP sought to control local territory in parts of Yemen, particularly in the south. As well, some of AQAP's most outspoken leaders in favor of global jihad were killed in American drone strikes, including top ideologue and propagandist to the English-speaking world Anwar al-Awlaki in 2011. As the breakdown of the Yemeni state transitioned into a full-on civil war by 2015, AQAP further morphed into a sectarian jihadi force, often working in (uncoordinated) parallel with the Saudis and Emiratis (and, by extension, the United States, even though drone strikes continued against AQAP targets) fighting Shia Houthi rebels who had taken control over parts of Yemen, including the capital Sana'a.[38] Although it is conceivable that AQAP may once again rediscover its core far-enemy ideology, those days appear to be long gone by now, and most of its leaders who espoused it are dead.[39]

There are other self-declared al-Qa'ida affiliates, none of whom carry with them the core "America First" ideology that distinguished al-Qa'ida and Usama Bin Laden from other jihadi groups. Rather, these are all jihadi groups fighting local battles but who found political or marketing advantage in declaring allegiance to al-Qa'ida. The Nusra Front (Jabhat al-Nusra, but which routinely reinvents itself with new names) was founded by ISIS in 2012 during the civil war in Syria, but the leader of Nusra, Abu Muhammad al-Jawlani, found it politically useful to declare allegiance to al-Qaida in 2013. He found ISIS wanted to micromanage the affairs of Nusra, but al-Qa'ida, being the weak shell of an organization it was, provided Jawlani a great deal more organizational autonomy. A similar story can be found in al-Shabaab, the Somali jihadi group. Its pledge of allegiance to al-Qa'ida in 2012 appears to have been a marketing and fundraising gimmick, where there is no actual command and control by al-Qa'ida in its operations. The al-Qa'ida affiliate in Algeria, al-Qa'ida in the Islamic Maghrib (AQIM), evolved over time to little more than a small criminal enterprise that raises money through kidnapping ransoms and drugs.[40] In 2014, Zawahiri announced the creation of al-Qa'ida in the Indian Subcontinent (AQIS), but this appears to have been more of a publicity exercise in relevance than the creation of an actual global jihad group on the ground.

In reality, after the death of Usama Bin Laden, the near destruction of al-Qa'ida central, and the morphing of previous affiliates into local jihad groups (to the degree those affiliates ever seriously espoused an "America First" strategy), there remained no more "America First" global jihad groups. The second wave of global jihad had largely come to an end. But with the demise of the second wave of global jihad in the years following its apex in 2001, two distinctive new forms of global jihad emerged essentially simultaneously. In particular, the third wave of global jihad, the ISIS caliphate wave, emerged as a far more powerful form of global jihad than the second wave ever was.

EVALUATING THE SECOND WAVE OF GLOBAL JIHAD

The enormous death and destruction witnessed by the world on September 11, 2001, belie the underlying reality that the second wave of global jihad was the smallest, weakest, and shortest-lived of any of the four waves. Al-Qa'ida's stature came more from its bloody sucker punch on 9/11 than from any inherent organizational strength or ideological appeal. At their height, al-Qa'ida and Usama Bin Laden had a run of fewer than four years, from the bombing of the US embassies in East Africa that began the "America First" violence in 1998, to their audacious and successful act of terror in the fall of 2001. During its heyday, al-Qa'ida could count its fighters in the thousands but not the tens of thousands. It recruited only a fraction of the fighters that ISIS brought in shortly after the demise of al-Qa'ida, and neither did al-Qa'ida come close to matching the ten thousand foreign fighters 'Abdullah 'Azzam and the first wave of global jihad had recruited to Afghanistan (although, in fairness, few of those fighters would have considered themselves part of any Jihadi International).

Even the collection of al-Qa'ida franchises often reflected the weakness of al-Qa'ida as much as the strength. It was precisely because of the lack of command and control that al-Qa'ida exercised over its franchises that Nusra, Shabaab, and others signed on. It could be good marketing, represent a better chance to raise money, and be affiliated with the deadliest terror strike in history, but nobody who affiliated with al-Qa'ida wanted to cede actual decision-making to Bin Laden or Zawahiri—and they didn't.

Why, then, was this second wave of global jihad so weak, unable to gain significant traction among the true believers in jihad, by comparison to the other three waves? The answer lies with the fundamental enterprise of Usama Bin Laden: attack America first and foremost. Even among jihadis, this goal was extremely controversial and some, like Abu Musab al-Suri, thought it bordered on the absurd (see chapter 4). It was an illusory aspiration, akin to a search for El Dorado, that simply did not appeal to very many young Muslim men. The liberation of occupied Muslim lands, or the rebuilding of the Muslim caliphate—or even an old-fashioned sectarian jihad against perceived Shia usurpers—these are the kinds of causes that can appeal to far more young Muslim men than a fantasy enterprise to take down the world's strongest military power. A far more appealing cause emerged with the destruction of the Iraqi state and the outbreak of civil war in Syria: an Islamic state and the reconstitution of the Muslim caliphate. Now that was a sexy cause that got people's attention! The third wave of global jihad was about to begin.

Chapter 3

CALIPHATE NOW!
2003–2017

THE SECOND WAVE OF GLOBAL JIHAD WAS LARGELY DESTROYED by 2003, with the remnant of al-Qa'ida central slowly petering out until the killing of Usama Bin Laden in 2011. By then, even the various al-Qa'ida franchises had switched from a far-enemy strategy (to the degree they ever bought into it) to fighting local regimes, or getting into profitable criminal activities instead. But even as the second wave of global jihad was dying out, a third wave was born from the US invasion of Iraq in 2003. The third wave of global jihad, embodied by ISIS, was starkly different from the first two. Instead of focusing on liberating occupied Muslim lands or fighting America first, this wave concentrated on defeating apostasy through the building of a puritanical state in the heart of the Middle East. Although ISIS had a long list of goals, its primary mission was to create a pure shari'a-based state in which apostasy itself—not apostate regimes but individual sin and immorality—would never be a temptation, and a fully pious Muslim life would thus be possible. In an Augustinian sense, ISIS sought to build a ferocious City of Man so that a virtuous City of God could emerge. Like the Taliban, Boko Haram, or the Khmer Rouge (see chapter 5), ISIS considered the display of Western cultural influence to be a major indicator of potential apostasy and social contamination.

While the prevalence of apostasy was the general crisis that informed ISIS's ideology, the specific crises that enabled it to gain power and infamy were the

US invasion of Iraq in 2003 and the subsequent civil war in Syria, which began in 2011. In both cases, Sunni Arab rights and privileges were tested. ISIS was based overwhelmingly in Sunni Arab communities that felt persecuted by Shia-based regimes in Baghdad and Damascus. In the case of Iraq, people who are both Sunni by religious affiliation and Arab by ethnicity make up less than 20 percent of the population. But this minority had dominated Mesopotamia for centuries. From the Ottoman Empire, through the British and Hashemite eras, the turbulent decade following the nationalist revolution of 1958, and the reign of the Ba'th Party, which took power in 1968, virtually the entire political elite and much of the economic elite of Iraq came from this Sunni Arab minority. The core of this population lies in areas to the north and west of Baghdad, including Mosul, Tikrit, Fallujah, Ramadi, and, before 2003, about half of Baghdad itself.

Sunni Arab privilege in Iraq decisively ended with the American invasion in 2003. The Shia (who are mostly Arab ethnically) constitute a substantial majority of Iraq's population, perhaps as much as two-thirds.[1] It was the Shia community who disproportionately benefited from the American occupation. The Iraqi state transformed into a hegemonic and revivalist Shia enterprise, particularly under the rule of Nouri al-Maliki (2006–2014), marginalizing and alienating the Sunni Arab community. It was in this context—turmoil, war, occupation, loss of privilege, rising Shia power—that parts of the Sunni Arab community radicalized, with jihadism the major ideological beneficiary.[2] Indeed, the two years following the American invasion saw the generation and publication of some of the most extremist jihadi ideas ever written, with much of it coming out of the Iraq experience.

The Sunni Arab experience in Syria was much the same as it was in Iraq, albeit with some important differences. Sunni Arabs had dominated the lands of Syria (*bilad al-sham*) for centuries, under periods of Ottoman, French, and nationalist rule. But they lost their position of privilege in 1963, when the Ba'th party staged a military coup and took power. The Ba'th-military alliance was dominated by minority groups, especially the 'Alawi and Druze communities, who had joined the army in large numbers under French mandatory rule as a means of upward mobility from the rural poverty in which most lived. Throughout the 1960s, the 'Alawi and Druze worked together to remove leading Sunni figures from positions of power; then the Alawis turned on the Druze to seize the most critical levers of power for themselves.[3] Because the 'Alawi branch of Islam is derived from Shia Islam, most pious Sunnis do not view the 'Alawis as true Muslims.[4] This animosity was made worse by the fact that the 'Alawi-Ba'thist regime was secular in its policies, much to the chagrin of Sunni fundamentalists. Thus the regime, which had been dominated by the 'Alawi Asad family since 1970, was anti-Islamic in the eyes of pious Sunnis for two reasons: its Shia origins and its secular, non-shari'a–based rule.

The Arab Spring events in Tunisia and Egypt in late 2010 and early 2011 set off a chain reaction around much of the Arab world. In the case of Syria, it reignited a low-intensity civil war from thirty years earlier, when the Sunni Arab majority had attempted to overthrow the 'Alawi minority regime. This new round of civil war, which flared to life largely due to the government's preference to fight a hot military conflict rather than a political battle, gave the Sunni Arab majority a second opportunity to take power from the 'Alawis.[5] The Syrian regime made the decision to redeploy most of its forces from the Sunni Arab crescent in eastern and northern Syria to the critical Damascus-Aleppo-Latakia triangle in the western quarter of the country. Without holding this crucial triangle that connects the two largest cities in Syria, and each of them to the major port city on the Mediterranean, the Asad regime would likely have fallen. It is not a coincidence that the fiercest fighting during the Syrian civil war occurred in and around Homs, the crux and focal point of this triangle of power: whichever party controlled Homs by extension controlled Damascus. As a result of the Asad regime's general withdrawal from most of the eastern areas of Syria, by the end of 2011 the large arc of Syria that is inhabited almost exclusively by Sunni Arabs—up the Euphrates River valley from the Iraq border to Raqqa, then stretching west through the rural areas of Aleppo province before ending in the Idlib province—was no longer under regime control, as various Sunni Arab groups, mostly salafi-jihadi in orientation, competed with each other for control of the area.

This evacuation of the relatively homogeneous Arab-Sunni areas of Syria created an opening that served as a lifeline for ISIS in Iraq. Attempts by ISIS and its predecessors to exert authority over large swaths of Iraq had had at best mixed success, and by the time the Syrian civil war broke out, ISIS had largely been defeated in Iraq. However, when the Asad regime essentially deserted eastern Syria, it saved ISIS from likely extinction in Iraq. This region in Syria became a safe haven in which ISIS could regroup and rebuild, enabling it eventually to take over northwestern Iraq and declare its Caliphate in 2014.

THE RISE AND EVOLUTION OF ISIS

ISIS stands for the Islamic State in Iraq and Syria, although ISIS used the traditional Arabic word "Sham" for Syria. Sham as a synonym for Syria is still in use today, although it lacks a specific territorial delineation. In that regard, it functions a lot like the phrase "holy land," referring to a general region but without consensus about exactly which lands are included.[6] The English for ISIS is a direct translation from the Arabic: al-Dawla al-Islamiyya f'il-'Iraq w'al-Sham. The acronym that comes from the Arabic name, Da'ish, was also commonly used for the group by both Arabic and English speakers, although ISIS itself forbade the acronym's use in its territory, preferring people refer to it simply as the Islamic State (al-Dawla al-Islamiyya). For the sake of simplicity, I primarily use the acronym ISIS in this book to refer to this group throughout its history, even though it went through many name changes over its evolution. The most famous earlier acronyms for ISIS were AQI (al-Qa'ida in Iraq) and ISI (the Islamic State in Iraq), which are also used briefly in this chapter. It is worthwhile to concisely look at that evolution prior to 2014, when ISIS stormed into the consciousness of the world.

The ISIS story began in late 1999, when a Jordanian radical from the provincial city of Zarqa traveled to Afghanistan and shortly thereafter began running a jihadi training camp near Herat in western Afghanistan named al-Tawhid w'al-Jihad. The camp came under the umbrella of al-Qa'ida, but Usama Bin Laden allowed Zarqawi operational autonomy and did not insist on any oath of allegiance.[7] The fighters produced here under Zarqawi's leadership formed the nucleus of what would become ISIS. Zarqawi's al-Tawhid w'al-Jihad group was not obviously a global jihad operation; instead, it was designed to overthrow local regimes in Jordan and elsewhere in the Levant that Zarqawi viewed as apostate. In its aims, Zarqawi's group was consistent with many other near-enemy jihadi groups around the Muslim world.

Zarqawi was already well-known to the Jordanian security services, as he had briefly spent time in Afghanistan in the late 1980s, came home as a committed jihadi, and spent much of the 1990s in prison in Jordan because of his militant activities. He was released from prison in 1999 as part of a general amnesty on the ascension to the throne of King Abdullah II. Zarqawi had radicalized further in prison, in part due to the influence of fellow inmate (and famous radical cleric) Abu Muhammad al-Maqdisi.[8] Upon Zarqawi's release, he immediately continued on the path of armed jihad. While living abroad, Zarqawi and his small band of jihadis were involved in the failed plot to bomb the Radisson hotel in Amman on New Year's 2000 and again in the successful assassination of a USAID official in Amman in 2002. Zarqawi traveled frequently in the region, primarily in the Levant, both to help plan attacks and for reasons of personal security. When the Americans invaded Afghanistan in late 2001, Zarqawi escaped to Iraqi Kurdistan, where some of his former pupils had set up operations to fight what they viewed as the apostate Saddam Husayn regime in Baghdad. After the US invasion of Iraq in 2003, Zarqawi stayed put, spending his last three years leading his band of followers in an attempt to gin up a sectarian war in Iraq against the Shia. Ironically, although he succeeded in his quest for a sectarian civil war in Iraq, the end result of the conflict was to further consolidate Shia power.

Zarqawi began his activities in Iraq as a free agent, not tied to any other group outside his own small operation. But a renewal of his relationship with Usama Bin Laden and al-Qa'ida awaited, in a marriage of convenience for both parties. Al-Qa'ida had been largely destroyed and was desperate to show its relevance in the new battlefield of Iraq. Zarqawi and his group were seen as the best available vehicle for al-Qa'ida to get a toehold in the Iraq fight against the Americans, even though al-Qa'ida did not share Zarqawi's extreme sectarian animus against the Shia. For Zarqawi, linking up with al-Qa'ida would provide him and his group significant name recognition and branding advantages, and perhaps some resources as well (which, in the end, were extremely limited). Zarqawi and Bin Laden, both headstrong authoritarian leaders, competed over who should pledge allegiance (ba'ya) to whom. By October 2004 each side had agreed to set aside their reservations about the other, and Zarqawi joined al-Qa'ida formally, with his operation in Iraq now going by a new name: Organization of Jihad in Mesopotamia (Tanzim Qa'idat al-Jihad fi Bilad al-Rafidayn), better known in the West as al-Qa'ida in Iraq (AQI).

Although AQI was technically a branch of al-Qa'ida for two years, it maintained operational independence under Zarqawi's command. This reflected Zarqawi's desire to control his own campaign according to his own ideology (more on that below). The marriage of convenience with al-Qa'ida was strained from the outset, with AQI focusing its attacks on Shia targets and on periodic gruesome beheadings of kidnapped Westerners, the videos of which were uploaded on the Internet. Bin Laden and his al-Qa'ida Central wanted Zarqawi to attack the Americans instead, which was something that AQI only sporadically attempted. The frustration grew so pronounced that Ayman al-Zawahiri wrote a letter of rebuke to Zarqawi in July 2005, warning him that his sectarian bloodlust and videoed decapitations were doing serious damage to the image of the jihadi cause in the Muslim world.[9] Zarqawi ignored the advice and instead broadened his campaign through a series of hotel bombings in Jordan in November 2005, killing sixty people, most of whom were Arabs. Al-Qa'ida sent another letter of rebuke in response, this one penned by 'Atiya 'Abd al-Rahman (also known as 'Atiyatullah al-Libi), who warned Zarqawi of the necessity of following the orders and strategic objectives of Bin Laden and Zawahiri, and not to stray into violence that did significant harm to the jihadi cause.[10]

Zarqawi's death in an American operation in June 2006 did not stop the souring of relations between al-Qa'ida Central and AQI and, in October 2006, AQI broke with al-Qa'ida to declare itself as the Islamic State in Iraq (al-Dawla al-Islamiyya f'il-'Iraq, or ISI). Oaths of allegiance (ba'ya) are personal, and with Zarqawi's death the formal link between his group and al-Qa'ida was broken, freeing up AQI to go its own way. This was the first time that an ISIS predecessor had taken a name that openly called for a territorial state. Other jihadi groups had avoided this because it entailed the need to defend a fixed territory, a task no jihadi group was able to do for any length of time. It is always advantageous for a guerrilla group to be able to attack, then fade away into the shadows, and then attack again; doing so makes it harder for military and security forces to find and defeat it. Drawing on a 2009 ISI document, scholar Mohammed Hafez suggests that ISI proclaimed an Islamic State in part to preempt Iraqi nationalists from agreeing to a federal plan for Iraq, and thus to keep them inside the ISI Sunni Arab coalition.[11] Such a declaration of statehood could prove to be an ingenious solution to overcome the natural tension that existed in the ISI coalition between Iraqi Sunni nationalists (often from the former Ba'thist regime under Saddam Husayn) and jihadis. As nationalists, the former were tied to the notion of a territorial state, and the latter were committed to shari'a rule. Thus a territorial state governed by shari'a could unite an otherwise fractious coalition.

However, without Zarqawi's charismatic (if thuggish) leadership, ISI stagnated, unable to hold territory and increasingly alienating the Sunni community it claimed to represent. In 2007, ISI's position was further weakened when the US military began working with Sunni Arabs in Iraq, particularly tribal groups, instead of seeing all Sunni Arabs as enemies. This counterinsurgency tactic is broadly and wrongly conflated with a later troop escalation known in American parlance as "the surge." Unlike the change in counterinsurgency tactics, which was effective, the troop escalation itself made only marginal difference in Iraq's overall trajectory.[12]

ISI was marginalized and near defeat in Iraq by 2010, when a skilled ideologue with a second-rate doctoral degree in Islamic theology and the nom de guerre of Abu Bakr al-Baghdadi took over the leadership position. Baghdadi had begun the process of stabilizing ISI when, a few months later in March 2011, ISI was given the gift of renewed purpose with the outbreak of civil war in next-door Syria. In due course, Baghdadi sent an exploratory team to Syria, which linked up with Syrian jihadis to form the Nusra Front in Syria (Jabhat al-Nusra f'il-Sham), led by Abu Muhammad al-Jawlani. The Nusra Front emerged over the course of 2012 as the best fighting force among the various Syrian rebel groups. In April 2013, Baghdadi announced that Nusra was indeed part of ISI and that he intended to merge their operational capabilities into a single unit. Frightened by the potential loss of operational autonomy that he had developed, and in a very Zarqawi-like move, Jawlani instead declared that Nusra was pledging loyalty to al-Qa'ida (to Ayman al-Zawahiri specifically). As a mostly expired organization that no longer had Usama Bin Laden, al-Qa'ida would not make many demands on Jawlani and Nusra, and would allow them essentially complete autonomy to fight in Syria however they deemed necessary.

ISI's loss of the Nusra Front proved only a temporary setback and perhaps helped the organization over the longer term. The Nusra Front was heavily involved in fighting in the western and northern parts of Syria, which was much more populated and strategically important than the lightly populated east. By contrast, neither the regime nor the various rebel groups paid much attention to the entirety of the Euphrates River valley in Syria. It was into this area that ISI moved, including Baghdadi, largely giving up its limited presence in Iraq, in order to grab the lands of Raqqa and the Euphrates River valley over the course of 2013. With its new presence in Syria, ISI changed its name once again, this time to the Islamic State in Iraq and Syria (ISIS, al-Dawla al-Islamiyya f'il-'Iraq w'al-Sham). During this period in 2013, ISIS began to seriously focus on state-building in the territory it controlled in eastern Syria, to create an area ruled by shari'a, free from apostasy and its temptations. ISIS largely avoided fighting with the regime in Damascus, prompting considerable speculation of backroom deals with the Asad regime.[13] Although clashes occurred from time to time, ISIS was more concerned with holding its territory and building its state, and Damascus was more concerned with defending the critical Damascus-Aleppo-Latakia triangle in western Syria; if the logistical and supply lines there fell, so would the regime. Eastern Syria was not a pressing issue for Asad, and it could be dealt with later.

From its headquarters in Raqqa, Syria, ISIS built a puritanical state. It had some popular support in this endeavor, to be sure, both for ideological reasons and for its ability to dramatically reduce the rampant everyday corruption to which most Syrians were subject. From this safe haven in Syria, ISIS launched a lightning strike across the Iraqi border in June 2014, capturing Mosul and other cities in Iraq's heavily Sunni Arab northwest. Baghdadi then proclaimed the Caliphate, marking the capstone of the rise and evolution of ISIS. This ascent to the apex of ISIS's power should neither be underestimated nor overestimated. For nearly three years, ISIS controlled a landmass the size of Great Britain, ruled over up to ten million people, had annual revenues of about $800 million, and recruited tens of thousands of ideologically committed fighters.[14] This is an accomplishment that far surpasses anything that any other jihadi group of any stripe ever did.

However, ISIS never conquered a serious adversary nor defeated the armed might of any state; rather, it filled a vacuum of essentially ungoverned lands in eastern Syria and northwestern Iraq. As noted, the Syrian army was concentrating its limited resources on the far more important battles in the western parts of Syria. Meanwhile, Mosul and other areas of northwestern Iraq were only lightly defended by a Shia revivalist regime in Baghdad that had done its best to alienate and marginalize the local Sunni Arab population. By 2014 this population was prepared to support any group that promised the protection of Sunni Arab rights and would fight Baghdad to get them. The minimal number of lightly committed "Iraqi" (really Shia) forces in the northwest melted away at the first signs of ISIS's arrival, hardly firing a shot to defend a part of the country they did not really view as essential to Shia hegemony. ISIS therefore expanded up to the limits of the power vacuum that it had helped to create but did not go beyond them. It never had a realistic chance to take Baghdad or southern Iraq, which have large Shia majorities, or to conquer a functional state's armed forces. Even a small and relatively weak state like Jordan would have overpowered ISIS easily had the Caliphate been declared in, say, the territory around Zarqa.

So although ISIS was the most successful global jihadi group by a significant margin, it is important not to overstate its success. The fact that no local state in the region outside of Iraq viewed ISIS as a serious existential peril should be contemplated when one rightsizes the threat ISIS posed. Indeed, some local states, such as Saudi Arabia and Turkey, indirectly assisted ISIS for a period of time, as it was seen as a useful tool against more important regional enemies. This is not to suggest that ISIS was a "JV team" in President Obama's unfortunate phrasing, but rather to note that most regional states prioritized other security threats as being more pressing than the threat posed by ISIS, even at its zenith.

THE IDEOLOGY AND IDEOLOGUES OF ISIS

Although the third wave was the biggest and easily the most successful of the four waves of global jihad, there was no one single ideologue who framed the totality of ISIS's ideology. All of the leading ideologues agreed on the major underlying principle of ISIS—building a territorial state under strict shari'a law—but they raised a number of distinct issues and arguments. To try to capture most of the important elements of the ISIS ideology, this section focuses on the ideas of three individuals: Abu Musab al-Zarqawi, who has already been discussed in his capacity as the founder of ISIS; Abu Bakr Naji, the pseudonym for the author of *The Management of Savagery*, the primary ideological justification for extreme ISIS violence; and Abu Bakr al-Baghdadi, the self-declared Caliph of the Islamic State.

Abu Musab al-Zarqawi

Zarqawi, from the large Bani Hasan tribe in Jordan, had only a rudimentary formal education, dropping out after finishing primary school. He had no secondary education or formal religious training but was self-taught and studied while in prison with jihadi cleric Abu Muhammad al-Maqdisi. Because of his lack of formal education, Zarqawi did not leave behind a large corpus of letters and documents from which to glean the finer points of his ideology. In addition to various statements he made, the most detailed document available that lays out his ideas is a long letter he wrote to Usama Bin Ladin in 2004.[15]

Zarqawi makes three broad contributions to the ideological development of ISIS, in addition to reflecting many other common themes found in the salafi-jihadi circles in which he traveled. First, his most fervent argument is to place a sectarian war with the Shia at the top of the jihadi agenda. His extreme sectarianism is not reflected in either of the first two waves of global jihad. Partly coming from Shia stock himself, Bin Ladin did not share Zarqawi's visceral hatred of the Shia, nor did he think it the appropriate strategy. Bin Ladin may have even contemplated some form of an alliance with Shia militants in fulfilling his primary desire to attack the Americans. For 'Azzam, the Shia were a tangential issue to liberating occupied Muslim lands. But for Zarqawi—and for the third wave of global jihad—extreme anti-Shia sectarianism took center stage. Zarqawi's views had both an emotional component, stressing the cultural contamination and evil that the Shia represented, and a strategic component, that unleashing a vicious sectarian war in Iraq would lead to multiple gains, including the reassertion of Sunni power, the marginalization of a defeated Shia community, and the defeat of the American occupation of Iraq. Zarqawi did not mince words:

> The Shia are the most evil of mankind. . . . They are the lurking snake, the crafty and malicious scorpion, the spying enemy and the penetrating venom. . . . They have been a sect of treachery and betrayal throughout history and throughout the ages. It is a creed that aims to combat the Sunnis. When the repulsive Ba'thi regime fell, the slogan of the Shia was "revenge, revenge, from Tikrit to al-Anbar." This shows the extent of their hidden rancor toward the Sunnis. The Qur'an has told us that the machinations of the hypocrites, the deceit of the fifth column, and the cunning of those of our fellow countrymen whose tongues speak honeyed words but whose hearts are those of devils in the bodies of men—these are where the disease lies, these are the secret of our distress, these are the rats of the dike.[16]

Zarqawi also took up the theme of dissimulation (*taqiyya*) to prove "the maliciousness and cunning" of the Shia. *Taqiyya*, defined as "prudence born of fear," is an old Shia theological argument that allows its followers to deny their sect when their lives or property are at risk. This was a practical bit of advice to a minority community mostly living among a majority Sunni population that often reviled and punished them. The Shia theological permission to dissimulate—to lie about one's faith under certain circumstances—is a common point of criticism among Sunnis, and Zarqawi referred to it often to paint a picture of how the Shia had manipulated and lied their way into positions of power in post-2003 Iraq. But his extreme sectarianism was more than a visceral hatred of the "rejectionists"; it was also a strategy to win back Iraq for the Sunnis, who could then implement a true shari'a state. His was an open strategy to provoke a sectarian war in Iraq:

> If we succeed in dragging them into the arena of sectarian war, it will become possible to awaken the inattentive Sunnis as they feel imminent danger and annihilating death at the hands of the Shia. Despite their weakness and fragmentation, the Sunnis are the sharpest blades, the most determined, and the most loyal; by contrast, the Shia are a people of treachery and cowardice. They are arrogant only toward the weak and can attack only the already injured. Most Sunnis are aware of the danger of the Shia and fear the consequences of empowering them. The Shia survived only because the feebleness of Sufi shaykhs and Muslim Brothers protected them.
>
> The Shia are the most immediate and dangerous enemy of the Sunnis, even if the Americans are also an archenemy. The danger from the Shia, however, is greater and their damage is worse and more destructive to the Islamic nation than that from the Americans, although there is a general consensus on the importance of killing Americans as the allies of the Shia.
>
> If we are able to strike the Shia with one painful blow after another until they are forced to engage us in battle, we will be able to reshuffle the deck of cards. Then, no value or influence will remain to the Governing Council or even to the Americans, who will enter a second battle with the Shia. This is what we want, and, whether they like it or not, many Sunni areas will stand with the mujahidin. Then, the mujahidin will have assured themselves land from which to set forth in striking the Shia in their heartland, along with a clear media strategy and the creation of strategic depth and reach among our brothers outside of Iraq.[17]

For Zarqawi, the Shia—through their lies, treachery and alliance with the hated Americans—represented the epitome of cultural depravity and of the contamination of the pure Sunni Muslim community. Only the extermination of the Shia was an appropriate solution to Zarqawi; negotiation and compromise were pointless and intolerable.

Zarqawi's second contribution to the ideology of ISIS can best be described with an old anarchist phrase: "propaganda of the deed." Zarqawi wanted his violent acts to be exemplary for other jihadis, to inspire his fellow Sunnis to do similar "heroic" actions. This was the point of putting videos of decapitations and planted roadside bombs (IEDs) online: to show the way forward for other potential jihadis. In this manner, Zarqawi was far less intellectual than other ideologues but much more of a man of action. He was the Rambo of jihadis, trying to inspire a mythology about his ferocity and bravery in battle through actions far more than through words. Like Rambo, Zarqawi wanted to be viewed not only as tough but also as cool, engaging in daring exploits that would cause other young Muslim men looking for excitement to follow suit. Even years after Zarqawi's death in 2006, ISIS adopted and promoted this same line of attack, the propaganda of the deed, promoting spectacular violence over words, undertaking what was cool and sexy without wasting much time in deep theological argumentation.

Third, Zarqawi took a big-tent attitude to recruitment. He argued for a mass-based approach that encouraged all Sunnis in Iraq to fight. An enduring split between jihadi ideologues is caused by the issue of vanguard-versus-populist approaches to violence, with Sayyid Qutb, Usama Bin Ladin, Ayman al-Zawahiri, and Muhammad 'Abd al-Salam Faraj among those arguing that small, vanguard-led violence is key to success, and Zarqawi, 'Abdullah 'Azzam, and Abu Musab al-Suri among those in favor of mass-based violence. Zarqawi invited all supporters to help in the cause and did not focus on creating a small, professional vanguard force in the Leninist tradition. ISIS continued Zarqawi's mass approach after his death in 2006.

Much of the rest of Zarqawi's ideology was consistent with common jihadi arguments, including his adoption of the *takfir* tactic of excommunication (including as a justification for the killing of Shia), his hatred of the Muslim Brotherhood and most clerics as sellouts, and his hostile views of Israel, Jews, and Christians. Like others in his circle, Zarqawi often quoted Ibn Taymiyya, the favorite medieval cleric of jihadis everywhere. But it is important to note that everything in Zarqawi's ideological pronouncements is consistent with a more traditional near-enemy jihad, intent on provoking a sectarian war to drive the Shia out of the power that had been handed to them by the US invasion of Iraq. Zarqawi accepted the argument of al-Qa'ida ideologues that the Americans should be attacked since they are an occupying power in Iraq; however, he made a point of painting the Shia as a greater enemy than the Americans. It would be hard to define Zarqawi as a true *global* jihadi. Moreover, the territorial state idea that would distinguish ISIS from other forms of global jihad is at best only nascent in Zarqawi's thinking. That idea would only fully bloom after his death. So although Zarqawi is rightfully seen—and was often remembered in ISIS propaganda—as the founding father of ISIS and the personification of some of its most fundamental themes, the movement evolved considerably in its ideology after his death in 2006.

Abu Bakr Naji

While Zarqawi embodied the notion of propaganda of the deed, it took more literate jihadi ideologues to lay out in detail the justification of and explanation for extreme violence, of murder as performative spectacle. Abu Bakr Naji was not a leader of ISIS per se, and his major writing was done in the immediate aftermath of the US invasion of Iraq and thus before ISIS became a serious movement. But without question, his views on the use and meaning of violence were deeply influential to those who would shortly seize the mantle of ISIS leadership. Three ideological innovations in particular, to which Abu Bakr Naji made considerable contributions, deserve attention: the use of extreme, performative violence; the focus on a territorial state; and the privileging of story-telling over deep theological argument.

In the post-2003 milieu many discussions and ideas were debated among jihadis about the role of extreme violence, but Abu Bakr Naji made the most impactful argument in his book, *The Management of Savagery*.[18] However, there were other major ideologues of extreme violence at this time, including Abu Ali al-Anbari in Iraq and Abu Musab al-Suri in Afghanistan.[19] Indeed, analyst Hassan Hassan argues that Anbari's influence on ISIS's radicalism was "more systematic, longer lasting, and deeper than that of Zarqawi."[20] Researcher Brian Fishman discusses many of the key ideologues during this period of ferment, focusing special attention on the role of the Egyptian jihadi ideologue Sayf al-'Adl.[21] Thus my discussion here is meant to be representative of multiple Sunni radical ideologues operating in the immediate post-2003 milieu who shaped the doctrine of extreme violence during this critical juncture. This was a period of intense ideological ferment among Sunni jihadis.

Abu Bakr Naji is likely a pseudonym for Muhammad Hasan Khalil al-Hakim, an Egyptian jihadi who spent his last years working in the Waziristan area of Pakistan that borders Afghanistan before being killed in an American drone strike there in 2008. More than the other ideologues, Naji laid out the logic and importance of extreme violence as well as the necessity of making sure one's enemies know that they will be subject to that very same extreme violence—savagery—if captured. Such savagery would provide two distinct benefits. First, and most important, the purposeful management or administration (*idara*) of savagery (*tawahhush*) would make lands contested. Regimes that, on paper, control a certain territory would find that they actually have diminished jurisdiction if the police, soldiers, and security personnel assigned to assert power instead shrink away in fear at the savage violence around them that they cannot control. The process of savagery turns territory from regime-controlled into contested lands and thus provides an opportunity for jihadi conquest.

This strategy is exactly how ISIS took over a third of Iraq suddenly in 2014. Their reputation for savagery was already becoming legend in the region, and the Iraqi security personnel would have been acquainted with the stories of ISIS barbarism. For example, Iraqi security personnel would have been familiar with ISIS's gruesome execution of two dozen policemen in Haditha, captured on video and distributed on the Internet.[22] Both the legion of bombings and shootings inside Iraq by ISIS in 2013 and early 2014, and the stories of savagery from inside Raqqa and other parts of ISIS-controlled Syria during the same period, appear to have greatly contributed to the (Shia) Iraqi soldiers essentially deserting Mosul and other parts of Sunni Arab Iraq when ISIS began its takeover push. ISIS militants were significantly outnumbered by Iraqi forces, yet they captured Mosul easily, as the Iraqi forces fled in fear after only a few days of light fighting. The first soldiers captured by ISIS forces in Mosul were hanged, set on fire, crucified, and torched on the hoods of their Humvees—a macabre display of savagery designed to send a message to other Iraqi forces.[23]

It worked. In short, through its administration of savagery, ISIS turned significant amounts of territory in Iraq into gray or contested regions where Baghdad no longer had real control. When the time was right, ISIS grabbed the territory for itself. Baghdad's purposeful marginalization of these Sunni Arab lands of Iraq only made the job easier, as ISIS found a population that was often supportive of its power grab, at least initially.

The second benefit of the strategic use of savagery was social control in the conquered areas while institutions of the new state were absent or nascent. In Raqqa, Mosul, and other areas of newly gained control, ISIS would make ferocious public displays of its wrath against its various enemies. "Paradise Square" in downtown Raqqa was used for all sorts of public beheadings, amputations, lashings and other punishments, and to display the severed heads of captured Syrian soldiers. Many of the most dramatic executions—purposeful violent spectacles—were scripted, filmed, and put out on the Internet or social media. This Stalinist form of social control for the twenty-first century effectively limited internal challenges to ISIS rule. This is not to suggest that ISIS did not have more than its share of ideologically committed true believers; it clearly did. But savage violence also played a key role in pacifying the broader public, as Naji argued it should.

Naji wanted to make clear to his fellow jihadis that the violence he spoke about did not concern Islam; it concerned war fighting and social control. The need for barbarism was not something one could read about in theological texts, but rather what was required to win territory and build a state. Jihadis, he argued, should not be soft and naïve about the need for savagery and its implementation. From Naji's *The Management of Savagery*:

> Those who study theoretical jihad, meaning they study only jihad as it is written on paper, will never grasp this point well. Regrettably, the youth in our Umma, since the time when they were stripped of weapons, no longer understand the nature of wars. One who previously engaged in jihad knows that it is nothing but violence, crudeness, terrorism, fear and massacring. *I am talking about jihad and fighting, not about Islam, and one should not confuse them.* A jihadi knows that he cannot continue to fight and move from one stage to another unless the beginning stage contains a phase of massacring the enemy and making him terribly afraid. However, there is also often a need for this violence in the other stages. A fighter cannot continue the jihad with softness . . .

since the ingredient of softness leads to failure. It is better for those who have the intention to begin a jihadi action and are also soft to sit in their homes. If not, failure will be their lot and they will suffer shock afterwards. Whoever wants to verify and understand what I mean should read biographies and histories and examine what happened to the modern jihadi movement. Regardless of whether we use harshness or softness, our enemies will not be merciful to us if they seize us. Thus, it behooves us to make them think one thousand times before attacking us.

Those who have not boldly entered wars during their lifetimes do not understand the role of violence and coarseness against the infidels in combat and media battles. . . . Today's youth are different from the Arabs at the time of the prophet. The Arabs used to fight and know the true nature of war.[24]

A second ideological emphasis for Naji, in addition to the focus on extreme, performative violence, was territoriality. This set the ISIS movement apart from other jihadi groups, who behaved as guerrilla groups not intent on controlling fixed territory, at least not until a distant future. ISIS ideologues, including Naji, emphasized the need for state building on fixed territory. According to Iraqi scholar Husham al-Hashimi, three other ideologues were essential in constructing the argument for Islamic statehood: Abu ʿAbd al-Rahman al-Iraqi, Nidham al-Din Rifaʾi, and ʿAbdullah ʿAbd al-Samad al-Mufti. The first two men are currently in prison, and the third is in hiding.[25] Thus it is fair to argue that Zarqawi himself was not the driving force behind creating a territorial state, but that he came to reflect this view in the last months of his life. The idea of declaring and implementing an Islamic state as soon as possible, and not waiting until a future when its survival would be guaranteed through a favorable balance of power, set the ISIS movement apart from al-Qaʾida (which saw such a move as dangerously naïve) and other jihadi groups.

A third ideological contribution by Naji and this cluster of ISIS ideologues was the avoidance of theology and the promotion of story-telling in its place. The two most important ideologues who advocated for this style of persuasion were Naji and the Egyptian Abu ʿAbdullah al-Muhajir.[26] Had ISIS sought to justify its actions primarily through sophisticated theological arguments, it would have been obliged to respond to counterarguments by ranking Muslim clerics. This was a losing proposition for ISIS, as there was little in the Qurʾan and *hadiths* that would lend itself to ISIS's view of the world and the actions it took. Rather, ISIS relied on stories—sometimes obscure ones—from Islam's long history to justify various bloodthirsty actions, including beheadings, crucifixions, and mass killings. Telling stories of cherry-picked actions by early Muslim warriors could be a more powerful teaching tool for ISIS recruits than deep theological studies. For the young and ill-educated, stories become a bumper-sticker version of a larger ideology.[27] For example, telling the story of early Muslim hero Khalid Ibn al-Walid's mass execution of Persian prisoners following the battle of Ullais in 633 CE, when Walid made a "river of blood" (at least in the storybook telling), is a more potent tool for teaching lightly educated Muslims than a deep-dive into Islamic just-war theory as it developed theologically over the centuries (which would prohibit such a mass killing of prisoners). Beheadings are likewise justified through a handful of historical stories, not through developed Islamic theology.

Journalist Graeme Wood was right to argue in his famous article in *The Atlantic* that ISIS takes Islam *very* seriously.[28] ISIS ideologues did not generally make up stuff out of whole cloth; rather, they tried to reference various stories from Islam's past to justify ISIS's actions. But what Wood missed in his otherwise valuable article was ISIS's emphasis on, and cherry-picking of, story-telling from Islam's history, rather than any persuasive theological arguments ISIS made. There was a good reason why ISIS's Caliphate was not accepted and recognized by a single ranking cleric in the Muslim world: those with actual deep theological knowledge of Islam recognized what a crackpot enterprise ISIS was: a fantasy land of violence more than a representation of orthodox Islamic theology and doctrine.

Abu Bakr al-Baghdadi

As the recognized and unchallenged leader of ISIS during the entire period when it could claim to be a territorial state, Abu Bakr al-Baghdadi was not only a major leader of the movement but also a major force in shaping ISIS's ideology. In this short summary, I focus on two issues in particular for which Baghdadi should be credited as the prime architect: the decision to declare a caliphate (which, as a marketing strategy, was a stroke of genius) and ISIS's use of apocalyptic ideological memes under Baghdadi's leadership. Born Ibrahim 'Awwad Ibrahim al-Badri Ali Muhammad al-Samarra'i circa 1971, Baghdadi came from the Samarra region in the "Sunni Triangle" north of Baghdad. His nom de guerre, Abu Bakr al-Baghdadi, is not from a traditional *kunya*, as he did not have a son named Bakr. Rather, the name appears to be a mixing of the name of Islam's first caliph, Abu Bakr, and Iraq's capital city—the combination of which was designed to lend weight and gravitas. After he declared himself caliph, he would often be referred to by his supporters as Khalifa Ibrahim, harkening back to his birth name. The truth of his claim that he descended from the Quraysh tribe (the tribe of the Prophet Muhammad) is open to debate but was a myth required to allow him to claim the title of caliph.

While Baghdadi was a mediocre student in high school, it appears that he ultimately received a doctorate in Qur'anic studies from Saddam University (now Nahrain University) in Baghdad, but even these studies remain somewhat enigmatic. Being a new university (established in 1987), it did not enjoy a reputation as a top university for Islamic studies, so Baghdadi's clerical credentials are not particularly august, even assuming that his degree was legitimate. Nor did Baghdadi publish serious works of Islamic scholarship, another requirement to be considered a top cleric. Thus it should not be a surprise that such a young, unaccomplished, and minor cleric garnered no clerical recognition of note for his caliphate; he was instead viewed more as an imposter.[29] One final note on this brief biography: Baghdadi was interred during most of 2004 by American forces in Camp Bucca in Iraq, which ended up being a place of introduction and indoctrination for much of ISIS's later leadership. He was killed in an October 2019 US operation while holed up in the Idlib province of Syria, just a few miles from the Turkish border.

As I have tried to stress, ISIS made no genuine attempt to be taken seriously by the leading members of the Muslim *'ulama* (clergy). Rather, ISIS was making a populist appeal to Muslims generally, especially young Muslim men, to join this legendary crusade. Credentials, expertise, recognition, traditional authority—none of these mattered very much, only the storybook tale that ISIS was imagining and implementing. The most incredible tale of all, the most charismatic and sexy step that ISIS and Baghdadi could undertake—even, or especially, in the face of universal clerical condemnation—was to declare a new caliphate, a fantastical shining city on the hill, with a mysterious, rarely seen, new caliph. So that is exactly what Baghdadi did from the pulpit of the historic Great Mosque of al-Nuri in the newly conquered city of Mosul in June 2014. ISIS's caliphate was the apogee of all the apocalyptic stories about the coming End Times and a chance for Muslims to gain dignity and slay all of their enemies—external and internal—in a gory culmination of history.

The declaration of a caliphate was an enormously powerful marketing move by Baghdadi, putting ISIS on the proverbial map perhaps even more than its recent military victories had. It was an act of chutzpah, doing something no other jihadi group had ever dared to try. The old caliphate in Istanbul had been abolished in 1924 by the new republican leaders in Turkey and, although there had been talk here and there of creating a new one, it had never come close to actually happening. While Islamists would often opine support for a reestablished caliphate in the future, the matter was mostly a nonissue in the Muslim world. Various jihadi groups, including al-Qa'ida, would periodically voice support for a reestablished caliphate someday, but that issue was not the most important animating issue for any group. Usama Bin Laden rarely mentioned it, focusing instead on his war against America. It is not that he rejected the notion, but only that it was well down his to-do list; there were more important matters to attend to first.[30] The main issue for this lack of immediate concern among jihadis (global and local) for a caliphate now was simply the presence of more pressing issues. There was a political concern as well: if a caliphate is declared without proper steps in place to protect its survival, then it would likely be defeated by its enemies, setting the idea back by generations.

By ignoring the concerns of others about a premature declaration of a caliphate, and just doing it, Baghdadi undertook a bold act of charisma that filled his followers and others with a sense of awe, wonder, and fear. It helped convince tens of thousands of foreigners from around the world to migrate illegally to Iraq and Syria to help this new caliphate survive and thrive, to "remain" (baqiya), in ISIS's own parlance. This act of charismatic authority was clearly not designed to convince leading Muslim clerics of the theological correctness of the decision but rather to create a buzz, a thrill, a calling for young Muslims seeking adventure and meaning in their lives, to join the caravan of the new Islamic state. Join they did, in droves, most not knowing much about Islam, but all eager to serve the new caliph and his wondrous, fantastical cause. About forty thousand foreign fighters from around the world made their way to the caliphate, including about five thousand from Western European countries.[31]

Let me add one final note on the utter bravado of declaring a caliphate. Other Islamist and jihadi groups have sometimes declared themselves an "emirate" with an "emir" as leader, using terms with a rich Islamic history. The Taliban in Afghanistan, for example, named their country formally the Islamic Emirate of Afghanistan, with Mullah Omar its longtime "emir." There is a significant difference between an emirate and a caliphate, however. The former claims sovereignty over all people who live within its territorial control but does not claim authority over others outside of its territorial control. Mullah Omar and the Taliban leadership did not claim legitimate authority over Muslims who lived outside of Afghanistan. A caliphate, by contrast, claims legitimate authority over *all* Muslims everywhere in the world, in addition to the people of all faiths who live within the territory the caliphate actually controls. By declaring himself caliph, Baghdadi was claiming as a matter of religious law that all Muslims in the world, or at least all Sunni Muslims, owed personal allegiance (*ba'ya*) to him as their rightful leader and must obey his orders. Baghdadi stressed this point in his June 2014 announcement of the caliphate when he said that he was "the Imam and Caliph for Muslims everywhere ... that it was incumbent on all Muslims to pledge allegiance to Caliph Ibrahim and support him."[32] So even while virtually all Muslims around the world rejected this command by the charlatan caliph, it was still a monumental summons to make in the first place, one that only solidified his standing among the true believers.

In the post-2010 period when Baghdadi led ISIS, he oversaw not only the caliphate itself but also the production of an ideological campaign based on a coming apocalypse. Ginning up an impending apocalypse was another ideological innovation, one that likewise stirred the imagination of the impressionable. Graeme Wood and, especially, William McCants have detailed the apocalyptic nature of ISIS, so I only highlight the issue briefly here.[33] Early Christians, believing that Nero's intense persecution signaled the coming End Times, created an apocalyptic theological strand, including the Book of Revelations found in the Bible. Much in the same way, early Muslims created an apocalyptic strand in dire protest against the usurpation of Muslim leadership by the Umayyad family in Damascus following their assassination of the Fourth Caliph, Ali, in 661 CE, and again a century later when the Umayyads were on the cusp of defeat at the hands of Abbasid insurgents (in present-day

Iraq). The principal Islamic texts, the Qur'an and the hadiths, both contain an apocalyptic End Times narrative similar to the one found in Christian tradition; however, ISIS drew many of its apocalyptic, end-of-the-world aphorisms from oral traditions passed down over the generations, in addition to using those found in the holy texts. These oral traditions presented a rich vein for ISIS ideologues to tap into, particularly given the anarchy and bloodshed in Iraq following the US invasion and occupation, and the generalized disarray around the Arab world as a result of the Arab Spring. The chaos was seen by some as the beginning of the end of the world, where Dajjal—the Antichrist equivalent in Islamic eschatology—may already be walking among men.

ISIS millenarian eschatology had five major themes, which, combined, represented nearly half of all its published propaganda.[34] First, ISIS ideologues from Baghdadi down stressed that the End Times are here now, not in some distant future, and it was a matter of months before the returning Mahdi, or messiah, would make his appearance to save the righteous Muslims. This gave the ISIS apocalypse a sense of urgency, that time was of the essence. Second, the imminent coming of the Mahdi meant that the great apocalyptical battle of the End Times at the town of Dabiq in north-central Syria pitting Muslim forces against "Rome" was likewise at hand. It was not a coincidence that it was in Dabiq that Muhammad Emwazi (aka Jihadi John) stood over the severed head of a US aid worker intoning that the first of the American "crusaders" had been killed in Dabiq and that ISIS awaited the rest so that they may meet a similar fate. The prophecy of Dabiq, with its Armageddon-like meaning for some Muslims, played a major role in ISIS eschatology, including ISIS naming its major propaganda magazine *Dabiq*. ISIS's joy at its capture of Dabiq, and its use of the town for apocalyptic ideological purposes, came to a sudden end in October 2016 when Dabiq was captured by Turkish-backed forces.[35]

A third theme in ISIS's apocalypse ideology is that the battle of Dabiq and the End Times more generally will usher in a new world of justice and the supremacy of Islam under the leadership of the Mahdi. In this cosmic war between good and evil, ISIS assures its followers that its side will win in the end, but not before grave defeats will badly thin its ranks. Those prophesied coming losses directly leads to the fourth major element, the recruitment pitch: it is imperative for all able-bodied Muslims to join the caravan, come to the lands of the caliphate now, to fight and win the apocalyptic battles that have already begun to occur. Without enough fighters, the caliphate could not survive, so such recruiting pitches happened frequently, including some done directly by Baghdadi. Finally, ISIS's apocalyptic discourse and imagery left no doubt that it was the leader of Muslims in this crusade: not al-Qa'ida, not apostate Muslim clerics or those in the "gray zone" (those trying to remain neutral in this cosmic struggle). It was ISIS and its newly minted caliph who were the center of the Muslim world, demanding Muslim obedience in the epochal fight against the armies of "Rome."

ISIS's ideological focus on the apocalypse diminished somewhat after 2014, as it divided its attention between End Times and state-building. But the prophecies of the coming apocalypse never went away from ISIS discourse and still remained in diminished form in the digital world after the ISIS territorial state was vanquished in 2017.

FROM THE APOCALYPSE TO STATE-BUILDING

The defining characteristic of the third wave of global jihad was its emphasis on state-building. 'Abdullah 'Azzam and the first wave were primarily concerned with liberating occupied Muslim lands. Usama Bin Ladin and the second wave of global jihad were focused on driving the far-enemy Americans out of the Muslim world as a means to weaken and eventually overthrow local near-enemy regimes. For both, building some sort of shari'a-based Islamic state would come in due course, but it was not the most pressing issue of the day. ISIS, by contrast, took an inside-out approach: the building of a true Islamic state today, free of apostasy and cultural contamination, would inevitably lead to the accomplishment of all other goals in due course, including defeating local apostate regimes (starting with the Shia regimes in Baghdad and Damascus) and driving out the United States and other infidel powers from the Muslim world.

It is worth underlining a subtle yet important distinction between ISIS and al-Qa'ida (one of many) regarding the core issue of apostasy, of Muslims abandoning true Islam in the eyes of jihadi radicals: al-Qa'ida wanted to overthrow apostate *regimes* in the Muslim world, while ISIS's focus was on eliminating *apostasy itself.* That is, ISIS's goal was far broader, seeking to remake all of Muslim society through its application of "true" shari'a, so that apostasy and the temptations that lead to apostasy were banished from all the lands of the caliphate. In that way, a truly pious Muslim life could be led. Apostasy is driven by temporal temptations, including listening to music, lax dress codes, smoking, shaving beards, wearing make-up, drinking alcohol, gender mixing outside of family members, homosexuality, chewing *qat* or consuming other drugs, the use of cell phones, noncondoned sexual relations, and any celebration of frivolous or non-Islamic holidays or occasions, among other vices—all of which were banned in the caliphate. Those participating in any of these activities could be punished with fines, lashings, incarceration, or other punishments, including death. In this way, ISIS was more akin to the Taliban, the religious police in Saudi Arabia (*mutawwa'in*), the guidance patrols in Iran (*gasht-i ershad*), and Salafi and other ultra-orthodox Muslims who seek to remake the public square so it would have no outward signs of anti-Islamic, Western, or apostate behavior.

ISIS viewed its attack on apostasy as an extension of the Apostasy (or *ridda*) Wars that followed the death of the prophet Muhammad in 632 CE. In the view of Abu Bakr, the prophet's successor, upon Muhammad's death apostasy became rampant in the previously united Muslim community throughout the Arabian Peninsula, as tribes turned their backs on Islam. Many claimed that their allegiance was made only to Muhammad, and with his death they became free agents again, not obliged to follow the tenets of Islam. Such challenges were not only about personal behavior but were viewed as a threat to the integrity of the new Islamic state, much like ISIS equated apostasy in personal behavior as a political threat to the new caliphate as well. Just as Abu Bakr put down the apostate challenges and reunited the Arabian Peninsula under the banner of Islam, so too did ISIS harshly suppress all signs of apostasy, which included political challenges to its rule.

The ISIS caliphate also represented a pre-Westphalian state. The Treaty of Westphalia in 1648 was a milestone in the evolution of the modern state system in Europe. It largely ended the nonstop religious wars that followed the Protestant Reformation of 1517 by recognizing the basic legitimacy of all states, no matter their religious or internal make-up. The inherent superiority or godliness of one monarchy over another gave way at Westphalia to a kind of grudging mutual acceptance among states and a recognition that their internal issues were not to be matters of deep interest to outside states. The logic of Westphalia undergirds the modern international system of states as well, although certain extreme exceptions (e.g., genocide) are widely viewed as requiring that Westphalian norms be put aside in favor of external intervention.

The ISIS caliphate thoroughly rejected the Westphalian system of modern states, and not just by its eradication of the border between Iraq and Syria and its rejection of all borders. ISIS also rejected the very notion that it should not interfere in the internal matters of other states: as the caliphate, all Muslims' concerns were its concerns. No artificial boundary between Muslim states had any legitimacy for ISIS, and it routinely acted both by word and deed to erase any such artificial distinction. ISIS customarily called for Muslims in other countries to rise up to overthrow their leaders and, to the degree it could lend material support, it helped Muslims try to do so. In other words, ISIS acted much like the religious states in Europe before the Treaty of Westphalia, rejecting the very legitimacy of any state other than its own. It is not a coincidence that ISIS never appealed to the United Nations or other individual states for recognition and an exchange of ambassadors. ISIS rejected the entire international system upon which such mutual recognition relied.

That said, ISIS still needed to act like a state *internally*, in that it had to provide various services to its population through specialized institutions. In this regard, ISIS had at best a mixed record. What ISIS did well was to reduce crime and official corruption. While reliable hard data are difficult to come by, all anecdotal accounts suggest that common crimes, such as theft and assault, dramatically waned under ISIS rule.[36] Such decline was almost certainly due to the *hudud* punishments implemented by ISIS: cutting off the hand of the thief, for example. In addition to such draconian punishments, criminals also risked being considered a political enemy of ISIS, depending on the circumstances. In that case, the punishment was public execution. Official corruption also declined dramatically, in part because of the harsh punishments inflicted and in part due to the presence of ideological true believers who very much thought of themselves as doing God's work in the caliphate. Other common forms of corruption declined, including the pervasive demand for petty bribes by police and other officials.

Scholar Aisha Ahmad has persuasively argued why Islamist regimes in unstable places tend to be preferred by many in business: Islamists tend to require less bribery, and one "tax" payment for goods entering their territory tends to suffice for their whole territory. In this way, some preferred Somalia under unified Shabaab rule to the previous fragmented, warlord-run country where every few miles a new tribe or clan or warlord set up its own checkpoint to extort transit fees on people and goods.[37] The same held true when the Taliban united most of Afghanistan away from fractious warlord rule. There is significant anecdotal evidence that ISIS behaved like the Shabaab and the Taliban during the height of its caliphate in the 2014–16 period, diminishing common corruption and bribes that locals had grown accustomed to under the previous rulers. When it came to governance, ISIS did "law and order" best, providing security (at least initially), reducing crime, and limiting corruption.

ISIS's extensive social engineering in other realms of governance was much less successful, however. Education under ISIS rule was a disaster. The primary "educational" activities for boys tended to be Qur'anic memorization and jihadi training. The degree of female education under ISIS varied widely by location, and girls often had no schooling at all. As a general proposition, ISIS, like the Taliban, did not believe girls should be educated; instead, they should be trained at home in how to take care of their future husbands and families. To the degree that textbooks were used at all, they tended to be highly unprofessional PDFs of various subjects, often using militaristic exercises (e.g., math drills counting Muslim versus *kuffar* soldiers on the battlefield). The "Diwan" (not ministry) of education tended to be used as "a dumping ground for unskilled or incapacitated fighters."[38] ISIS sometimes focused on the bizarre at the expense of real education: for example, replacing in mathematics classes the universal symbol for addition (+) with a (z) so as not to use a symbol similar to the Christian cross and thus imitate infidels.[39] In all cases, militaristic indoctrination replaced actual education; in some cases, young boys actually participated in the execution of some prisoners, with the executions videotaped and uploaded online. The youth under ISIS's control lost years of education, in addition to suffering psychological problems as a result of their indoctrination in, and exposure to, perpetual extreme violence.

Other realms of governance—such as public works, street maintenance, water, and electricity—did not markedly decline in the early months of ISIS rule.[40] ISIS tried to keep the current technocrats in their respective positions as long as there were no obvious political problems. So, for example, sewage system operators were kept in place when ISIS took over an area, preventing a collapse in the processing of sewage. But three factors prevented this early relative success from being sustainable over time. First, ISIS could not keep up with replacing the technocrats that it did lose, as the volunteers from abroad almost always came to fight and were not well-trained technocrats who could run a sewage system, for example. ISIS lost so many doctors that it allowed medical students with only three years of study to be licensed to practice. The same brain drain was evident in other fields that required technocratic knowledge. Second, ISIS's constant ideological need for war and fighting to expand the caliphate put greater stress on the system of governance, especially the provision of services. Endless war takes its toll on all governance. Third, and related: ISIS's system of taxation and revenue generation was not sustainable and more closely approximated a Ponzi scheme than a sustainable governmental system.

ISIS never published a budget, so information about its system of taxation, revenue generation, and expenditures is to some degree informed guesswork, although some captured documents corroborate the general gist of its finances. During its three-year apex, from 2014 through 2016, ISIS generated on average about $800 million in revenues per year, but the actual amount and sources of revenues varied significantly.[41] Taxes and fees were always the leading revenue source, typically accounting for about half of all revenues. They were in sharp decline (by about half) by 2016, as the gradual immiseration of the population under ISIS's control became more acute. The sale of oil constituted about 25 percent of revenues, but this also declined as US and allied air strikes reduced oil supplies. Looting, fines, the sale of confiscated property, revenues from kidnappings, and the sale of antiquities on the black market combined to make up about 25 percent of ISIS revenues, but these were also in steep decline by 2017 as the supplies of these items had begun to dry up.

The evidence suggests that ISIS did not have a sustainable system of taxation and revenue generation, as it (a) relied on the sale of items that were of limited supply, and as the supply dried up, so did revenues, and (b) it relied on a level of taxation that could not be sustained by an increasingly impoverished population. But given the demands for basic services in its territory and given its need for endless, apocalyptic war, ISIS was stuck: it simply did not have a sustainable system of revenue generation that could last indefinitely and help generate economic growth within the confines of its policy decisions. As scholar Mara Revkin has shown, ISIS (like other radical groups) often collected taxes for ideological reasons, not for economic ones, meaning revenues were not designed to boost economic output so much as to satisfy ideological goals.[42] While ISIS supporters could point to this or that anecdote of successful governance for a while, its basic governmental and fiscal models were broken from the start and doomed to collapse over a fairly short period of time, particularly as external pressure on the caliphate ramped up substantially in 2016. Even without its military defeat, it was just a matter of time before the ISIS state went bankrupt.

JIHADI COOL

What made ISIS so much more popular than any other global jihadi group, and arguably more successful than any jihadi group of any stripe? Why would forty thousand mostly young men take the risk of illegally slipping across international borders to join a dangerous fight in Iraq and Syria? Why would tens of thousands of other local Sunnis willingly, even enthusiastically, join the cause, at least until ISIS's fortunes began to fall? The secret to ISIS's success lay in its unique merging of the traditional with the hip, of orthodox Sunni Islam with memes of *jihadi cool*.

Much of ISIS's messaging was profoundly traditional, which expanded its potential support base with Sunni Muslims who saw nothing particularly radical about ISIS, at least in its earlier years. A major traditional theme for ISIS was communal sectarianism: to defend Sunni Islam against the "rejectionist" (*rafida*) Shia, who had been empowered by the US occupation of Iraq and were using their newfound power to advance their own interests and settle scores with the Sunnis. This theme was singing to the choir among Iraq's Sunni Arab community, which was in need of a champion to protect its communal interests. It did not have to be ISIS that rose to be the community's champion, but as the fortunes of Iraq's Sunni Arabs sank lower and lower in the face of a recalcitrant anti-Sunni regime in Baghdad, ISIS took advantage of that opportunity. It was nearly the same story in next-door Syria, where the Sunni Arab community was at war with the 'Alawi Ba'thist regime in Damascus. In the case of Syria, multiple groups claimed to be the Sunni Arab community's champion, although all of the most powerful contenders were hardline salafi-jihadi groups: the Conquest Front (Jabhat al-Nusra), the Free Men of Syria (Ahrar al-Sham), the Army of Islam (Jaysh al-Islam), and ISIS.

ISIS left the other groups to fight in the more densely populated western part of Syria, while it focused on conquering eastern Syria: lands that the Syrian military had largely vacated.

A sectarian jihad to defend Sunni rights against Shia apostates is about as traditional a message as one could have. This was not a fanciful global jihad to attack America or liberate some faraway occupied lands, but a real-life fight for Sunni rights in the heart of the Middle East. Such a framing of the issue allowed young Sunni men from Liverpool or elsewhere to proudly "serve" the cause without risking the stigma of radicalism from others in their community at home. The clear dedication in word and deed to Islamic traditions, mores, and laws—or at least to ISIS's interpretation of them—also constituted a powerful, if traditional, meme. Graeme Wood famously called ISIS "very Islamic," and it was this powerful construction of tradition that ISIS propagated that attracted many young men who were not particularly radical in their world view.[43]

But ISIS's construction of tradition was married to a hip, cool message that set it apart from al-Qa'ida and other jihadi groups. I have stressed that ISIS did not concern itself with convincing theological arguments that would persuade ranking clerics of the rightness of its actions. Rather, it wanted to appeal to young men seeking adventure and meaning in their lives, who grew up listening to hip hop and other forms of pop culture, played gory video games, and perhaps had a few scrapes with the law. What leading ISIS ideologues such as Zarqawi, Naji, and Baghdadi embodied is what I described earlier as *propaganda of the deed*—letting one's actions speak for themselves. The message was this: Come to the caliphate not because we are theologically correct, but because we are cool, because you can do these ultra-hip things with us that are unimaginable in the real world. Zarqawi's theological or political arguments could not be repeated by most recruits, but they had seen him decapitate "infidels" and fire off his M-249 machine gun in the desert wearing his jihadi garb and New Balance running shoes. Baghdadi declaring himself caliph, having the guts to do what no other jihadi leader was willing to do, was the epitome of cool. To do it wearing chic black garb designed to evoke memories of earlier caliphs, adorned with the bling of a Rolex watch, just added to the coolness factor.[44]

The caliphate became a dark Disneyland for Jihadis, a place where they could fulfill all of their most ghoulish dreams, as though they were living out some real-life version of *Mortal Kombat* or *Manhunt* video games. In the caliphate, like in the video games, there was no accountability required. No matter how gory or how macabre, violence that advanced the interests of the caliphate was celebrated, not punished. There was no limit except for the imagination on ways to kill various infidels, apostates, enemy soldiers, or just hapless victims of kidnapping whose ransoms were not paid. The executions were always videotaped in high-definition color, with melodic Qur'anic chanting (*nashid*) typically added for effect, and then distributed to ISIS's morbid fans online and through social media to get maximum exposure. Drown caged prisoners in a pool with underwater cameras to catch all the action? Shoot a rocket-propelled grenade into a car with prisoners locked inside? Slowly and dramatically burn to death a prisoner locked in a cage? Execute prisoners with anti-aircraft guns? Have "lion cubs"—that is, indoctrinated young boys—shoot lines of prisoners? Use a knife to behead a prisoner? All of these gory deaths and more were part of the ISIS message of grisly cool, of mimicking those video games but this time for real—and being celebrated for it. Actions that would turn the stomach of most Muslims viscerally appealed to a small subset of mostly young men for whom all of this was an incredible adrenalin rush, the coolest, most awesome spectacle imaginable. ISIS was jihadi cool.

In addition to the opportunity to prove their manhood through battlefield heroics, all ISIS fighters were also promised bountiful sex—a factor that should not be overlooked in examining ISIS's appeal to young men. The sex could come from a promised wife or wives recruited from around the world or from concubines or sex slaves passed on from man to man. Indeed, ISIS went out of its way to identify what kinds of women were most suitable for which category. Teenage Muslim girls, preferably virgins, were idealized as brides, and ISIS actively tried to recruit such girls to join them in the caliphate. On the far other end of the spectrum were women and girls who were neither Muslim nor from protected groups (Jews and Christians) and thus who could be used as sex slaves in ISIS's view. It was this distinction that prompted the use of Yazidi females as sex slaves by ISIS. Yazidis are Kurds who practice a folk form of pre-Islamic Zoroastrianism. Thousands were captured and enslaved, and most of the men were executed, when ISIS overran the Mount Sinjar region of northwestern Iraq in August 2014. ISIS wanted to institutionalize the practice of such sex slavery, issuing "Fatwa Number 64" to parse out the details for its internal members.[45] ISIS also justified and detailed its enslavement of Yazidi women to the wider world in its propaganda magazine, *Dabiq*.[46]

Dangerous exploits, unaccountable and macabre violence, and bountiful sex, all in the service of a brand new caliphate—what could be more attractive to a stratum of young men in search of an adventure, who wanted to be heroes in a cause bigger than themselves and have fun doing it? This was cool, jihadi cool, for tens of thousands of young men. This is not to suggest that all ISIS recruits fit the jihadi cool recruitment pitch. Some earnest young men joined to fight the oppressive regime of Bashar al-Asad in the belief that doing so was their duty as Muslims. Rarely, whole families migrated to the caliphate, making the allure of bountiful sex for young men less applicable. The point is not to suggest a single profile of all ISIS recruits, but rather to argue for the prominent role that jihadi cool played in attracting many young men to the cause.

THE FALL OF ISIS

It was only a matter of time before Iraq's military forces would recover, regroup, and rout ISIS. A recognized state, even a dysfunctional one, will nearly always have access to more resources and military might than a group, even one controlling a chunk of territory for a short period. Baghdad also had access to the military might of both the United States and Iran, something ISIS could not come close to matching. ISIS's lightning expansion in 2014 was stopped by late summer when US and allied bombing of ISIS positions began. But ISIS was really stopped when it reached the limits of the ethnosectarian vacuum created by Baghdad's neglect of the Sunni Arab population centers in northwestern Iraq and started to butt up against Shia-majority areas, beginning in Baghdad. ISIS never had a realistic possibility of controlling large Shia areas of central and southern Iraq as those populations would have been constantly in active armed resistance. But Iraq needed to rebuild and retrain its broken military first, with the billions of dollars the United States had spent on that endeavor after 2003 having already been wasted.

During the first two years of its caliphate, ISIS had a nearly free hand to rule as it saw fit in the territory it controlled. While some skirmishes occurred, from the declaration of the caliphate in June 2014 to the reconquest of Falluja by the regime in June 2016, neither Baghdad nor Damascus had the combination of capability and desire to confront ISIS. The exception to this relative calm was Tikrit, where two battles to retake the city occurred, with the second one leading to its successful capture by Iraqi forces in 2015. But Tikrit proved to be a problematic victory: it was accomplished mostly by an ill-trained Shia militia (the Popular Mobilization Forces, or al-Hashd al-Sha'bi), who then rampaged through Tikrit in bloody retaliation against the civilian population for all that ISIS had done against Shia personnel. Such behavior slowed further attempts to defeat ISIS due to the need for much greater training and professionalism. It also hardened Sunni sentiments in Mosul and elsewhere against the notion of being "liberated" by Shia at all.

But over the course of 2016, the strategy of reconquest started to crystalize. In what could be called the Obama Doctrine, the strategy of ISIS rollback involved the combination of overwhelming US airpower (ISIS had no air force nor any effective anti-aircraft capabilities) and local ground forces working with a small number of US special forces to coordinate ground attacks with air strikes. US airpower was assisted by numerous European (especially France and the United Kingdom) and Arab partners in a display of just how many countries ISIS had alienated by that point. The Iraqi army did most of the ground fighting and suffered the most casualties within the anti-ISIS coalition. In a parallel effort, Iran was also assisting Iraq in defeating ISIS, led by General Qassem Soleimani and the Quds Force of the Revolutionary Guards. The Quds Force is Iran's primary regional military actor, as it works with its allies in Iraq, Syria, and Lebanon, and Soleimani earned the reputation as a brilliant tactician for Iran's elite special force. Iran focused on recruiting and training the Popular Mobilization Forces, giving it an informal division of labor with the United States: the Americans worked with Iraq's formal military, and the Iranians worked with the militia forces.

The battle to retake Mosul began in October 2016 and was not completed until July 2017. At the beginning, ISIS was able to field about five thousand of its most hardened, ideologically committed fighters, who had had plenty of time to set booby traps, dig tunnels, and stake out the best ambush sites inside Mosul. Iraqi forces were much more numerous, but overwhelming numbers are of marginal significance in urban warfare; the defense has the advantage. The slow, grinding, street-by-street fight gradually sapped ISIS of its fighters but also led to the deaths of about ten thousand civilians.[47] The Obama Doctrine of using the combination of US airpower, indigenous ground forces, and small numbers of US Special Forces to coordinate the effort was continued by the Trump administration when it came to office in January 2017. Although the rules of engagement were loosened, the same formula was kept in place for the final battles in Iraq and those in Syria. In the case of Syria, the indigenous force with whom the Americans partnered was the Syrian Democratic Forces (SDF), which consisted primarily of the Kurdish YPG (People's Protection Units) militia and some local Arab forces.

The battle for ISIS's notional capital city, Raqqa, Syria, began even before Mosul had completely fallen. When SDF troops captured Raqqa in October 2017, the ISIS territorial state—the caliphate as a landed entity—ceased to exist. The third wave of global jihad effectively ended when the thing that made it distinctive—its territorial state—no longer existed. ISIS still had some thousands of fighters who held out in a few patches of territory in Syria along the Iraqi border until early 2019, before being routed by the SDF. But the territorial state was already finished and unlikely to be reconstituted in the future. The defeat of ISIS as a territorial state, and thus the defeat of the third wave of global jihad, did not mean the end of ISIS as a jihadi group. ISIS may not have much command and control over its fighters anymore, but emerging from ISIS's defeat were thousands of ideologically committed fighters, now dispersed, who will represent a deadly terror threat well into the future. In addition, while ISIS as *state* has been defeated, ISIS as *idea*, has not. We have not seen the last of the ISIS effect yet.

EVALUATING THE THIRD WAVE OF GLOBAL JIHAD

The third wave of global jihad began as a result of the US invasion of Iraq in 2003 and ended with the fall of Raqqa in 2017. It was easily the largest and most impactful of the four waves of global jihad. "Largest" can be measured in various ways, including the amount of territory controlled by ISIS during its peak years (the size of Great Britain), the number of people who came under its jurisdiction (up to ten million), the extent of its financial resources (over $3 billion in total ISIS revenues), and the number of foreign fighters it attracted (approximately forty thousand). In fact, the four waves of global jihad together have attracted a grand total of about one hundred thousand fighters, both foreign and local, the large majority of whom fought with ISIS.

Part of ISIS's success was attributable to its more traditional form of local and sectarian jihad. In terms of extreme Sunni fundamentalism, ISIS was quite traditional in some ways: fighting foreign invaders in the heart of the Middle East and working to overthrow apostate regimes in Baghdad and Damascus. Even the most radical aspect of ISIS—the declaration of a caliphate—fits in with a long history of multiple claimants to the office of caliph.[48] Indeed, ISIS quite consciously patterned much of its behavior after early Saudi state-building attempts, primarily those from the nineteenth century.[49] Of the four waves of global jihad, ISIS had the least claim to a global agenda but the greatest ability to recruit; these two phenomena are closely related.

A reasonable question suggests itself: Given this focus on tradition, why should ISIS be classified as a *global* jihad group at all? There are three reasons. First, ISIS recruited both men and material globally, particularly the estimated forty thousand fighters from at least eighty-six countries. Second, ISIS had a global vision: to bring 1.7 billion Muslims under its authority and sovereignty as a caliphate. Third, ISIS had global reach, from terror attacks in Europe and elsewhere, to alliances with its affiliates around the Muslim world. In these important ways, ISIS was indeed a global phenomenon. ISIS's impact will long outlive the actual caliphate, both as a group and as an idea. The destruction of the territorial state, and the mopping up of the remaining ISIS villages in Syria along the Iraq border that was completed in March 2019, still left thousands of ISIS fighters dispersed in Iraq and Syria, many of whom will likely continue the fight. As long as the Sunni Arab communities in Iraq and Syria feel marginalized and discriminated against, such fighters will find a largely receptive social base in which to live and operate. The jihadi fish will find a welcoming sea, to borrow Mao's observation. The structural conditions that allowed the third wave of global jihad to prosper have not been addressed, making it likely that the violence will continue. ISIS as guerrilla group or series of cells has already begun to materialize in the absence of its territorial state.

The third global jihad wave of fighters will likely bleed into the fourth wave of lone wolf and small cell stochastic violence, as is discussed in chapter 4. That is, as ISIS fighters go home or otherwise move on from the caliphate, some will likely continue to undertake acts of violence even without logistical support from ISIS or any other group. These fighters will maintain the inspiration of global jihad and act on their own to advance the cause. The ISIS wave of global jihad will also leave two indelible ideas percolating in jihadi circles for many years to come. First, ISIS invented the notion of jihadi cool, and it was a stroke of marketing brilliance. Other jihadis, at least the smart ones, will learn this lesson if they want to become relevant. "Jihadi cool" means the propaganda of the deed is more important than deep theological argumentation; "just do it" might as well have been the ISIS motto. Using outrageous action and pop culture both to attract recruits and resources, and to frame the message of jihad, will likely become the new normal for the most successful jihadi groups. To the degree that groups can successfully merge tradition with jihadi cool, as ISIS did so successfully, they will become more powerful.

Finally, ISIS has opened the Pandora's box of a new caliphate, forever changing the ideological terrain of global jihad. The caliphate bell cannot be unrung, and that idea will be central in how future jihadi groups position themselves ideologically. Are they part of this notional caliphate? Do they reject the idea and, if so, why? Can jihadi groups return to the old normal of saying a caliphate is a long-term goal but not something that is urgent? Jihadi groups will be compelled to deal with this issue ideologically. Beyond jihadi groups, the idea of a reborn caliphate has captured the imagination of many Muslims around the world: such a place would be led not by the blood-soaked leaders of ISIS, but by a real caliph, much like the Catholic Pope, who would be a moral religious leader. In broader Muslim circles such discussions have begun to occur, again, about the possibilities of a reestablished caliphate appropriate for the twenty-first century and a Westphalian world. If such a development ever comes to pass, ISIS and the third wave of global jihad will be able to claim some credit for that eventuality.

Chapter 4

PERSONAL JIHAD
2001–2020...AND BEYOND

THE FOURTH WAVE OF GLOBAL JIHAD BEGAN AT NEARLY THE SAME time as the third wave, but for very different reasons, in a different part of the world, and with a vastly different ideology. The fourth wave would also long outlast the ISIS caliphate. The third wave was launched with the US invasion of Iraq in 2003 and had as its primary mission the construction of a puritanical territorial state—a caliphate—that would banish apostasy and make a true and pious Islamic life possible under shari'a. By contrast, the fourth wave had its origins back where global jihad first began, in Afghanistan, with the collapse of the Taliban "emirate" at the end of 2001 and the killing or capture of many of the global jihadi fighters who had been based there. The specific crisis that launched the fourth wave was the defeat of the Taliban, but the broader crisis was the looming defeat of global jihad itself, given its unfolding destruction from the end of 2001 into 2003 (by which point the George W. Bush administration had diverted most military resources away from Afghanistan to fight its mistaken war in Iraq).

The fourth wave of global jihad was about the survival of the movement, of keeping hope alive until strategic circumstances improved. Those involved in this wave are not interested in state-building; instead, they have focused on stochastic (inspired) violence through networked, decentralized individuals and small cells, taking full advantage of modern communication technologies to advance the cause of global jihad. If the third wave was mostly about the territorial caliphate, the fourth wave has used *jihad fardi* (personal jihad) as its primary method of operation. The goal of the fourth wave of global jihad is to stitch together small and episodic violent acts of personal jihad into a broader and sustainable *system* of global Islamic resistance.

Usama Bin Laden had made Afghanistan his home since 1996, and it was here that he worked to rebuild the old al-Qa'ida into a force for global jihad. Although the Taliban itself should not be considered a global jihadi group, it was a clear enabler of Bin Laden's passion to attack America, as al-Qa'ida's strikes on US embassies in Africa in 1998 and on the USS *Cole* in Aden Harbor in 2000 demonstrated. Because of that close relationship between al-Qa'ida and the Taliban—including intermarriage—Bin Laden's terror attacks of September 11, 2001, immediately put the Taliban's rule in Afghanistan at risk. To harbor a fugitive responsible for the deadliest attack on US soil since Pearl Harbor in 1941 was to invite an American military response that would not be limited to just al-Qa'ida, which is precisely what happened. The Taliban regime never seriously engaged the American demand for immediate extradition of Bin Ladin and al-Qa'ida's other leaders and instead engaged in a series of stalling tactics designed to buy time. On October 7, 2001, US military action commenced, aided by a large international coalition, and two months later the Taliban surrendered its last stronghold, Kandahar.

American and allied forces continued to pursue al-Qa'ida leaders, most of whom had gone into hiding initially in Waziristan and other remote locations along the Durand Line, which divides Afghanistan from Pakistan. Over time, many leaders (including Bin Laden) relocated to areas in the heart of Pakistan. The megacity of Karachi, with all of its chaos and unruliness, proved a particularly popular locale for al-Qa'ida leaders and related jihadis. One by one, many of these leaders were arrested, often by Pakistani forces, and turned over to the Americans. The global jihad community in 2002–2003 was not such a large force that it could withstand a sustained decapitation effort, and it found itself facing an existential threat to its very survival. Global jihad as both *idea* and physical *movement* was in a perilous position because of Bin Laden's foolish gambit. All of its leaders apart from Bin Laden and Zawahiri were either dead, captured, or on the run by 2003. No one was in a position to reconstitute any kind of effective centralized organization to carry on the cause. The main concern for al-Qa'ida militants and their fellow jihadi travelers was not fighting for the cause, but rather fighting for their lives.

It fell to an accomplished ideologue from Syria, Abu Musab al-Suri, to think through how global jihad could survive this existential threat. What kind of strategy could be constructed and adopted that best fit this desperate period and that would allow global jihad to survive until its strategic situation improved? Abu Musab al-Suri put his voluminous thoughts to paper and published his answer online in 2004 in a lengthy book titled *The Call for Global Islamic Resistance (Da'wat al-Muqawama al-Islamiyya al-'Alamiyya)*.[1] Suri's book was central to giving rise to the fourth wave of global jihad and helping define its characteristics. The fourth wave is a durable form of violence based on stochastic personal jihad, and it has already outlived the ISIS territorial caliphate and all other waves of global jihad.

THE LIFE OF ABU MUSAB AL-SURI

Born Mustafa bin 'Abd al-Qadir Sitmiriam Nassar in Aleppo, Syria, in 1958, Suri was radicalized from a young age. He quit his studies in mechanical engineering at the University of Aleppo early, in 1980, to join a growing revolt, led by a radicalized local branch of the Muslim Brotherhood and like-minded jihadis, against the regime of Hafiz al-Asad. Suri's personal role in the uprising is not well-known, although he is thought to have fought in the climactic battle in Hama in 1982, when regime forces flattened the old city and defeated their challengers. Suri was forced to flee Syria, eventually making his way to Spain, where he married a Spanish woman and took Spanish citizenship. Spain remained his primary place of residence through 1994, although he spent considerable time in Afghanistan and Pakistan. He made his first visit to that region in 1987, when he went to Peshawar, Pakistan, with an eye toward fighting in the Afghan jihad. It was then that Suri met and began a relationship with 'Abdullah 'Azzam. Suri subsequently met Usama Bin Laden, with whom he struck up a long-term relationship.

Suri published his first book in 1991, in Peshawar. Titled *The Islamic Jihadi Revolution in Syria*, it was a nine-hundred-page "lessons learned" treatise on the failed uprising in Syria a decade earlier. This book initially set Suri apart from many other jihadi ideologues for his ability to be self-critical, identifying mistakes made by his own side in the war, and suggesting means to fix those mistakes in a future conflict. It appears the publication of this book, more than his actual participation in the uprising itself, made him a wanted man in Syria and may have ultimately led to his (presumed) death. In 1994, Suri moved to London, then the center of jihadi thought in Europe. He was an active journalist and writer in extremist circles, even helping to establish a journalistic center that provided a base from which to engage Western journalists. It was through this center, for example, that Suri arranged a famous television interview for CNN analyst Peter Bergen with Usama Bin Laden in 1997.

Late in 1997, Suri left London permanently for Afghanistan, where he continued his writing and helped train future militants. He opened his own jihadi training camp near Kabul in 2000. The name of Suri's camp, al-Ghuraba', was a reference to a prophetic hadith about the sturdiest earliest Muslims who left the safety and comfort of their tribes to be part of the Muslim community—a distinct linguistic encouragement for Muslims everywhere to leave the comforts of home and gather with the heartiest and most pious Muslims. What set Suri apart from other Arab jihadis in Afghanistan was that he worked closely with the Taliban, including its Ministry of Defense, rather than staying in an Arab cocoon as did most Arab fighters. Over time, Suri fell out with Bin Laden, whom he thought to be a strategic novice and excessively impulsive. Suri openly criticized both the American embassy bombings and the 9/11 attacks as strategic blunders of the first order. He viewed Bin Laden as a dictator for the way he ran al-Qa'ida, referring to him as a "pharaoh." Although Suri is often described as an al-Qa'ida member, in reality he was a free agent, a global jihadi ideologue and fighter who marched to his own (often sordid) drummer.

Suri's movements following the American invasion of Afghanistan in 2001 are shrouded in mystery. He was likely in residence in Pakistan for most of the time until his arrest in 2005. It is speculated that his close ties to the Taliban led him to reside in Quetta, where the Taliban's headquarters in Pakistan is located. Taliban members were protected by Pakistan's ISI (Inter-Services Intelligence, the nation's premier military intelligence unit), which had helped build up the Taliban's capacity as a useful client regime in Afghanistan. During this period in 2003 and 2004, Suri wrote his magnum opus, *The Call for Global Islamic Resistance*, which was published online in 2004. Suri was ultimately captured by Pakistani forces in 2005 and turned over to the Americans. From there, the trail goes cold. He was not transferred to the US base in Guantanamo Bay, Cuba, although he may have been one of the "ghost prisoners" the United States held in Diego Garcia. It appears that Suri was at some point rendered to

Syria, where he was a wanted man. While various jihadi sources report from time to time that Suri is in prison in Syria, the fact of the matter is that if he had been rendered to Syria, he would almost certainly be dead today. Syrian policy during its civil war, beginning in 2011, was to either release or execute its prisoners rather than spending the resources to hold them long term. Suri wasn't released, so if he was rendered to Syria, he is almost certainly dead.

PERSONAL JIHAD AND THE IDEOLOGY OF THE FOURTH WAVE

Seeing his life's work being destroyed all around him in 2001–2002, Suri wrote from a place of desperation. His participation in the armed uprising in Syria in the early 1980s as a college student had been crushed in Hama, forcing him to flee his native country. From his perch in Europe in the 1990s, he had worked closely with the Armed Islamic Group (known as the GIA for its French acronym) in Algeria, only to see the Algerian military win that gruesome civil war. Suri's allegiance to and work for the Taliban in the Islamic Emirate of Afghanistan since 1997 were in shambles by the end of 2001, with the Taliban overthrown by the Americans and with the foreign jihadis who had worked in Afghanistan (like Suri) dead, captured, or on the run, all (in Suri's view) because of the strategic stupidity of Usama Bin Laden. These were desperate times for the global jihadi cause that had had Afghanistan as the center of its universe, and a Plan B was now desperately needed.

Suri was global jihad's most prolific ideas man, and capturing the totality of his strategy in a few pages here will, by necessity, not do it justice.[2] I have chosen to highlight what are the most important and salient elements of Suri's strategy for a new wave of global jihad, including ideas that have significantly evolved within the jihadi community since his capture. Suri's overarching theme was to produce a *system* that could be sustained over time, rather than a hierarchical *organization* that could be easily destroyed. The components of his system consisted of stochastic, individualized violence; a networked and narrative-driven strategy; and plenty of both actual and ritualistic bloodshed. I treat both the overall system and its three component parts in turn.

"A System, Not an Organization!" (*Nizam, La Tanzim!*)

Considering the local jihadi vanguard organizations present throughout the Middle East since the 1960s, Suri recognized how fruitless such organizations

were. Security services had little trouble capturing one or two members, tor-
turing them until they divulged all they knew, including the names of other
members, then rounding up those members, and so on until the whole group
was destroyed. The destruction of secretive, vanguard local jihadi groups occurred mostly in the 1990s, as Suri argued:

> [when state] programs for fighting terrorism were able to disband those organi-
> zations security-wise, militarily defeat them, isolate them from their followers,
> damage their reputation, dry out their financial sources, make their members
> homeless, and put them in a state of constant fear, starvation, and poverty,
> bereft of members. This was a reality that I knew, as other old jihadis like me
> knew as well.... But I look upon methods as means, and not as idols never to
> be altered. We should use those methods that have given us a proven bene-
> fit, and leave behind those methods that are no longer useful. Otherwise, time
> will pass us by.... This earlier emphasis on secretive jihadi organizations led to
> complete failure on all levels.... Gradually, those secret organizations vanished
> and disbanded, and small groups of the remaining jihadis became refugees and
> fugitives, scorned upon here and there, hardly producing anything.

Suri detailed the destruction of local jihadi groups in Algeria, Egypt,
Lebanon, Libya, Morocco, Syria, and Yemen—all of which occurred in the
1990s, well before "the September events" (as Suri referred to 9/11) gave local
security forces a free hand to finish off such jihadi groups. The defeat of jihadi
organizations "was repeated in every Arab and Islamic country," even when
pitted against "the weakest security and intelligence regimes." States and their
coercive apparatuses had little difficulty rolling up hierarchical jihadi organizations. Looking forward, Suri saw the future as even bleaker for jihadi organizations: "If the methods of the hierarchical, local, secret organizations
completely failed in confronting the local security regimes in recent decades,
just imagine how much more we will fail in confronting the security apparatus
of the New World Order and the onset of the worldwide war to fight terrorism
with all its security, military, ideological, political and economic means....
If we insist on continuing these same methods under these new [post 9/11]
circumstances, it will be like committing suicide and insisting on failure."

The end of the Cold War spelled doom for many jihadi (and other militant)
groups, Suri argued, as it closed the political gaps that such groups were able

to use to survive and even thrive. Bin Laden's misguided terror attacks of 9/11 furthered the catastrophe: "We can blame nobody but ourselves when 80% of our forces were eliminated in only two years of repercussions following September 11th." Suri concluded that "the times have changed, and we must design a method of confrontation that is in accordance with the standards of the present time." His new method emphasized a total system of confrontation that was not based on specific hierarchical organizations. The al-Qa'ida type of hierarchical organization had been shown to be ineffective in dealing with the new circumstances of the twenty-first century, as it could be just as easily defeated as were those old local jihad groups in Egypt and elsewhere. A new and global system that was not dependent on an easily-defeated organization was needed: *nizam, la tanzim* (a system, not an organization). Suri's system for the survival of global jihad during a period of desperation had three main components.

Personal Jihad (*Jihad Fardi*)

Suri's *nizam* (system) relied on stochastic violence: violence that is carried out by an individual or small group that has been inspired to engage in that violence by another person or organization. That is, using modern mass communication, calls to violence will increase the *probability* of localized violence but without any increase in certainty where or by whom the violence will be carried out. Suri called his version of stochastic violence "personal jihad" (*jihad fardi*). Personal jihad is better known in the West as "lone wolf" attacks by individuals or small cells. These personal jihads are inspired by calls to violence by various global jihadi groups or leaders but the violence is undertaken independently, with no financial or logistical support from any outside group such as ISIS or al-Qa'ida: only inspiration and encouragement. Scholar Marc Sageman has referred to this phenomenon as "leaderless jihad."[3]

Suri takes no credit for the concept of personal jihad, suggesting it has a long tradition in the Muslim world dating back to the time of the Prophet Muhammad. In more recent years, Suri notes a number of examples of personal jihads, including the assassination of the radical rabbi Meir Kahane; the first attack on the World Trade Center in 1993 by a small cell around Ramzi Yousef; a Jordanian soldier who opened fire on Israeli students "who were mocking the Muslim prayer"; and numerous other acts of violence by single individuals or small groups. Suri argues that personal jihads have been very successful in most ways, because they have the element of surprise, are often spontaneous, and are extremely difficult to stop. Because they are carried out by one person or a small cell, often by individuals not known previously as security risks, such attacks are exceedingly challenging for police and security forces to detect ahead of time and prevent. This type of durability represents the strength of personal jihad. By contrast, the historical weakness of personal jihad is that the attacks tend to have little political coherence or broader demonstration effect. They tend to be isolated acts of violence that fade from public memory fairly rapidly. Thus, for Suri, the answer in turning personal jihad from a successful but small and episodic form of political violence into something that can be sustained and enlarged over time is to ensure that it is part of a *system*—a system of global Islamic resistance.

According to Suri, personal jihad must take place under the condition of an absolute commitment to the Islamic nation (*umma*). One's tribe or ethnicity or country of origin should make no difference; the only identities of importance are one's commitment to God and to each other as Muslims. This is the cause that must tie together all acts of violence, all acts of personal jihad, in the name of the universal Islamic community and its global resistance against those who seek to harm Muslims. He explained it this way:

> It is absolutely necessary to have a sense of commitment to the Islamic Nation and its world, in the geographical, political and military dimensions and in every field. Whoever looks at these established borders, curved and strangely twisted as they are when they draw the maps of our countries, see the drawings by the pens and rulers of the infidels in the ministries of the colonial powers. It is strange, then, that these false borders that wrongly divide Muslims have been engraved in the minds and hearts of the majority of the sons of this Islamic Nation.... We must open the minds and hearts of the Islamic Nation's youth so that they feel commitment to the Islamic Nation as a whole, and not to arbitrary states. This is fundamental to our religion and faith, but also to our politics and our strategic military concept.

Suri's military theory for the fourth wave of global jihad relies foundationally on two elements. First, of course, is personal jihad, which he openly refers to as terrorism—*jihad al-irhab al-fardi* (personal terrorism jihad). Indeed, Suri embraces the word *terrorism* (*irhabiyya*), arguing that Muslims should reject America's definition and moral judgment about such violence. According to Suri, under the right circumstances, terrorism can be praiseworthy: it can be violence "by the righteous who have been unjustly treated, and to remove injustice from the oppressed.... Ours is the terrorism of a people defending themselves against the servants of Satan. This is praiseworthy terrorism. Terrorizing our enemies is a religious duty, and assassinating their leaders is a Prophetic tradition."

In addition to personal jihad, Suri's military theory relied on the use of networks (more on that below), which could withstand the pressure of security forces far better than organizations. Networks have been empowered in the age of the Internet, a reality that jihadis could take advantage of. Network forms of organization become essential given the weakness of the global jihad community, although certainly do not represent an end state for the movement. According to Suri, only after enough personal terror attacks based on network forms of organization will the time again be ripe to conduct more organized and open warfare to seize and control land (one can hear echoes of Abu Bakr Naji's "savagery" argument here):

> The jihad of individual or cell terrorism, using the methods of urban or rural guerilla warfare, is fundamental for exhausting the enemy and causing him to collapse and withdraw.... The personal terrorism jihad and small cell warfare pave the way for other forms of warfare, the "open front" jihad to seize control over land in order to liberate it and establish shari'a rule.... But without confrontation and seizure of land, a state will not emerge for us, and that is the strategic goal for the Resistance project.

But Suri maintained that the "open front jihad" had failed to date, that seizing land in open armed confrontation with the Americans or others had not worked and was at this point a distant dream. That left his focus on the tactic of networked personal jihad. Personal jihad was not a small vanguard operation: it was for every Muslim. It was an Everyman's Jihad, the "battle of the Islamic nation, not the struggle of an elite." In particular, it was a form of violence that could include the mostly excluded youth in the Muslim world "who want to perform the duty of jihad and resistance by contributing with some kind of activity, but without being required to commit themselves to membership responsibilities of a centralized organization." Mission was more important than bureaucracy.

A final point on Suri's big-tent approach to personal jihad is in order. Like 'Azzam before him, Suri had grown immensely frustrated with Arab Salafi-jihadis who found all sorts of arcane theological reasons to not cooperate with otherwise like-minded jihadis, particularly the non-Arab Taliban. In fact, Suri coined the term "Salafi-jihadi" and he did not mean it as a compliment. These were people he considered to be so doctrinaire and puritanical on matters of theology that they had lost sight of the bigger struggles that faced the Muslim community, and had isolated themselves from their fellow jihadis. That kind of puritanism within the ranks only fragmented the jihadi community and weakened it, in Suri's judgment. The animosity was shared. Salafi-jihadis did not trust Suri because of his broader education and familiarity with ideas outside of the Islamic tradition, which were concepts of knowledge rejected by Salafis. That Suri read and quoted guerrilla warfare practitioners such as Mao Zedong, Che Guevara, Fidel Castro, and Vo Nguyen Giap made him untrustworthy in the eyes of those same Salafi-jihadis for whom there is no worthwhile knowledge outside the corpus of Islam. For Suri, in the global jihadi struggle against powerful enemies, it was not prudent to exclude whole categories of jihadis from potential cooperation based on minor points of theological disagreement.[4] It was for this same reason, again following 'Azzam, that Suri mostly rejected the *takfiri* school of jihad, less on principle and more for the weakness and division it caused among Muslims.

Networks and Narratives

Suri's next critical argument focused on making a coherent whole out of otherwise disparate, one-off acts of personal jihad. In the absence of an organization, what tied the system, the *nizam*, together to make it coherent and meaningful? The answer: networks and narratives. Instead of an organization, the global jihad would be held together through decentralized networks of individuals and small cells. This would provide far greater security to the members of the networks. No money changed hands; no orders were given; there were no promotions or demotions. Such a network was not possible on a global scale in 1963, which Suri used as the base year for his historical narrative, but, as he noted, it is certainly possible in the twenty-first century, given the

Internet and other new information technologies. Jihadis can communicate digitally without ever meeting each other and learn from each other via networks of like-minded individuals. There was no organization to be rolled up by security forces, no names that could be divulged under torture (unless the jihadis were very sloppy), no camps to raid or arms caches to discover. Networks and netwars were a form of conflict and violence made possible by the advent of widespread digital technology.[5] Indeed, when Suri was captured in 2005, he had only had a glimpse of the kind of networked power that digital technology has made available today. He could speak of the Internet but could only imagine social media, encryption technologies, and 5G cellular communications. The technologies that allow jihadi and other networks to thrive have outpaced law enforcement's ability to deal with them.

Perhaps even more important than the information technology that would allow Suri's "system" to operate, was the presence of a narrative that would link together the acts of personal jihad around the world into a coherent and compelling story for other jihadis to follow and for their enemies to fear. Suri typically used the word *culture* (*thiqafa*) to describe the construction of a global jihadi narrative. The production of a broad and unified jihadi narrative would help to

> spread the culture of the resistance and transform it into an organized strategic phenomenon, and not merely a collection of unconnected actions; to spread the ideology of the resistance, its program, its legal and political bases, and its operational theories so that they are available for the Umma's youth who strongly wish to participate in the jihad and resistance.... This will help build the resistance units into a "system of action" in which all efforts are coordinated so as to confuse the enemy, exhaust him and inspire the spirit of the Umma so that more Muslims may join in the resistance.

Suri stressed the idea that there would be no organizational bonds linking the members of the global Islamic resistance, "except for the bonds of a program of beliefs, a system of action, a common name, and a common goal"—that is, a common grand narrative—and that "every unit consisting of one person or more is regarded as an independent unit." Every attacker must be savvy about reporting his objectives to the media, to spread the word of the intent of the action in the name of global Islamic resistance. "The idea" of this strategy, this grand narrative to be employed at the individual level, according to Suri, "is to transform the individual jihad into a phenomenon which embraces the efforts of everyone under a single name, for a single goal, and with a single slogan, organized under a single program." This is how otherwise random acts of violence get unified under a single narrative of global jihad. Such a compelling narrative that stiches together disperse acts of violence can thereby make the overall impact of rather minor violence seem greater than the sum of the parts.

The narrative that unites jihadis in purpose in the absence of organization, and that explains and justifies their acts of violence, also contains an understanding of the hated Other, the various cultures of apostasy that the jihadis are fighting. As Suri put it:

> The American Jewish-Crusader invasions today are dependent on destroying the Muslims' religious, moral, cultural and ideological foundations. Among the methods of doing this is the spreading of a culture of decay, depravity, adultery and immorality, and of unveiling, nakedness and the mingling of sexes, and other types of social corruption. Many mass media and propaganda outlets have embraced this corruption, and they have employed many thinkers, artists, literary men, and the like to propagate it. One of their greatest tools today are satellite TV channels which are financed by the millionaires of debauchery and corruption, that is, rich Gulf Arabs and Saudis.... This is a rotten torrent and sweeping epidemic of a culture of corruption, licentiousness, and depravity.... It is therefore necessary, legally, logically, and rationally, that these institutions and their most important men, advocates, and leaders become targets for bombs, destruction and assassinations.

Thus Suri called for a system of violent personal jihads, united through networks and a grand narrative (a *wiki-narrative*, as I discuss below). Suri was not calling for surgical strikes and limited violence. Rather, through his arguments and actions, he advocated for extreme violence directed primarily against soft targets: civilians.

Extreme Violence

Like Abu Bakr Naji, writing at the same time, Abu Musab al-Suri emphasized the need for prodigious and bloody violence. As noted above, Suri took pride in repeatedly using the term *terrorism* to describe the violence global jihadis needed to inflict on their enemies. But even before writing *The Call for Global Islamic Resistance*, he was a practitioner and close confidant of terror. In the 1990s, one of Suri's journalistic portfolios was the bloody civil war in Algeria, and there is evidence that he was close to the GIA—the most bloodthirsty of all the participants in that most gruesome of conflicts. Before there was ISIS, the GIA undertook a similar style of over-the-top blood and gore, of performative slaughter, although without the benefit of social media on which to share live videos. The GIA took its bombing campaign to Paris in 1995, which may have been what convinced Suri to leave the continent permanently for London so that he could more easily escape suspicion.

Being a close student of Algeria and an avid reader, Suri would have certainly come across the writings of Frantz Fanon, and in particular Fanon's 1961 book *The Wretched of the Earth*, which is in many ways the most radical expression of the 1954–62 Algerian revolution against France. France's colonialism in Algeria was probably the most extensive colonial project in history. Over the course of its 132-year domination, France utterly shattered Algerian society with pervasive violence, both overt and institutional. French suppression of the Algerian revolution likewise reflected the violence that lay at the base of French control, as General Paul Aussaresses, one of the chief architects of French repression, would later famously detail.[6] In allegorical form, Fanon wrote of the importance of bloody revenge against one's oppressor, a sort of ritual purification of the soul that comes from killing one's oppressor with one's own hands. It seems that Suri may have adopted a Fanon-like fascination with the ritualized killing of one's perceived oppressor.

In addition to Suri's early ties to the bloody GIA (before he later broke with them), he appears to have had an operational hand in two of the grisliest terror attacks in Europe, which occurred in Spain and London. The 2004 train bombings in Madrid killed nearly two hundred people and injured about two thousand, making them the deadliest terror attacks ever in Spain. Although Suri was not formally charged, he was widely believed to have played a role in the attacks. He wrote about the Madrid attacks in detail in his book, justifying them as a significant strategic success because of their impact on the Spanish elections and Spain's subsequent decision to withdraw its small contingent of forces from Iraq. It is also widely suspected that Suri played a planning role in London's "7/7" suicide terror attacks in July 2005, which killed fifty-six and wounded nearly eight hundred bus and subway riders. In addition to his suspected planning role in various acts of terror, Suri wrote of the need for extensive and extreme acts of violence, focusing primarily on the soft targets of civilians. His enemies list in *The Call for Global Islamic Resistance* is extensive. His theory is one of terrorism, of instilling fear in the civilian population of enemy countries. To quote Suri:

> The theory of terrorism is based on deterring the enemy with fear.... The Resistance is basically at war with the invader campaigns, and it must deal with them by using the methods of terrorism and confrontation.... The resistance must be able to confirm that its arms are long and able to reach everyone who allows himself to be seduced into joining the aggression against the Muslims and the Islamic resistance fighters, or to support their invader enemies. Generally most of our enemies, and especially the apostates, the agents, the hypocrites, the corrupted, and those bragging about their so-called culture and development, are a group of cowardly rats, starting from the biggest of their kings, presidents, and princes, and to the smallest of their writers, their media figures and their sycophants with all their fantasies. Most of them will be deterred if one sets an example of striking or severely punishing a few of them.

According to Suri, civilians (particularly Americans and their allies) are legitimate targets. He calls for the "mass slaughter of the population by targeting crowds in order to inflict maximum human loss. This is very easy since there are numerous such targets, such as crowded sports arenas, social events, large international exhibitions, crowded market-places, sky-scrapers, crowded buildings.... There is a large number of easy targets." Suri's idea of personal jihad was adopted by others in the global jihad community, especially ISIS. Indeed, after the US-led bombing of ISIS targets in Iraq began in the late summer of 2014, ISIS leader Abu Muhammad al-Adnani called for ISIS's supporters in America and France to kill their "infidel neighbors" wherever they were without waiting for instructions or permission:

> [Kill them] from your place, wherever you may be. Do not ask for anyone's advice and do not seek anyone's permission. If you are not able to find an IED [bomb] or a bullet then smash his head with a rock, or slaughter him with a knife, or run him over with your car, or throw him down from a high place, or choke him, or poison him. If you are unable to do so, burn his home, car or business.[7]

Suri was perhaps the most dangerous of all global jihadi ideologues. He was smart and could engage in self-criticism; he did not wear an ideological straitjacket that comes from an inability to learn from mistakes and change tactics as needed. He had a sort of Machiavellian cold-bloodedness to him in his calls for extreme violence; it was nothing personal, just what was needed to accomplish the goals of global Islamic resistance. But there was also a ritualistic flavor to Suri's violence, likely born from Fanon's influence. Suri argued that it was important for jihadis to slaughter their political oppressors and cultural contaminators in large numbers—not just for the specific goals it would accomplish but also as a means for Muslims to free themselves from the very demons that had possessed them for so long. Gruesome, bloody violence against one's perceived oppressors—intimate, face-to-face shedding of their blood—was not just a political and "military" undertaking but the ultimate act of self-liberation.

PERSONAL JIHAD AS A FORM OF STOCHASTIC TERROR

Abu Musab al-Suri was one of the world's first ideologues of stochastic terror in the information age, a form of violence made possible through information globalization in the digital era. As noted, stochastic violence is inspired by others but not specifically directed or given logistical support. It typically takes the form of "lone wolf" attacks by true believers who are inspired to kill by others, but who carry out attacks all on their own. The violence is "stochastic"—a mathematical term of probability—because it is both predictable and random. When a group like ISIS puts out a call using mass media for its followers in the United States to kill infidel Americans without waiting for permission or assistance, it is statistically probable that some number of such attacks will occur in response, but it is also random in that there is no way to know which specific lone wolf will take up the call to arms and which specific victims will be targeted. Stochastic terror means that we can predict a general increase in extremist violence under circumstances of external inspiration, but we have little ability to predict the specific details.

Global jihadis are not the only source of stochastic violence. As discussed below, I note violence by white nationalists in Norway, New Zealand, and Virginia that was similarly stochastic. The perpetrators of those killings were motivated by outspoken ideologues, from Donald Trump (in the Virginia and

New Zealand cases) to other leading Islamophobes, but took it upon themselves to carry out the murders without any logistical support from those leaders. When such leaders implore their followers through various forms of mass media that "something must be done" to stop some dire problem, it is predictable that some of their followers will take up arms. To date, neither Suri nor ISIS nor similar ideologues have left any mystery about their calls for mass murder, but their actions are stochastic when they have used mass media to inspire violent acts without providing any direct support for any particular action.

The discourse of "lone wolf" attacks by motivated individuals operating under the radar and not as part of organized groups was started in the 1990s by white nationalists, especially Tom Metzger and Alex Curtis. Metzger was a former Grand Wizard of the Ku Klux Klan (KKK) and is the founder of the White Aryan Resistance, while Curtis likewise has been active in the KKK and other white supremacist groups. The information age, especially the advent of the Internet and social media, has made stochastic violence much more likely, as opinion shapers can easily get messages and narratives out to millions of followers (and anybody else) in seconds. While white nationalists have been early and eager users of new information technologies to spread their narratives and influence action, ideologues of every other cause, including global jihad, have learned to do the same.[8] Right-wing terror expert David Neiwert has referred to this same phenomenon of stochastic terror as "scripted violence." Quoted in a 2018 article, he explained:

> Scripted violence is where a person who has a national platform describes the kind of violence that they want to be carried out. He identifies the targets and leaves it up to the listeners to carry out this violence. It is a form of terrorism. It is an act and a social phenomenon where there is an agreement to inflict massive violence on a whole segment of society. Again, this violence is led by people in high-profile positions in the media and the government. They're the ones who do the scripting, and it is ordinary people who carry it out.[9]

In practice, stochastic violence is almost always stochastic *terrorism*. In the large majority of cases, lone wolf attacks target civilians randomly chosen from broad categories ("infidels," "immigrants," "Muslims," "Jews," "Americans," "anyone walking down the street at the moment," etc.). The same has been true for stochastic, fourth wave violence done by global jihadis in the West:

nearly all have attacked randomly selected civilians, meaning they can be more narrowly seen as acts of terror. Terrorism relies on the fear created by the random selection of its targets: if you are in the wrong café at the wrong time, you could be the next victim. Not all forms of political violence are acts of terrorism. For example, assassinations of political leaders may be acts of war, depending on who carried out the attack, and are certainly criminal acts of homicide, but by definition they would not be acts of terrorism since their victims would not be randomly selected civilian targets. Fourth wave jihadi stochastic violence, like white nationalist stochastic violence, may not *necessarily* be terrorism in theory, but it almost always turns out to be the case in practice. Soft targets are so much easier to hit, and such attacks are much more effective at inducing fear and terror into a hated population, which is the point of terrorism.

Stochastic violence somewhat alters our understanding of the manner in which ideology functions. Typically a political ideology affords three elements: *description, prescription,* and *conscription.* That is, a political entrepreneur will construct an ideology that describes a problem, prescribes a particular solution to that problem, and tries to persuade people to join the caravan (i.e., conscription) to help implement the solution. All of the ideologues described in this book undertook this exact process. For example, Usama Bin Laden constructed an ideology that described a problem (American support kept apostate regimes in the region in power), proposed a solution (attack the Americans to drive them out of the region, making apostate regimes vulnerable), and sought to recruit fighters and resources to his far-enemy cause.

But the fourth wave of global jihad does not rely on a particular ideologue to make the case for the cause. Specific, individual ideologues are too easy for states to assassinate, meaning reliance on them is not sustainable. Suri has not been heard from since 2005, presumably killed by the Syrian regime. The most important English-language inspiration for stochastic jihadi violence was the American cleric Anwar al-Awlaki who had a deep digital presence online. His own radicalization in the years after the 9/11 attacks ultimately led him to AQAP in his ancestral homeland of Yemen, where he was killed by an American drone strike in 2011, along with fellow radical American ideologue Samir Khan.[10] Abu Bakr al-Baghdadi was the target of numerous assassination attempts until finally being killed in 2019. Living, breathing ideologues of global jihad tend to have a short life expectancy.

Rather, the fourth wave relies on a community narrative that keeps getting reshaped and remolded as the wave unfolds, depending on which lone wolf is doing what kind of violence. It is a kind of *Wikipedia* for ideological construction: always changing and evolving, although remaining within broad parameters agreed to by the jihadi community. The shared narrative of global jihad is the ideology, but it is always being tweaked by its community of adherents, rather than by an authoritative ideologue with a position of power and influence. In the fourth wave of global jihad, the *charismatic leader* has given way to the *charismatic narrative*—something that has only become possible with the information age. This community-driven narrative formation among global jihadis may be understood as a *wiki-narrative*, given its ever-evolving content.

Suri's notion of personal jihad (*jihad fardi*) should be understood as foundationally a form of stochastic violence, inspired by a narrative of global jihad and by various groups and leaders, but undertaken by individuals and small cells without any direct assistance from outside actors. The lone wolves have been inspired to take up the mantle of violence by ISIS, al-Qa'ida, or others, or perhaps psychologically snapped upon reading about Israeli violence toward Palestinians or after visiting an old family home in Chechnya where anger against Russia still seethes—or any one of hundreds of other potential triggers. But in every case, the broad narrative will be the same: Islam is under attack by the West and Muslims must respond. They must violently fight back: for honor, for dignity, for survival.

Suri knew the accumulation of lone wolf pinprick terror attacks by themselves would never represent an existential threat to any Western state, nor even a strategic threat, but only a deadly nuisance. This is why he spent so much time focusing on the importance of networks and media narratives, trying to use new technologies to make sure jihadis could network in cyberspace and that they would each build on the narrative of global Islamic resistance, one after another. This connectedness, Suri hoped, would create an impact much bigger than the disconnected attacks that personal jihad had represented in his historical review. Such uncoordinated attacks can be compelling and hard to stop, but as one-off events they lose their power over time and are mostly forgotten. Networks and narratives in the information age can sustain these lone wolf attacks, building their power by connecting them, one and all, at least until times are better for global jihad and more classical open-front warfare might be able to succeed. At least, this is what Suri hoped would happen with his strategy of personal jihad.

FOURTH WAVE ATTACKS IN THE WEST

It is not always possible to distinguish stochastic, fourth wave global jihadi attacks from those that are planned and implemented by groups such as ISIS. Attackers sometimes ignore Suri's recommendations by not leaving behind a video or other media message that unambiguously states why the violence was undertaken or who (if anyone) helped with the logistics of the attack. In some cases, ISIS has been quick to claim credit for attacks it may not have had anything to do with, although its messaging has typically used a particular vocabulary for the attacks that surprised ISIS but that may have been inspired by global jihad in some form. Such militants have often been referred to as "soldiers of the Islamic State," but this pattern has not always held true.

A variant of fourth wave attacks has only begun to occur but will no doubt intensify for the next several years: the lone wolf ISIS returnee strike. By the time the ISIS state collapsed in 2017, there were up to ten thousand living foreign fighters with varying amounts of training. Of those, many stayed with ISIS as it transformed itself back into a guerrilla group, centered mostly in Iraq. Others went home to Europe and elsewhere at different points completely disillusioned by ISIS, with its cherry-picked interpretations of Islam, maladministration, and grotesque violence. But some ISIS fighters have already returned or will return to their homes around the world, still ideologically committed, and will need little if any encouragement from others to undertake acts of terror. They are already highly radicalized. This variant form of lone wolf or small cell violence will almost certainly be more deadly on average than the more typical stochastic jihadi attacks, given the training and knowledge such returnees already possess.

The Easter Sunday 2019 terror attacks in Sri Lanka appear to fit this variant form of fourth wave attacks: led by men who had fought with ISIS and returned home radicalized, who needed no logistical entanglement from the organization to carry out their bombings. There is a parallel here with the so-called Arab-Afghans who returned to their home countries after 1989 and in some cases carried out violent attacks in the absence of any coordination with a larger organization. They were plenty radicalized already. Some generalizations can be made about violent attacks made under the banner of global jihad since 2014, the year ISIS proclaimed a caliphate. Four generalizations stand out. First, the vast majority of such attacks have occurred in the Middle East and North Africa, not in the West, and that is where most deaths have occurred as well. So global jihadis have primarily killed fellow Muslims.[11] Second, the attacks in the Middle East and North Africa have been much more likely to have been planned by ISIS or an affiliated group and thus would not constitute a stochastic, fourth wave attack. Third, and related, the deadliest of the terror attacks, regardless of their locations, are almost always planned and organized by a group, not by an individual. The institutional expertise accumulated in groups like ISIS is reflected in their ability to murder much larger numbers of people than a lone wolf attack typically can. Finally, the global jihadi attacks that have been carried out in the West since 2014 are much more likely to be stochastic in nature than a group operation, even if the deadliest such attacks typically have been planned by a group. Family ties have become increasingly important in such terror attacks.[12]

Deaths from global jihadi terror attacks in North America and Western Europe, combined, in the five-year period from 2014 to 2018, numbered just under four hundred.[13] To put that figure in perspective, it represents about the same annual average for deaths in the United States from bathtub accidents.[14] In the United States and Canada all global jihadi attacks since 2013 appear to have been stochastic, including the four most notorious.[15] During the 2013 Boston Marathon, two Kyrgyz-American brothers, Dzhokhar and Tamerlan Tsarnaev, set off two homemade pressure cooker bombs near the race's finish line. The bombs went off twelve seconds apart, killing three people and injuring more than two hundred others. Over the next several days, the brothers killed two police officers and badly injured another. Following a firefight with the police, Tamerlan was killed, and Dzhokhar was captured, convicted, and sentenced to death. All evidence suggests the Boston Marathon bombing was stochastic in nature and done under the banner of global jihad. The brothers had self-radicalized, mostly over the American wars in Iraq and Afghanistan, and were inspired to action by the various radical jihadi literature they had read online. Indeed, they built their bombs based on an al-Qa'ida instruction manual published on the Internet.

The San Bernardino, California, shootings two years later also appear to have been stochastic. Inspired by ISIS, the husband-and-wife pair, Syed Rizwan Farook and Tafshin Malik (he a native-born American and she from Pakistan), had recently radicalized online and ended up shooting to death fourteen co-workers who were attending an office holiday party. Both attackers were killed in the ensuing chase and shootout with police. Omar Mateen, the shooter in the June 2016 Pulse nightclub attack in Orlando, Florida, had a similar story. Also a native-born American, he self-radicalized late in life, inspired by ISIS. In the midst of the attack, during which he shot to death forty-nine people, Mateen called 911, as Suri would have wanted, to let it be known that he was performing the slaughter for ISIS. Mateen had unresolved problems with his own latent homosexuality, which added another layer to his motivation for the terror attack. The fact that the Pulse nightclub catered to the local gay community only furthered the psychological complications for Mateen's motive. The last of the four most notorious stochastic jihadi terror attacks in the United States occurred in October 2017, when twenty-nine-year-old Sayfullo Habibullaevich Saipov drove a rented pick-up truck into a crowd of pedestrians and bicyclists in New York City, killing eight people. Saipov had immigrated from Uzbekistan in 2010 and had a history only of a bad temper, not political radicalism. He was self-radicalized, apparently inspired by ISIS, but had no logistical connections with any group. His weapon of choice—a vehicle driven into a crowd of pedestrians—has become a favored weapon by stochastic terrorists, in part at the urging of ISIS.

In addition to those four deadly events, there have been a dozen other terror attacks in the United States and Canada, which typically left one or two people dead, often including the perpetrator. These include the first specifically ISIS-inspired stochastic terror event in the United States, which occurred on September 26, 2014, when a worker in Oklahoma beheaded a coworker in the name of global jihad, before being killed himself. In October 2014 two Canadians were killed over a twenty-four-hour period in Montreal and Ottawa by two ISIS-inspired lone wolves, and two more were killed in 2018 in Toronto when a gunman opened fire on Danforth Avenue in Greektown, apparently inspired to do so by ISIS.

Three of the deadliest jihadi terror attacks in Europe during this same time frame were not stochastic because they were planned and executed by groups. The January 2015 assault on the *Charlie Hebdo* magazine's offices in Paris that killed twelve people was organized by AQAP out of Yemen, and the Paris terror attacks in November 2015 that left 130 people dead and scores more wounded were planned and implemented by ISIS. Four months later, at the Brussels airport, another terror attack left thirty-two dead in the name of ISIS, which appears to have played a direct planning role. None of these three large jihadi attacks was stochastic, but essentially all other global jihadi attacks in Europe during this period were stochastic in nature. These include the July 2016 truck attack in Nice, France, that killed eighty-four pedestrians who were out celebrating Bastille Day; a similar truck attack against pedestrians at a Christmas market in Berlin, Germany, in December 2016 that left twelve dead; a horrific May 2017 attack in Manchester, England, mostly against female "tweens" and their parents at an Ariana Grande concert, murdering twenty-two; a truck and stabbing attack a month later near the London Bridge that killed eight; and another truck attack on the popular La Rambla pedestrian mall in Barcelona, Spain, that left thirteen people dead. As in North America, there were a dozen other stochastic terror attacks in Europe during this same time frame that usually killed one or two people at a time in the name of ISIS and the global jihad.

EVALUATING THE FOURTH WAVE OF GLOBAL JIHAD

While Suri's strategy for stochastic, lone wolf terrorism in the name of global jihad was taken up in spades by ISIS as its caliphate began to shrink, and to a lesser degree by other groups, it is not so clear that his tactic of a wiki-narrative that would stitch together all these attacks to make the whole greater than the sum of the parts was particularly successful. Did Suri's strategy of instilling fear and terror in enemy populations while enhancing the networked power of those engaging in personal jihad really work the way he had intended? By some measures, jihadism has enjoyed a meteoric rise over the past two decades. There are far more armed jihadi fighters today than there were on September 11, 2001, although it should be noted that most of that increase was due to hot wars fought in Afghanistan, Iraq, and Syria.[16]

Organized groups such as ISIS and Boko Haram account for the large percentage of all jihadi fighters. By contrast, the number of jihadis who have undertaken stochastic violence has been quite small, measuring in the hundreds, not in the tens of thousands. Yet it is impossible to know how many potential stochastic radicals actually exist, who may snap at some point in time, convinced by the evolving wiki-narrative that it is time for them to take up arms (or trucks) against random Westerners. In all the stochastic acts of terror across various ideological communities, the perpetrator had previously caught the attention of law enforcement only in a handful of cases. Most lone wolves strike without notice or warning, and the degree of their radicalization is only known in hindsight.

Suri's fourth wave strategy has been the most durable of all forms of global jihad. Organizations and territorial entities can be defeated by superior military force. Stochastic, inspired jihadi terror undertaken by an individual or small cell, by contrast, can never be fully and finally defeated, only contained and limited. Suri's focus on a system instead of an organization (*nizam, la tanzim*) to structure global jihad was a brilliant strategic insight. His recognition of the likely success of personal jihad (*jihad fardi*) by comparison to more traditional military or large guerrilla-war tactics was likewise a smart observation on the balance of military power and the nature of the security state in today's world. His focus on the centrality that media and narrative construction (the wiki-narrative) must play in digitally uniting jihadis in common cause and carrying forward the goals of global jihad demonstrated an astute awareness of the uses that information technologies can play in the twenty-first century. In all of these ways, Suri produced a strategy that can survive many potential means of state detection and repression, particularly in the open societies of the West.

But it seems that Suri likely overestimated the force-multiplying impacts of the Internet, social media, and the wiki-narrative. He was right that his narrative media strategy would produce more stochastic violence, but to date, it has not had the enormous synergistic effect that he had hoped for. Dozens of people are being murdered in Europe and North America every year on average from stochastic jihadi violence, but it is a smaller number than are being murdered by stochastic white nationalist violence and only on par with those dying annually in bathtub accidents. Barring dramatic change, fourth wave global jihad will likely remain a durable threat, but one that should be understood as being at the level of deadly nuisance more than as an existential or even significant strategic threat.

Conclusion

MOVEMENTS OF RAGE

THROUGHOUT THIS BOOK I HAVE ARGUED THAT GLOBAL JIHAD has gone through four distinct iterations, or waves, since the 1980s, each wave launched by a particular set of crises and each wave having its own distinctive ideology. The first wave had its beginnings with the Soviet invasion and occupation of Afghanistan (1979–89), which was also the original crisis that launched global jihadism as a phenomenon. For 'Abdullah 'Azzam, the godfather of global jihad, the specific crisis of the Soviet occupation of Afghanistan underscored a broader crisis facing the Muslim world: the occupation of Muslim lands by infidel powers around the world, including Palestine, Kashmir, Mindanao, in Central Asia, and elsewhere.[1] 'Azzam's answer to this broader crisis was to do around the world what he had helped to do in Afghanistan: to create a Jihadi International of pious, strong Muslim warriors who would work with local Muslim populations to free their lands from infidel occupation. 'Azzam was assassinated in 1989, and the Saudis' rejection of his idea, as presented to them by Usama Bin Laden in 1990 as a means to liberate Kuwait from Iraq's occupation, effectively ended the first wave of global jihad.

Radicalized, in part, by that rejection and seeing an ever-growing American military footprint in Arabia since 1990, Usama Bin Laden launched a second wave of global jihad in the mid-1990s. The specific crisis that motivated Bin Laden was the looming defeat of the jihadi campaigns in Egypt and Algeria to seize power from what he viewed as apostate regimes. The expanding US military footprint and the durability of local apostate regimes both had the same underlying source for Bin Laden: an America at war against Islam that was determined to control Muslim resources and diminish Muslim dominion. Bin Laden understood Muslim weakness through the lens of a far enemy that kept propping up local apostate regimes against the will of pious Muslims and increasingly practiced direct domination of the Middle East through an archipelago of US military bases.[2] Thus the second wave of global jihad was initiated; its aim was to drive the Americans out of the Middle East and thereby make local apostate regimes vulnerable to overthrow by righteous Muslims. The terror attacks of 9/11 represented the apex of the "America First!" wave of global jihad. By 2003 al-Qaida as a centralized organization had been virtually destroyed, and the killing of Bin Laden in 2011 essentially spelled the end of the second wave of global jihad.

But two new and distinctive varieties of global jihad were launched in the early years of the twenty-first century. The third wave, embodied by ISIS and its self-declared caliphate, had as its origins the twin crises of the US invasion and occupation of Iraq beginning in 2003 and the civil war in Syria that began in 2011. The broader crisis for ISIS was not the local apostate regimes that so concerned many *takfiri* jihadis who sought to overthrow them. Rather, ISIS was focused on eliminating apostasy itself through state-building. A proper Islamic theocratic state where Muslims could lead a pious life under shari'a was not possible in a Middle East awash with sin and immorality. ISIS's solution, filled with apocalyptic End Times ideology, was to build a pre-Westphalian Islamic state in the heart of the Middle East, call it a caliphate, and banish apostasy and its temptations so that Muslims could live an abundantly righteous and godly life. Never mind that ISIS was cherry-picking its own idealized version of Islam, or that it accomplished what it did more by appealing to a sense of *jihadi cool* than to orthodox Islamic theology. Like other theocratic undertakings where God is at stake, the ISIS caliphate was drenched in the blood of all who disagreed with its vision. The destruction of the territorial caliphate in 2017 with the fall of Raqqa, the nominal ISIS capital in Syria, brought the third wave of global jihad to an end. While the idea of ISIS and a reestablished caliphate remain potent, and their remnants as a jihadi group will continue on its murderous path for years to come, the territorial state is what made the third wave distinctive, and that is not likely to be replicated any time soon.

The fourth wave of global jihad was born out of desperation, when the so-called Islamic Emirate of Afghanistan under the Taliban was destroyed, and the global jihadi community that had gathered in Afghanistan was being killed, captured, or put on the run. The broader crisis was existential: Could global jihad survive this onslaught and live to fight another day? It fell to the Syrian jihadi ideologue Abu Musab al-Suri to chart a strategy for the survival of global jihad. Suri was the most shrewd of all global jihad ideologues, and his strategy of a decentralized network engaging in lone wolf attacks—personal jihad (*jihad fardi*)—and making full use of the Internet and other new information technologies has proved to be a very durable form of global jihad. Inspired, stochastic violence is extremely difficult to stop, even if the number of people it actually kills is small. Suri emphasized the need for a system instead of an organization (*nizam, la tanzim*), as the latter had always proved too easy for superior powers to destroy. He also understood the need to construct a narrative that would stitch together otherwise disparate acts of violence, thereby making the whole effect greater than the sum of the parts. That narrative would not be the work of any one leader, but rather would continuously evolve within the jihadi community, making it a kind of wiki-narrative. The fourth wave of global jihad does not represent an existential threat or even much of a strategic threat, but it is a durable and deadly nuisance.

In this concluding chapter I seek to position global jihad among the universe of cases of violent social movements. In other words, is there a distinctive form of violent social movement across cultures and continents to which global jihad rightfully belongs? Is global jihad so unique and distinctive that it cannot fruitfully be compared with other violent social movements around the world? Is global jihad sui generis or part of a more common response to the vagaries of modernity over the past century? As this conclusion shows, the phenomenon of global jihad shares too much in common with other violent groups to be seen as sui generis or in a universe of cases by itself. In order to properly situate global jihad among that universe of violent contemporary social movements, I compare global jihad groups to other forms of violent groups using the standard, if competing, forms of categorization of violent social movements to show that these usual categories fail to capture the totality of global jihad.

I then turn to the concept of "movements of rage" to suggest that global jihad can be more profitably understood to be a variant form of this rather rare type of political violence.[3] Movements of rage are social movements that, in pursuit of their political objectives, call for extreme nihilistic violence—violence out of all proportion to any reasonable strategic goal—against what their adherents view, in part, as sources of cultural corruption. Within *national* movements of rage, educated urban elites are considered to be the primary source of cultural contamination. Such national movements of rage seek to kill or violently marginalize the educated strata, who are typically found in the capital city. I refer to this assault on the educated, "corrupted," strata of society as *gnosicide*: spasms of violence against those who are seen to possess modern knowledge and sensibilities. For global jihadis, the primary source of social contamination and communal weakness in the Muslim world is seen as the West, along with the "faux-Muslims" who represent a fifth column of corruption within Islam. Global jihad is a variant form of a movement of rage in that it focuses its ideological activities at the global level rather than at the national level.

A primary comparative advantage for using a movement-of-rage approach is that it can insightfully link together both religious and secular groups that are ideologically and sociologically very similar in a way that a religious terrorism or "cosmic war"–type approach cannot. Thus it can help us see patterns of shared ideology, sociology, and politics that foundationally inform what at first glance seem quite different groups—for example, Maoists in Cambodia, Brownshirts in Nazi Germany, Boko Haram in Nigeria, and even elements of white nationalism in Trump's America, to name a few. Global jihad fits well into the comparative patterns found in movements of rage around the world over the past century. Understanding global jihad as a variant form of a movement of rage does not suggest that these groups are somehow apolitical. Far from it. I have spent the previous four chapters detailing the intensely political nature of each wave of global jihad. Rather, it is to highlight the role that extreme, almost unhinged, violence against noncombatants plays in the ideology of global jihad, and how those civilian targets are not viewed as mere tactical enemies to be overcome, but as symbols of cultural corruption and moral depravity. Moreover, a movement-of-rage approach helps situate the ideology of global jihad as not one of progress, equality, or even justice, but rather one of "killing and smiting of necks" in Usama Bin Laden's useful formulation.[4] It is an ideology that is profoundly nihilistic, in the way that the word *nihilism* properly applies to political groups (and not to philosophy).

REVOLUTIONARY MOVEMENTS AND ENLIGHTENMENT IDEALS

The obvious comparison for the global jihad movement is with the whole spectrum of other violent, revolutionary movements in the modern era. But such a comparison is significantly flawed based on the fact that virtually all such movements in the modern era have been based on some version of Enlightenment ideals of human progress, be they from the political Left, Right or Nationalist Center. The most common form of revolutionary violence from the Left centered on Marxism. Karl Marx himself, the various Leninist groups that staged revolutions seeking to come to power, and Communist parties operating around the world in the twentieth century viewed their ideology as explicitly scientific, as the forward progress of humankind from servitude in feudal days, to exploitation under capitalism, to egalitarianism and prosperity under Communism. Their ideology represented the advance of humankind within the parameters of scientifically valid theory, they claimed. In other words, Marxism was founded on the Enlightenment ideals of science and human progress. Even the mainstream Maoist variant of Marxism, which held the peasantry as the proper revolutionary class in nonindustrialized societies, was similarly seen by its adherents as bringing human progress based on a scientific understanding of history. Their societies would be richer, healthier, and more equal once their form of Communism was enacted—a claim that helps explain the broad appeal of Marxism for more than a century.

Most historically recent violent, revolutionary movements on the Right, especially fascism, have been similarly based to a significant degree on Enlightenment ideals. Fascism competed with Marxism throughout the first half of the twentieth century to be the dominant challenger to the liberal world order. And while the word *fascism* has become a verbal insult in today's world, its ideological pull remains strong to this day. Fascism is also an ideology of progress, of "making the trains run on time" in the famous phrase describing (not very accurately) Benito Mussolini's modernization of the Italian rail system in the 1920s and 1930s. In the same vein, the fascist Mussolini left a lasting urban legacy for "modernizing" Rome as part of "la Terza Roma," the rebirth of

Rome for a modern Italian empire. Drawing on Italy's "rational architecture movement," neighborhoods were bulldozed in favor of huge new boulevards and giant monuments to the greatness of Italy. Indeed, the destruction of the Spina neighborhood next to the Vatican in favor of a massive new boulevard leading up to Saint Peter's square was famously initiated by Mussolini himself in 1936, putting a pickax to a Spina roof to begin the demolition. Hitler had an even grander vision for what a new, modern Berlin ("Germania") was to look like, courtesy of Albert Speer, with imposing monuments and broad, modern boulevards. Similar views of progress and modernity can be found in most any fascist movement over the course of the past century, including contemporary variants.

Fascism is a modernist, progress-oriented ideology, although not a liberal one. Fascists believe that excessive freedom undermines their ability to construct the good society, so they advocate for harsh law-and-order policies and the restriction of individual rights. Indeed, society is not seen by fascists as an amalgam of individuals with inalienable rights, but rather as a corpus, a single body of people working in unison for a common purpose. Dissent, in this view, is not normal but represents a form of disease inflicting the corpus; it must be stamped out. Because of its overarching corporatist view of social homogeneity, fascism shares a natural bond with organized religion, which also discourages individual freedom in favor of social uniformity under religious principles. This is the reason that the Catholic church was a strong, if usually quiet, supporter of fascist regimes in Italy, Spain, and Germany. The strong corporatist view of fascism also encourages the elimination or marginalization of those who don't quite "fit in" with society: Jews, for example, or the Roma, or people with disabilities, or homosexuals. Thus, while coming from a Right political perspective that emphasizes social conformity and order, fascism is similarly modern in its focus on development and material progress. Like Marxism, fascism is based on Enlightenment ideals of human progress but with a strongly corporatist and conservative hue.

A third common form of violent political movement over the past three centuries comes from the broad political Center and revolves around either national liberation or liberal nationalism. The post–World War II era saw the advent of decolonization by European countries from around the developing world. Although some decolonizations occurred without serious bloodshed, many more undertook significant violence in order to achieve their aim of national liberation. The 1954–62 Algerian revolution of national independence against French occupation was a particularly bloody decolonization event, but far from unique. Kenya's struggle against the British included the Mau-Mau revolt and its bloody suppression. More contemporary wars of national liberation include Eritrea's fight to be free of Ethiopian rule, South Sudan's long war for liberation from Khartoum, the Palestine Liberation Organization's often violent struggle to create a Palestinian state free of Israeli occupation, and the Irish Republican Army's effort to liberate Northern Ireland from British colonization (as they see it). In all cases of struggles for national liberation, the goal is Enlightenment-based: to advance the freedom and independence of a people seeking equality with the other nations of the world as part of the forward march of human progress. No more Orientalist paternalism of a White Man's Burden, in Rudyard Kipling's expressive formulation, but freedom and equality for all nations was the new standard of progress.

Liberal nationalism also adopted violence if the advance of history called for it. The French Revolution of 1789 threw off monarchy and adopted a modern republic in the name of human progress under the banner of "Liberté, égalité, fraternité." The American Revolution of 1776 was an early iteration of decolonization, but it likewise clearly adopted the principles of the Enlightenment in the face of British monarchical repression. The American Civil War (1861–65) was actually far more revolutionary in its content than the US war for independence, advancing both human freedom by ending slavery and advancing human progress by replacing plantation agrarianism with modern industrial capitalism throughout the United States. The African National Congress (ANC) led an effort not to detach from South Africa but to liberate all of South Africa by making it a more perfect union for all of its citizens—an effort that came to fruition with the election of Nelson Mandela in 1994 as president of a new South Africa. These examples involved nationalist ideologies that were based on Enlightenment ideals.

Having a revolutionary movement based on Enlightenment ideals typically either limits violence to strategically important targets or accepts large violence in the name of greater progress. The national liberation movements noted above did not have as their goal to kill as many civilians as possible. The goal typically was not to utterly destroy the global "system" but rather to advance progress of one sort or another. The ANC, the IRA, the PLO, and virtually any other violent national liberation group could have easily slaughtered far more people than they actually killed, but they saw violence as something to be employed tactically, in service of a strategic goal, not as a good in its own right. Compare this approach with the 1994 genocide in Rwanda, where the goal of the Hutu "combatants" was to slaughter as many ethnic Tutsis as they could find.

When revolutionary movements that are based on Enlightenment ideals have engaged in massive violence, they have always justified the slaughter in the name of those same Enlightenment ideals: to create a more progressive, modern society. For example, Joseph Stalin killed off millions of peasants in the USSR (especially in Ukraine), many through the collectivization of agriculture. But the justifications that seeped through the initial denials were always based on modernizing the USSR: assisting the drive to heavy industrialization and creating a more egalitarian and productive agricultural sector by ridding society of feudal Kulak obstructionism. Scholar James Scott has deftly recounted the ostensibly modernizing projects in many states that ended in fiasco, although not typically on such a grand scale as happened under Stalin.[5] Fascists likewise have justified horrendous violence based on the notion of human progress. The Brownshirts aside, Nazis did not slaughter Jews for enjoyment but rather to advance the progress of the German nation under the banner of science, in this case eugenics. In this view, ridding Germany of "inferior" human beings would bring further greatness and progress to the Fatherland. British scholar Eric Hobsbawm has adroitly captured the vast violence of the twentieth century done in the name of human progress.[6]

As the preceding four chapters should have made clear, the broad ideology of global jihad is not based on Enlightenment ideals, but rather the implementation of violent goals under the banner of religion and a highly regressive version of Islam at that. The political goals are impeccably rational—liberating lands, driving the Americans out of the Muslim world, abolishing apostasy through state-building, creating a system of global Islamic resistance—but they are not informed by ideals of human progress, science, and reason. Rather, the ideologies of global jihad are ultimately based on the concern of expanding the width and depth of religion and piety in the Muslim world, inherently regressive goals in an Enlightenment framework. The first wave focused on expanding the width of Islam by bringing old territories back into the Muslim fold; the second wave focused on deepening Islamic piety through a strategy that would weaken apostate regimes and create the conditions for their overthrow by true Muslim warriors. The third wave combined both: deepening Muslim piety through the creation of a state designed to abolish apostasy and then expanding that state to all corners of the Muslim world through a new caliphate. The fourth wave is far more defensive in nature but still seeks the same basic goal of advancing Islamic triumphalism (or their version of it) through unconstrained violence.

A subset of the study of revolutionary movements focuses on terrorism. Terrorism is, of course, a tactic typically used by weak actors in asymmetric conflicts to try to level the playing field against a much stronger force. Although there is no single definition of terrorism adopted by all analysts, most definitions of terrorism look something like this: an act of violence against random civilians for political ends. In this definition, terrorism has four defining characteristics. First, it is a violent act. Second, the target set consists of randomly selected victims from a broad society. If a group knows the name(s) of the person or people they are targeting, it is not terrorism. That would be an assassination, and perhaps an act of war, but it would not fit into the key consideration of terrorizing a whole society, that any random individual from that society could be the next victim. Third, the targets of an act of terrorism must be civilians, or at least noncombatants in some definitions. Targeting uniformed military or security personnel of the society one is violently opposing is not terrorism (but again, it may be considered an act of war in some cases). And fourth, the violent act must be in pursuit of a political goal. An act of violence that has no known political purpose is a criminal act, not a political one, so should not be considered terrorism per se. For example, the deadly 2017 Las Vegas shooting at a country music concert that killed fifty-eight people and wounded hundreds more appears to have had no political content; instead it was an abhorrent criminal act of mass murder, perhaps merely for the entertainment of Stephen Paddock, the shooter. The attack was many things, but it was not an act of terrorism as far as we know.

A great many acts of violence by global jihad groups fit this definition of terrorism. But the problem here is a conceptual one. There are *acts* of terror to be sure, but is it analytically sound to classify violent groups as either terrorist or nonterrorist? The short answer is no. All violent groups in modern times have undertaken acts of terror; some do it more often, some less often. But all have done it, including groups many Americans like to consider "good guys": many Irish Americans were raised in adoration of the IRA, but the IRA has committed acts of terror; many Jewish and evangelical Americans revere Israel, but Israel was founded in large measure through successful terrorism, as Georgetown scholar Bruce Hoffman has so ably argued; African Americans (and others) are proud of the work the ANC did to bring freedom to South Africa, but some of their actions constituted terrorism; most Arab Americans (and many others) support Palestinian self-determination and respect the history of the PLO in leading this cause, but the PLO has also committed acts of terrorism.[7]

Compiling lists of terrorist groups is frankly more about the politics of those writing the list than about the groups it seeks to describe. Virtually every group that has committed violence—even popular ones—has also committed acts of terror, so should be on such lists. Terrorism lists try to create distinctions where there is no real analytical difference, only differences in political popularity. Certainly ISIS would qualify for any terrorism list, but that sheds little light on its ideology or sociology. For example, the distinction I made above about violent or revolutionary groups informed by Enlightenment ideals as a first test to situate global jihad comparatively would be lost if all such groups simply get lumped together for having committed terrorism. Terrorism as a defining group characteristic, as opposed to a description of a particular act of violence, is not a very useful analytical category.

A REACTION TO REPRESSION AND EXCLUSION?

Another common and insightful comparative framework is to focus on regime types out of which violent groups tend to emerge. Repressive regimes that are unable or unwilling to absorb common grievances in a regular institutional framework are far more likely to produce opposition groups that are radical and violent. This has been a truism all over the world, and the largely Arab regimes that gave rise to ideologues of global jihad (as well as other forms of violent dissent) are mostly prime examples of closed and repressive regimes that seek to prevent ordinary and nonviolent dissent, and thus invite violent and radical responses instead. I noted in the introduction that Egypt's military coup in 2013 against the first democratically elected president in Egypt's history, and its subsequent quashing of all forms of dissent, has only invited more radicalism and more violence in response. Finding ways to include all political stripes into a more liberal and inclusive polity will typically dampen political violence.

The best recent comparative framework for understanding regime types and their propensities to encourage or discourage political violence has been developed by the scholars Douglass C. North, John Joseph Wallis, and Barry R. Weingast.[8] Their concept and description of "limited access states" deftly captures how some regimes seek to limit political and economic orders to themselves and thus prevent potential new elites from emerging, as would happen in more open systems. The economic pie is not likely to expand much in limited access states, but extant elites may continue to enjoy all of it. But they will also create significant opposition in the process, some of which likely will take up arms. My colleague Robert Springborg has taken the concept of limited access orders and applied it to regimes of the Middle East and North Africa to show why and how regimes that have closed political and economic systems also have the most violence directed against them by their opponents.[9]

Such a regime-type comparative framework has much to offer, particularly at the meta-level, in predicting the growth of violent movements of opposition to closed regimes. What it cannot do well, however, is to predict the *types* of violent groups that are likely to emerge: jihadi? Leftist? Ba'thist? global jihadi? fascist? other? Since this book is specifically about the iterations and ideologies of global jihad, and not other forms of violent dissent that may be directed against a closed and dysfunctional regime, a regime-type approach would not be the right tool to use to predict or explain the emergence of this specific type of violent group. It is enough to say that open and well-functioning regimes in the Arab world would produce far less violent reactions of any stripe. The creation of open and accountable regimes was the goal of many of the Arab Spring protesters in 2011, a movement that has been effectively quashed for the time being by regimes opposed to opening up their political and economic systems. Thus a comparative framework that centers on regime type and activities to predict the growth of oppositional political violence is a very good way to forecast general rises or declines in political violence, but it is not a very good approach to distinguish between different specific *types* of politically violent groups and movements, such as global jihad.

COSMIC WAR?

Another comparative framework that more usefully captures elements of the global jihad phenomenon centers specifically on religious violence, and especially postmodern religiopolitical violence. Sociologist Mark Juergensmeyer has evocatively captured this idea with his concept of "cosmic war."[10] A similar early articulation of how modern religious violence fits into the broader history of terrorism was made by UCLA scholar David C. Rapoport in his influential article on the four waves (no relation to my delination) of modern terrorism: anarchists, anticolonial, New Left, and, since 1979, religious.[11] An analogous observation is made by scholars who work on "post-modern terrorism," a term coined by Walter Lacquer, or the similar concept of "new terrorism," most commonly associated with Bruce Hoffman.[12] Like Juergensmeyer, these authors insightfully demonstrate the rising influence of religion (as well as changing technology that enables violence) in recent political violence to suggest that contemporary political violence is less constrained than were earlier generations of political violence that were usually based on secular political goals (nationalism, socialism, fascism, etc.). These scholars generally note the political nature of even much religious violence, particularly the organized acts of violence. I would add that if violence is a *political* act, it is also a *rational* act within the parameters of the ideological world view of the people who carry it out. Others have pointed out that there is nothing particularly new about political violence carried out by religiously informed groups.[13]

Juergensmeyer, like other scholars, explores how religious violence is more unconstrained in its killing than previous forms of political violence but also how such violence should be viewed as rational. "What makes religious violence particularly savage and relentless," Juergensmeyer writes, "is that its perpetrators have placed such religious images of divine struggle—cosmic war—in the service of worldly political battles."[14] Similar to the way I use the concept of nihilism (see below), Juergensmeyer does not argue that religious violence, even at the "cosmic" level, is inherently irrational, but rather that "acts of religious terror" can serve both as "tactics in a political strategy but also as evocations of a much larger spiritual confrontation."[15] Thus, as a political tactic, such violence is rational in that it is consistent with the ideological world view of those who perpetrate it. It advances their political cause: at least, they *think* it will.

It is important for both analysts and policy makers not to dismiss out of hand religious-based violence as done by "crazies" that are inherently "irrational." Plenty of pundits have erroneously described Iranian policy under the Islamic Republic as undertaken by irrational actors. Nothing could be further from the truth. Americans might not have liked it, but Iran consistently outwitted American decision-makers in Iraq following the US invasion in 2003, which is why Iran today is the most influential foreign power in Baghdad, at a fraction of the cost the Americans spent. Disdain for the actions of another party or state should not to be confused with rationality.

A "cosmic war" comparative approach to the rise of religious violence in recent decades captures many of the key elements of global jihad: calls for unconstrained violence in the name of God, often married to rational, political goals. It could be sufficient to end this comparative inquiry here, placing global jihad as a form of religious terrorism or cosmic war that can be seen across different cultural and religious traditions. But such a stopping point leaves analytical weakness. First, there are nonreligious forms of political violence that seem pretty similar to global jihad in their calls for unconstrained, nihilistic violence in the name of some cause. The highly secular anarchist movement in Russia in the nineteenth century, for example, shared important ideological and sociological attributes with global jihad that not all other religious group do.[16] Self-styled anarchists are still present in the world's rich democracies and are more likely than other ideological groups to engage in egregious and wanton destruction of property in realization of their ideological goals. In short, a broader and more provocative comparative understanding of global jihad should focus on violent groups, both religious and secular, that share fundamental ideological and sociological characteristics. A movement-of-rage comparative analysis provides just such a broader understanding of global jihad.

NIHILISM, VIOLENCE, AND RATIONALITY

The word *nihilism* gets used and abused in discussions over political violence, mostly because the word has multiple meanings. The *Oxford English Dictio-*

nary (OED) lists five different meanings for nihilism, while Dictionary.com lists six. *Merriam-Webster* (M-W) provides two definitions for *nihilism*, but this concision has the advantage of focusing on the two most used and often confused meanings of the word: as a *philosophical* concept and as a *political* idea. The philosophical concept of nihilism is bound up with existentialism, a philosophy that "the world has no real existence, [that rejects] all notions of reality" (OED) or "that existence is senseless and useless, [that] denies any objective ground of truth" (M-W). The word *nihilism* is derived from the Latin *nihil*, meaning "nothing," thus fitting the philosophical use of the word precisely. Danish theologian and philosopher Soren Kierkegaard (1813–1855) is widely credited with being the original proponent of this new philosophical school. Other major philosophers and writers of the nineteenth and twentieth century are often described as existentialists, including Friedrich Nietzsche, Martin Heidegger, Fyodor Dostoyevsky, Jean-Paul Sartre, and Albert Camus.

The second major definition of nihilism is political: "negativity, destructiveness, hostility to accepted beliefs or established institutions" (OED); "a belief that conditions in the social organization are so bad as to make destruction desirable for its own sake" (M-W); "total rejection of established laws and institutions; anarchy, terrorism, or other revolutionary activity; total and absolute destructiveness, especially toward the world at large and including oneself" (dictionary.com). This understanding of nihilism is also a nineteenth-century invention, founded on the notion of a total rejection of the established sociopolitical order. The meaning was coined in reference to the writings of Mikhail Bakunin and the actions of his fellow Russian anarchists. In the political sense of the word, nihilism invites not *meaningless* violence but rather *extreme* violence, the root-and-branch destruction of society. This is where the analytical confusion is sometimes seen. For some scholars, the word *nihilism* will imply irrationality or literal meaninglessness (from the philosophical usage). Thus, for these scholars nihilistic violence is irrational and pointless, just a lashing out at anybody for no purpose. It is, quite literally, meaningless existential violence.

But defining nihilistic violence when applied to political groups as "meaningless violence" makes little sense. Groups with a political agenda do not commit meaningless violence; there is always a point to it, even if to broadly terrorize a society. I can think of no act of violence by a political group that would be usefully categorized as "meaningless." Abhorrent, grotesque, illegal, even a miscalculation, yes; but "meaningless"? No. Only individuals or apolitical groups can undertake violence that has no meaning, no point to it. An example of a truly meaningless act of violence was the 2017 slaughter in Las Vegas by Stephen Paddock, noted earlier. There appears to have been no cause, no justification for the mass shooting, not even an attempt to gin up an excuse by Paddock. There was no note or video left behind, no history of political activity, no last-minute phone call to claim the killings in the name of some cause. It appears to have been slaughter for the sake of slaughter, nihilism as pure meaningless violence.

I contend that global jihadis call for nihilistic violence in the political (not philosophical) sense of the word. That is, global jihadis promote extreme (not meaningless) violence generally designed to destroy what they see as a corrupt and rotten system. Such violence is nihilistic in the sense that it is so extreme as to have no sense of proportionality, or little direct connection between the strategic goal sought and the level of violence called for. That is, I am not using the word *nihilism* to mean or to imply irrationality, as violence conducted by global jihad groups, as with other movements of rage, is purposeful and rational; there is an intent to achieve certain political ends. I have laid out in detail in the previous chapters the global political ends that ideologues of global jihad have sought to achieve. Whether one agrees with them, these ideologues calling for mass violence are not crazy, idiotic people. The same applies to other movements of rage as well. Elements of white nationalism also constitute a movement of rage, but they are not usually simply crazy. For example, read the long manifesto by Brenton Tarrant, who murdered fifty-one Muslims in two mosques in Christchurch, New Zealand, in March 2019. It is conspiratorial in tone, simpleminded in argument, and often factually wrong, but it is not the ravings of a deranged lunatic. It reads instead like the work of a cold, evil, calculating murderer. In other words, it reads a lot like something Usama Bin Laden would write.

Rather, I use the term *nihilism* to refer to extreme violence that is *unconstrained* yet *compartmentalized* against specified, large categories of people. It is violence designed to destroy on a large scale, not surgical violence designed to usher in a better society. Let us examine each of these characteristics in turn. Nihilistic violence is *unconstrained* in that it seeks to inflict maximum casualties against the specified enemy. Norms, institutions, and teachings that might otherwise limit and constrain the violence are disregarded in favor of maximum killing. Again, this is made more feasible by the advance of technology, where small numbers of people can inflict large-scale levels of casualties that would not have been possible centuries earlier. As an example, the 9/11 attacks were planned and implemented by only a few dozen people who had a small budget of about $500,000, which is less than the cost of a single US Army jeep.[17]

But I argue that the rationale for unconstrained violence is fundamentally different from old-fashioned communal violence between tribal, ethnic, sectarian, or other corporate groups. Those forms of violence were typically (but not always) constrained in various ways where the whole of the corpus Other was not typically exterminated by design. Unconstrained violence is typically linked to the advent of modernity, and not just because of technological changes but also because of the types of societal warping brought on by modernity. The advent of modernity everywhere tended to rip apart larger familial structures in favor of smaller ones, produce massive dislocation from the countryside to the cities, and destroy traditional social hierarchies.[18] It is not a coincidence that both the coining of the term *genocide* and its practice in various places were by-products of the twentieth century, the first full century to experience the technological effects of the industrial age. Murder on a mass scale became much more feasible. It is also not a coincidence that the leaders of the various movements of rage in the twentieth and twenty-first century were neither from wholly traditional society nor from fully modern elements of society, but were instead hybrids of both. The leaders of the Khmer Rouge in Cambodia were educated in France, the Nazis in the modern universities of Germany and Austria, and ISIS in Europe or secular universities in Iraq.

In what ways did leaders of global jihad preach unconstrained violence? There was clear variation among the ideologues on this issue. Perhaps the one most constrained by traditional norms was 'Abdullah 'Azzam, the architect of the first wave of global jihad. As a trained scholar from the prestigious al-Azhar seminary in Cairo, 'Azzam was more prone to give deference to Islamic just-war notions than were nonclerical ideologues. But even as a hybrid ideologue combining traditional norms with modern extremes, 'Azzam was the person primarily responsible for the construction of a "cult of martyrdom" in Islam (detailed in chapter 1). 'Azzam glorified death in the path of armed jihad, wrote of miracles occurring on the battlefield where Muslims could defy death and experience *tawhid* (the fullness of God), and he encouraged all able-bodied Muslims to participate in battle and welcome death if that is what God has in store.

'Azzam never explicitly accepted suicide operations, but his general ideological architecture paved the way for its adoption in the Sunni Muslim world in the 1990s (in the Middle East, suicide operations had only been undertaken by Shia radicals in the 1980s). Subsequent waves of global jihad were marked by an ideology of even more untethered violence. Usama Bin Laden and Ayman al-Zawahiri issued a *fatwa* in 1998 that called for the mass murder of all American civilians wherever possible anywhere in the world by all able-bodied Muslims, and then oversaw an operation on 9/11 designed to kill as many innocent civilians as possible given the technology available. ISIS went further, not only calling for mass murder of civilians on a regular basis, but also using as propaganda videos its staged executions of numerous prisoners, killed in the most cruel ways imaginable, from the immolation of a caged Jordanian pilot to the drowning of men in a cage with underwater video cameras there to capture the gruesome death throes for ISIS's worldwide and ghoulish Internet audience.

Perhaps the most unconstrained of all the global jihadi ideologues when it came to violence was Abu Musab al-Suri, the architect of the current fourth wave of global jihad. He both advocated for and likely helped design the slaughter of soft targets—civilians—in Algeria, Madrid, London, and perhaps elsewhere. For Suri, the bloody destruction of one's enemy constituted a ritualized cleansing of cultural corruption, much like Franz Fanon's depiction of the necessity for the ritualized killing of one's colonial oppressor.[19] Suri was realistic that his theory of "personal jihad" would likely not lead to mass slaughter, at least not right away, but that did not mean he rejected such slaughter on moral grounds. Far from it. Suri, like other global jihads, expressed interest in acquiring nuclear weapons, and there is no reason to believe that such groups would not seek to use a weapon of mass destruction were they to acquire one. Traditional deterrence techniques, effective against states, are not likely to be as effective against nonterritorial and unconstrained movements of rage.

Nihilistic violence is both internally rational and unconstrained. But it is also *compartmentalized* in that violence is not to be used against just anybody, only against specified large groups of people.[20] Movements of rage in general have specific enemies that they target: the people they view as the prime contaminators of the pure society. Localized, national-level movements of rage have mostly targeted Westernized, modern elites (more on this below). Global jihadis have also compartmentalized their target sets, and that compartmentalization also goes to the issue of rationality. While global jihadis may be nihilistically violent, they are not irrational in their targeting. The first wave targeted the infidel occupiers of Muslim lands, and the second wave all Americans and their allies (especially Jews). The third wave, by far the largest, was more complicated, targeting a series of enemies both internal (Shi'a, enemy Sunnis, military and police forces, and captured American and British civilians) and external (mostly random Western civilians attending cultural events in Europe). Still, even here, the violence was targeted with a certain rationale—it was not *meaningless*. Abu Musab al-Suri's fourth wave of global jihad is similarly compartmentalized in that it calls for the killing primarily of Western civilians, although other targets are not excluded. Thus there is a randomness as to *which* civilians happen to be at the wrong place at the wrong time, but there is a compartmentalization of general targets, not a random targeting of all humans everywhere.

In sum, the large majority of global jihadi violence, both as called for in the ideological pronouncements detailed in this book and in the actual acts of violence carried out, has been nihilistic but not irrational. The violence is compartmentalized to certain target sets, but within those target sets it is unconstrained, with a call for maximum carnage. The violence is not accidental or simply criminal but is rather a political act, part of a broader global strategy to advance what these ideologues view as the interests of the righteous Muslim world. As this book has demonstrated, the strategy has varied depending on the particular wave of global jihad, from liberating Muslim territory, to driving the Americans out of the Muslim world, to banishing apostasy through puritanical state-building, to keeping hope alive for global jihad during particularly trying times. In all cases, the violence had a strategy behind it, as is the case for the violence found in other movements of rage.

It needs to be emphasized that such violence is not the same as old-fashioned communal violence, of Hindus killing Muslims over a rumor of a cow being slaughtered, for example; rather, it represents a form of violence that arises from modern conditions, both sociologically and ideationally. Ideologues of global jihad are not old-fashioned tribal or other corporate-group leaders. They tend to be relatively highly educated in secular subjects from secular universities. Indeed, jihadis of all stripes tend to be well above average in terms of educational achievement, as social scientists Diego Gambetta and Steffen Hertog have shown in their book *Engineers of Jihad*.[21] More than once I have said only half in jest to my students: "Show me an unemployed engineer, and I will show you a jihadi." All of the global jihadi ideologues described in this book were well-traveled, including in the West, and well-educated, including doctors of theology and philosophy, medical doctors, business majors, engineers, and journalists. Only Zarqawi did not have the educational credentials of other such ideologues, but rather got his education primarily while in prison. None was a usual tribal or other traditional corporate group leader. All fairly easily straddled the worlds of Islam and Western modernity.

This sociological characteristic of the cadres of global jihad also provides an interesting entrée into the well-known debate between scholars Gilles Kepel and Olivier Roy over the origins of jihadis more generally.[22] Briefly stated, Kepel argues that the origins of jihadism writ large are ideational, that they stem from an ideological shift in the interpretation of Islam by a strand of Muslims. Kepel's argument mirrors Max Weber's famous discussion on the origins of modern capitalism, which Weber maintained came from the development of ideas of Protestant Puritanism by a strand of Christians, found most strongly in the new movement of Calvinism centered in Geneva. For Kepel, it was a similar shift in the interpretation of Islam by some—an ideational change—that birthed modern jihadism. Roy takes a sociological approach instead of an ideational one in understanding the rise of modern jihadism, suggesting certain sociological categories of individuals are more prone to violence under any ideological banner. Jihadism just happens to be the primary contemporary ideology of violent extremism, the "flavor of the month" so to speak, so those people tend to migrate to jihadism. The allure of permitted violence under jihadi ideology helps explain the large number of converts, at least in European jihadi circles.

While I will not pretend to settle this debate, a movement-of-rage understanding of global jihadism would strongly suggest that the sociological origins that Roy focuses on have more explanatory power than an ideational change. Movement-of-rage cadres have a distinctive sociology, which trumps an ideational change because movements of rage are found in different cultures, different religions, and different continents. Leading cadres of movements of rage generally share the same sociological background, but they do not share the same religious or political philosophies from which an ideational change can launch a social movement. "Movements of rage" is a comparative framework that has broader explanatory power across more cases than an ideational change type explanation within one religious tradition. Having contemplated both different comparative approaches to understanding global jihad, and major components of the nature of violence called for by ideologues of global jihad, let me now more precisely identify and define a theoretical approach to understanding the global jihad phenomenon: movements of rage. This theoretical approach can link together in interesting and insightful ways a category of violent movements around the world over the past century.

DEFINING A MOVEMENT OF RAGE

For Ken Jowitt, the originator of the theory of movements of rage, such a movement represents a total and violent rejection of Western modernity.[23] It is defined as a neomillenarian amalgam of charismatic leadership and apocalyptic ideology, combined with a strategy of nihilistic violence. Those three specific items—leadership, ideology, and violence—are discussed in more detail below. But first, some context is needed. Jowitt comes from the Weberian school of social science and views much of world politics through the lens of the rise of Western liberal capitalism, which he considers to be the most novel and powerful form of social organization in world history, and reactions to that rise. Modernity for Weber, as for Jowitt, involves a number of historically rare characteristics, including the use of the individual over the corporate group as the principal societal unit, market-based industrial economies, and open, secular political systems. For specific historical reasons, this amalgamation arose first in Europe and is thus intrinsically linked with European ("Western") sensibilities. Modernity and Westernization are not synonyms, but there is clear overlap when it comes to the shape of political, economic, and social institutions. This new phenomenon—modernity—proved so powerful that it allowed a few European countries to conquer much of the world in the nineteenth century and then to export globally in highly uneven ways those same notions of modernity.

Consistent with this Weberian view of the world, much of history over the past two centuries has focused on how societies have come to terms with European modernity—including in Europe itself. Fascism and Communism, for example, each rose as competitors to Western liberal capitalism, but each was defeated in turn. This was the point of Francis Fukuyama's famous, if controversial, essay, "The End of History," which was written after the end of the Cold War: various forms of communal or tribal conflict will continue here and there, but the major ideological challengers to Western liberal capitalism were all defeated. Political evolution had reached its apex.[24]

It should be stressed that such modernity was not viewed by Weber as an unalloyed good. Better efficiencies due to increasing rationalization would produce more effective bureaucratic outcomes and prosperity, but the concomitant secularization of society would result in an increasingly cold, bureaucratic, and meaningless existence. Weber termed this problem "the iron cage" of modernity. Books and essays about escaping Weber's iron cage of modernity could fill a library.[25] I briefly discussed the philosophical school of existentialism earlier in this chapter in my discussion of nihilism. The same set of concerns that worried Weber about the loss of sacred meaning with modernity informed the existentialist philosophers' discussions about the meaninglessness of modern life. The rise of the profane and the loss of the sacred in a cold modernity have been the source of much philosophical and political thought for more than a century.

For Jowitt, movements of rage fall at the far, fringe end of the spectrum of responses to the rise of Western liberal capitalism. Many around the world embraced Western liberal capitalism, as they do today, although few embraced the colonialism that often accompanied its export around the world. Others embraced a form of liberal capitalism but tried to meld it with forms of cultural authenticity and identity, often with mixed results. Many in the world today embrace the economic elements of modernity but push back on the political liberalism that modernity implies: Putin, Erdogan, Modi, Bolsonaro, Xi, and Trump are prime examples. Traditionalists, such as the Jewish Haredim or Salafi Muslims, rejected liberal capitalism but focused on piety, not violence, in response. But at the far end of the spectrum, as an "ideal type," are people who reject and fear Western modernity and resort to nihilistic violence as a form of radical purification to cleanse society from all its manifestations.

Those who join movements of rage are typically not the poorest and most marginalized in society, but rather those people who are not allowed to fully benefit from the fruits of modernity due to the perceived corruption of elites. Like Pol Pot of the Khmer Rouge, they tend to hail from provincial cities and do well in an educational meritocracy, but are not from the families and classes of national elites, and are thus excluded from what they view as their rightful place. Their response is to blame those corrupt, Westernized elites in the capital city for holding them back and, Samson-like, choose to destroy the whole corrupt system. Movements of rage rarely get very far past the murder of some cultural elites and perhaps some hapless policemen who get in the way. But the rage is genuine, designed to annihilate the whole political and social edifice, rather than surgically murdering a few.

In my discussion of movements of rage, I have tried to do justice to the totality of Jowitt's vision within his Weberian framework of modernity and tradition. That said, I believe it is possible to identify and define such movements of rage without getting into the contested and controversial notions of modernity and tradition. Certainly, many participants in movements of rage have no problem using the most modern and lethal technologies that they can obtain in order to inflict maximum damage on their targets. Even if the specific Weberian framework is removed, there is still something important and unique about the kinds of movements that Jowitt has identified. But to better capture that uniqueness, I have chosen to coin the term *gnosicide* to home in on what is truly specific about these movements: their primary goal, as part of their apocalyptic millenarianism, is the mass murder of knowledge itself. The carriers of knowledge, the educated urban elites, seen as invidious fifth columnists who spread cultural contamination, are targeted for annihilation.

As the name implies, *global* jihad is not a *national* movement, and thus its ideological animus is not primarily directed against insidious and corrupt national elites (although there is a clear element of that as well). Rather, I suggest a novel approach to understanding global jihad, where the same set of dynamics one sees in national-level movements of rage get applied to a global-level movement of rage. Put another way, movements of rage at the national level focus their rage on the contaminated *national* center of power;

movements of rage at the global level—like global jihad—focus their rage on the corrupting *global* center of power. Global jihadi ideologues do not limit their criticism of the United States and the West to policy differences, such as those dealing with the Israel-Palestine issue, the support of "apostate" regimes in the Arab world, or the military footprint of the United States in the Middle East. Rather, their writings invariably view the United States in particular and the West in general as the most important source of cultural corruption in the Muslim world, beyond just political differences.

This argument about the cultural contamination of the Muslim world is not new: it was a major theme for Hasan al-Banna and Sayyid Qutb, and, as mentioned in the introduction, Iranians even had a specific phrase, *gharb zadeghi*, for their countrymen who were seen to be "drunk on the West." But global jihadis are the first Muslims to use the notion of cultural corruption, in addition to their political goals, as a justification for war against the global centers of contamination and the United States in particular.

HISTORICAL EXAMPLES OF NATIONAL-LEVEL MOVEMENTS OF RAGE

After detailing the more common form of national-level movements of rage, I will return to the concept of a global-level movement of rage.

The Khmer Rouge in Cambodia

Severe instability marked Indochina in the aftermath of World War II. The long period of French colonialism seemed to be coming to an end. Suddenly Paris reversed course and reasserted its imperial mastery of the area, only to be driven out of the region after being defeated at the battle of Dien Bien Phu in northern Vietnam in 1954. Within a few years, the United States began to replace France as the primary imperial power in Indochina, although both the Soviet Union and China were likewise heavily involved in the series of conflicts and small wars being fought in the region to fill the power vacuum left by France. This political disarray allowed a small group of Paris-educated radicals, led by Pol Pot, Ieng Sary, Hou Yuon, and Khieu Samphan, to gradually gain power in Cambodia's countryside and eventually conquer the capital city, Phnom Penh, in 1975.

But the Khmer Rouge (an anglicized version of the French for "Red Khmers") were no ordinary band of conquerors.[26] Within days of gaining control over

Phnom Penh, they began to empty the capital city of its inhabitants, whom they considered to be the reviled "New People" of Cambodia. Professionals, writers, artists, and intellectuals of all kinds were either exterminated or imprisoned in labor camps. Anyone thought to be touched by modern sensibilities—evidenced by such characteristics as speaking a European language, wearing Western clothing, or being educated beyond rudimentary schooling—was targeted either for execution or forced labor. Even those who wore eyeglasses were victimized, as eyewear somehow suggested literacy and education. Those sent to the labor camps often had a death sentence that was only delayed; lacking the agricultural skills required to survive the harsh conditions of the camps, many starved to death.

Because Phnom Penh was the epicenter of Cambodian modernity and thus, in the view of the Khmer Rouge, the epicenter of cultural corruption, it became a ghost town, with its population either murdered or exiled. Non-Khmer ethnic minorities and non-Buddhist religious minorities were also targeted. As quasi-Marxists, the Khmer Rouge were not religious at all, but they did have an idealized devotion to the mixed Buddhist-Hindu Khmer empire (whose capital was Angkor) that ruled from the ninth through the fifteenth centuries, so they tended to spare Buddhist clerics.[27] By the time the Cambodian genocide ended in 1979, the Khmer Rouge had exterminated about two million people—about a quarter of the country's population—roughly half by direct execution and the other half from famine as a result of their ruinous agricultural policies. The murdered represented Cambodia's "best and brightest": those people with the educational wherewithal needed for the country's economic, political, and social development. The slaughter of the educated, its *gnosicide*, set Cambodia's development back by generations.

The ideology of the Khmer Rouge is typically described as extreme Maoism. That is, it was a form of Marxism that reversed Marx's emphasis on urban workers as the primary revolutionary class and instead substituted the peasantry as the vanguard of socialist revolution. However, what stands out about the ideology and practice of the Khmer Rouge was not arguments about the finer points of Marxism, but rather the nature and extent of violent rage inflicted on the population. Three elements in particular are worth noting. First was the sheer extent of the violence. Killing roughly two million people is murder on a massive scale, and it may well have continued were it not for Cambodia's military defeat at Vietnam's hands in 1979. A second element of note was the choice of targets. The Khmer Rouge did not much traffic in old-fashioned communal violence that pits one corporate group (tribe, clan, sect, etc.) against another; instead, they primarily targeted the entire urban, educated stratum of society. It was a form of *gnosicide*, a word that combines the Greek word for *knowledge* with the Latin suffix meaning *killing*. Gnosicide is the killing of knowledge or, more accurately, the purposeful extermination or violent marginalization of the educated classes. Much of the killing perpetrated by the Khmer Rouge was directed at the best-educated elements of Cambodian society, most of whom lived in Phnom Penh. Third, the Khmer Rouge's ideology can be described as neomillenarian: they believed that cataclysmic and immediate social change would bring about a type of secular nirvana, a heaven on earth, that was entirely rural, agrarian, and self-sufficient. I say "neo" as this was a new and very secular kind of millenarianism, which is typically associated with religious ideologies.

In addition to these three foundational characteristics of the Khmer Rouge's rule from 1975 to 1979, its leadership had a noteworthy sociology. Specifically, its leaders mostly came from middling elites, not from traditional national leadership strata. As young men, they did well enough in school to earn scholarships to study in France. Pol Pot, for example, was born and raised in Prek Sbauv, a rural village outside the city of Kampong Thom, a provincial capital. His father was a successful farmer, and Pol Pot was a good student, earning that coveted scholarship to France. Like other leaders of similar movements, Pol Pot was both charismatic and from nontraditional origins.

The Red Guards in China

The Khmer Rouge's orgy of violence was not unique in history. Indeed, just a decade earlier in nearby China, a similar kind of gnosicide had been carried out by the Red Guards under Mao during the Cultural Revolution. Indeed, it is likely that the Khmer Rouge drew inspiration from the program of the Red Guards. China's Cultural Revolution, which began in 1966, was primarily an effort by Mao to fully regain power after the humiliating disaster of the Great Leap Forward, a violent and hare-brained development scheme that led to the deaths of perhaps forty-five million people, mostly from man-made famine. Mao did not create the Red Guards, who were self-motivated student militants pushing for radical change in China, but he did ride on their coattails for several years, until their disruption was threatening to careen out of Mao's control.

Like the Khmer Rouge who followed in Cambodia, the Red Guards practiced gnosicide, killing or otherwise attacking the educated classes of China. Such intellectuals were seen as a source of cultural contamination and presumed guilty of intellectual elitism and "bourgeois tendencies." Beijing was seen by the Red Guards—and confirmed by Mao—as the epicenter of corruption and the concomitant return of bourgeois capitalists striving for power, even from within the Communist Party. The mark of "bourgeois tendencies" was to be educated, and thus it was the urban educated who were primarily targeted. Thousands of Chinese intellectuals were killed by the Red Guards during the Cultural Revolution, most between 1966 and 1968, including the beating to death of high school teachers and principals, university professors, artists, and others among the urban intelligentsia. To cleanse Beijing (and to a lesser degree other major cities) of the pollution of modern education, about seventeen million young urban high school and college graduates were sent to rural areas to be "reeducated" under the rubric of the "Down to the Countryside" policy. Similar to the gnosicide in Cambodia, many of those sent to the countryside ended up dying from starvation as they were unprepared to survive in such conditions. Altogether, perhaps between one and two million people died during the Cultural Revolution, most during its first three years.

Perhaps most tellingly, the Red Guards were charged with implementing the destruction of the "Four Olds": old customs, old cultures, old habits, and old ideas. Under this policy mandate, universities and schools were shuttered for years, most from 1966 until 1972. Museums were ransacked, libraries burned, and shrines and historical artifacts plundered and destroyed by the fanatical Red Guards. The gnosicide in China resulted in fewer murders than occurred under the Khmer Rouge a decade later, but it was just as clearly a vengeful attack on those with knowledge, those "enemies within" that carried with them cultural and political contamination that most clearly manifested itself through the fact of their education.

Bouts of gnosicide have occurred from time to time in other Leninist regimes, beyond Cambodia and China. Extreme interpretations of Maoism, with its emphasis on agrarian revolution, are prone to gnosicide, given their antipathy to urban life and the educated, who tend to populate cities far more than villages. In addition to the Khmer Rouge and the Red Guards, other examples of Maoist gnosicide include the Simba rebellion in Congo in 1964, the Khalq faction of the People's Democratic Party of Afghanistan in the 1970s, and the Shining Path of Peru in the 1980s. In each of these cases, there was an extreme ideology of purification and attacks on symbols of modernity or the West were encouraged. The fifth column of cultural contamination—educated urbanites—were particularly suspect. While urban and not Maoist, the neo-Marxist Tupamaros movement in Uruguay in the early 1970s can in part be similarly categorized, given its target list of urban elites and Westerners as well as the antimodern tint to its ideology.

In each of these cases, the movement's ideology sought to destroy the system, root and branch, and blamed the most educated and modern strata of society for the woes of the community. In each case, the educated, Westernized strata of society were seen not just as an impediment to progress but also as the embodiment of cultural corruption. As such, those strata were attacked, violently and often with abandon. In most cases, these movements of rage came from the fringe, led by parochial elites upset with an established order that prevents them from achieving the status they believe they have earned. As fringe movements, movements of rage tend to be weak, rarely actually coming to power, and generally remain on the margins of society, radical and dangerous, but a deadly nuisance more than a major political and military threat. During the few times such movements actually gained power the results were terrifying, as the Khmer case demonstrates.

Movements of Rage in Western Industrialized Societies: Nazi Brownshirts and White Nationalism

Most movements of rage form in the ex-colonial world, so their ideology is informed in part by their long and often brutal experiences with colonialism. But this is not always the case. The primary example of a powerful movement of rage in the heart of modern, industrial society is the Nazis, and in particular the Brownshirts (*Sturmabteilung*, literally Storm Detachment) of the Nazi movement in the 1920s and 1930s. Consisting mostly of semiliterate, often rural, and marginalized elements of German society, the Brownshirts were fundamental in the rise to power of Adolph Hitler and the Nazi Party. They were the militia movement of Nazism, acting as thugs and enforcers at rallies and other gatherings of Nazi leaders, especially those led by Hitler. They likewise embodied an inchoate ideology of cultural pollution inflicted on the pure German (or Aryan) people by cosmopolitan elites—and in particular, by the Jews. As argued earlier, fascism itself does not represent a movement of rage by the marginalized but is rather a progress-oriented ideology that falls well within the parameters of Enlightenment ideals. Mussolini, Franco, and other fascist leaders were well regarded by those who wanted development and progress with a clear conservative, law-and-order hue. The Nazi coalition that came to power in Germany was not a single movement of rage, since the coalition included major industrialists, the Catholic Church, much of the military officer corps, and others. The Brownshirts were only a part of that coalition, but they were willing accomplices to and major cheerleaders for the extermination of the urban and cosmopolitan elements that they considered to be corrupting German society.

White nationalism is a contemporary example of a movement of rage that also formed in the industrialized West. Not all white nationalists should be considered part of a movement of rage, but critical elements of the movement writ large are certainly consistent with the model. Those characteristics include: virulent antielite rhetoric that posits a juxtaposition between an imagined "real America" and the corrupt "coastal elites"; rhetoric hostile to cosmopolitan Others who contaminate the true America (this was the meaning of the chant in Charlottesville, Virginia, in 2017 that "Jews will not replace us"); a harkening back to a golden era when societal contamination was minimal and life was better (e.g., when blacks, Jews, and women "knew their place"); and barely disguised calls for violence against both external enemies (e.g., illegal migrants) and fifth-column internal enemies who insidiously corrupt and weaken the body politic (e.g., liberals). A college education is now viewed negatively by such white nationalists: a 2017 Pew survey found that 58 percent of conservatives in America view colleges and universities negatively, a sharp rise from 45 percent from just one year earlier. Certainly, most conservatives are not white nationalists, but it is a fair hypothesis that most white nationalists in the Pew survey viewed colleges and universities negatively. Universities are considered sources of cultural corruption. The Pew survey represents an early indicator for the potential of future gnosicide, however unlikely it is to actually occur. Like the Brownshirts before them, such white nationalists typically are more rural and less-educated than the societal norm, and there is no shortage of radical ideologues that seek to manipulate their feelings of exclusion, of being passed by—of being "replaced."

The Taliban in Afghanistan and Boko Haram in Nigeria

The Muslim world has seen its share of groups intent of gnosicide, seeking to destroy the sociopolitical order and rid society of cultural contamination embodied by corrupt, Westernized elites. There were elements of this view found in some of the small jihadi groups of the 1970s, discussed in the introduction. But perhaps the best-known movement of rage in the Muslim world—at least before ISIS—was the Taliban in Afghanistan. As with other such movements, the Taliban was born out of chaos: in this case, the destruction of much of Afghan society by the Soviet occupation of the 1980s. Millions were made homeless and turned into refugees, and the social and political institutions that could in theory have helped to address societal problems were destroyed. The Soviet withdrawal in 1989 left behind a broken country, which turned into a large turf war between competing tribal, ethnic, and sectarian warlords. Out of this chaos, a movement of seminary students promising law and order gradually gained strength as they brought a measure of stability to the areas they controlled. By 1996 the Taliban (which means "students") had gained control of Kabul and about three-quarters of Afghanistan, essentially the lands of the Pashtun ethnic group.

What set the Taliban apart from most other Islamist movements was the austerity and violence of its ideology, and its focus on the cultural contamination embodied in Kabul. The Taliban's leaders were not from Kabul, and they viewed the capital city and the Westernized elites who inhabited it as foreign and corrupt. Although the Taliban did not depopulate Kabul as the Khmer Rouge did Phnom Penh, they enacted policies to rid Kabul of all of its foreign, especially Western, influences—from the playing of music to the shaving of beards to the education of girls (all *haram*, or forbidden). The internal rhetoric of the Taliban was a discourse primarily of cultural pollution from the West, with the corruption of Kabul the principal target of their anger. Violence, often justified under the banner of shari'a, was their principal mechanism for social control. Indeed, the austere totalitarianism of the Taliban was primarily an exercise in puritanism under the flag of Islam, based on the pervasiveness of cultural contamination by Afghan elites who had imported impure, Western tendencies—much like the "bourgeois tendencies" targeted by the Red Guards in Mao's China.

A second example of a movement of rage in the Muslim world was Boko Haram in the state of Borno, Nigeria, especially in the years before it decided to join up with ISIS. Formed in 2002 by Muhammad Yusuf, Boko Haram grew more violent over the years. Yusuf was killed by security forces in 2009 and replaced by Abubakar Shekau. In 2015 elements of Boko Haram allied with ISIS, leading to a formal split in the group by 2016, with part still loyal to Shekou and others following Abu Musab al-Barnawi, a son of Yusuf and a supporter of the links with ISIS. Like the Taliban, Boko Haram (a nickname given to the group by the local population) often targeted people and institutions viewed to be carriers of cultural corruption. Boko Haram rejected all forms of Westernization and specifically targeted secular schools. The name Boko Haram itself is an amalgamation of Arabic and Hausa words that mean "Western education is a sin."[28]

Schools for girls have been a prime target by Boko Haram. In 2014, 276 girls—most of whom were Christians—were kidnapped by Boko Haram from a school in Chibok; many were never returned, forcibly converted and "married" off to Boko Haram fighters, similar to the way ISIS treated non-Muslim girls it had kidnapped. By 2015, Boko Haram had kidnapped more than two thousand women and girls, sometimes forcing those females not given as wives or sex slaves to fighters to carry out suicide attacks.[29] Officials and other elites in the provincial capital of Maiduguri have regularly been targeted by Boko Haram, as have Western tourists, who have been kidnapped and held for ransom. In 2011 the United Nations, which is often seen by jihadis as a purveyor of Western ideals, fell victim to a Boko Haram suicide car bomber that targeted its building in the Nigerian capital city Abuja, killing twenty-one and wounding dozens more. Since its founding in 2002, Boko Haram has killed at least twenty-thousand people and perhaps as many as one hundred thousand, and has displaced perhaps a million more.[30] For several years, Boko Haram rivaled and sometimes surpassed ISIS as the most-deadly terror group in the world.[31]

Boko Haram's ideology is an often inchoate and simplistic depiction of the world, not a well-thought-out doctrine.[32] Its level of violence is rarely consistent with a clear political strategy but rather constitutes nihilistic extremism in its rage to eradicate corruption from a society it views as having been contaminated from the pure Islamic Salafi nirvana it imagines. Other than the police and security forces it fights, the targets of Boko Haram's violence are mostly the cultural symbols of that social contamination. Elimination of that supposed corruption, and especially Western education, is the primary driver of Boko Haram's violence.

CHARISMATIC LEADERSHIP, APOCALYPTIC IDEOLOGY, NIHILISTIC VIOLENCE

To make the case that global jihad is a variant form of a movement of rage, focused at the global level instead of the national level, let us return to the three foundational elements of movements of rage: charismatic leadership, apocalyptic ideology, and nihilistic violence. Charismatic leadership in the Weberian understanding is not to be confused with popularity. Rather, Weberian charisma is hard and fear-inducing. Charismatics challenge potential adherents to fulfill their destiny through sacrifice for the greater good.

Although the concept of charisma had religious origins, its political use can be seen in both secular and sectarian movements. Chairman Mao and Ayatullah Khomeini were charismatic political leaders, one as an atheist and the other as a member of the Muslim clergy. They both instilled fear and passion in their followers, many of whom would gladly have given up their lives for the cause. They both challenged their followers in hard and unforgiving ways; they both instilled a sense of awe and inspiration in how others viewed them. But they both had to deliver the goods, to show their followers at the end of the day that they had a form of divine blessing about them. Showing a type of mandate from heaven applied equally to secular charismatics. For Mao and Khomeini, this started with winning social revolutions against long odds and taking power. Khomeini's supporters could whisper about the return of the missing Twelfth Imam, the imam in occultation (*al-imam al-gha'ib*), a story akin to the Christian story of the Second Coming of Jesus. Mao's Communist followers could speak of his Mandate of Heaven (*tian ming*).

Having such a charismatic leader is a requirement for any social movement, including a movement of rage, to get off the ground. Movements are not born with institutions in place that can carry them forward. They need powerful leaders to survive the early, tough years in the wilderness. Movements of rage rarely get past that charismatic leadership phase, and indeed the premature death or removal of a charismatic leader of a movement of rage can effectively end the movement. In this way, movements of rage are much like cults in their leadership structure, where the life or death of one man can dramatically alter the political landscape. More institutionalized movements can survive the assassination of their leaders; nascent movements of rage cannot.

A second and more interesting aspect of movements of rage is their apocalyptic ideology. Most political ideologies, even those espousing violence, exist for a specific political purpose: to take power, to drive out an occupier, to advance social justice, to further the interests of this or that group in society. The ideology of a movement of rage is not about any of those Enlightenment-based programs but rather about cleansing society from contamination. Such a goal is not the basis for a complex ideological argument about class or nation, liberation, or the advancement of justice. Rather, by definition, such ideologies are poorly formed, inchoate, and rudimentary. Cleansing society of the contamination brought by educated elites does not require sophisticated argumentation and evidence. What possible persuasive logic could advance and defend the idea of exterminating Jews from Europe, of killing intellectuals of all stripes in Cambodia, or of violently rejecting the very notion of education in Nigeria? The language used is cataclysmic, claiming that the very existence of the "real" and "authentic" society is at stake given the contamination brought by elites, be they Westernized in outward appearance, showing "bourgeois tendencies," or simply too educated. No sophisticated ideology can justify gnosicide, so the ideological underpinnings of movements of rage always remain underdeveloped. To the extent that they exist, such ideologies hold out the promise of a utopian community freed from cultural corruption, but the appeal remains at a rudimentary conceptual level.

The apocalyptic ideology of a movement of rage may be nested inside a broader Enlightenment ideology of human progress. The ideologies of both the Khmer Rouge and the Red Guards were nested inside a broader Leninist (Maoist) movement that espouses the science of and progress in human history. The Nazi Brownshirts were nested inside a broader fascist coalition that likewise espoused a conservative vision of the forward march of human history. White nationalists in America are mostly nested inside the Republican Party, another coalition of conservative interests. Nesting inside a broader political coalition appears to give movements of rage a longer shelf life than they would have by existing independently.

Finally, movements of rage follow a strategy of nihilistic violence. Such a strategy has three components: *violence* that is *nihilistic* in nature and that emanates from a purposeful *strategy*. While movements of rage have half-baked ideologies, their pursuit of their enemies can be focused and fearsome. Movements of rage are inherently violent and will always take up arms against their perceived enemies. That violence is nihilistic in nature, in that it is extreme and out of all proportion to a strategic goal. It is not irrational or meaningless violence but rather vastly excessive violence that is unconstrained by usual norms and institutions. The leading cadres of movements of rage live and work in the space of upheaval between the modern, usually Westernized world, and the traditional world of their ancestors—at least, as they have imagined it. Although they are motivated by both worlds, they are constrained by neither.

THE FOUR WAVES OF GLOBAL JIHAD AS GLOBAL MOVEMENTS OF RAGE

Since most nascent social movements must have strong, often charismatic leadership to survive, the two elements that really set movements of rage apart from other violent actors are the combination of their apocalyptic ideologies and their strategies of nihilistic violence. Because of the distinctiveness of this combination of cataclysmic ideology and nihilistic savagery, movements of rage are legitimately seen as a distinctive form of violent social movement. I have suggested up to this point, with some examples, that global jihad in most cases should be viewed as a variant form of movements of rage that focuses on the *global* center of corruption rather than on a national center of cultural contamination.

There is an undeniable view among the ideologues discussed in this book that the West represents a clear-and-present danger to Islam via an insidious cultural contamination and societal corruption. This observation about the importance of cultural contamination to global jihad ideologues does not detract from the fact that all global jihad groups have been intensely political in pursuit of their objectives. But it does suggest that we miss something very important about global jihad groups by viewing them as just another violent political movement, just like so many others. It is important not to see global jihad as a unique, or sui generis, form of political violence, but one that is comparable to other extreme forms of violent social movements in the world over the past century. I conclude this book by taking a final dive into each of the four waves to identify the characteristics that make each, to varying degrees, a movement of rage.

The First Wave as a Movement of Rage

Of the four waves of global jihad, the first wave is the hardest case to make for a movement of rage, even if Abdullah 'Azzam's ideology was steeped in extreme violence. The case is made harder perhaps because the first wave was so limited in scope. With 'Azzam's assassination in 1989 and the failure of his idea of the Jihadi International to take root outside of Afghanistan, there is not enough evidence to conclusively say this had the makings of a movement of rage. Certainly 'Azzam was a charismatic leader; frankly, he was a more influential leader of Arab mujahideen for most of the Afghan war than was either Bin Laden or Zawahiri. His memory is still revered in jihadi circles to this day. As to ideology, 'Azzam was certainly radical, especially in his view of the necessity of permanent armed jihad as the only means to experience *tawhid*, the complete unity of all things under God. 'Azzam was concerned primarily with liberating lands that had historically been under Muslim rule from infidel occupiers, much like driving the Russians out of Muslim Afghanistan. Unlike every other ideologue of global jihad studied in this book, 'Azzam was much more careful in delineating legitimate targets of violence from illegitimate ones. This relative concern with just-war concepts was almost certainly a by-product of his formal training as a cleric at the prestigious al-Azhar seminary and university in Cairo, which set him apart from the vast majority of jihadi ideologues.

That said, 'Azzam was primarily responsible for creating the ideological justification for a cult of martyrdom that has marked various jihadi groups in recent decades. His explicit encouragement of seeking martyrdom in a jihad is only a short step away from advocating for suicide operations. Thus, like other radicals from other causes, 'Azzam advocated for significant political violence, although not the kind of millenarian and apocalyptic framing of violence used extensively by ISIS. It may well be true that had his vision of a Jihadi International ever really materialized outside of the realm of ideas and Afghanistan, it could have morphed into a broader movement of rage. Given what happened in subsequent waves of global jihad, one cannot dismiss this possibility.

The Second Wave as a Movement of Rage

By contrast, the second wave of global jihad (i.e., far-enemy targets) more clearly fits the criteria for a movement of rage. Usama Bin Laden emerged in

the 1990s as a charismatic leader of global jihad, partly for the constructed mythology of his role in winning the Afghan war, but primarily for his willingness
to give up a life of luxury—he came from the richest nonroyal family in Saudi
Arabia—and instead devote his life to a cause that meant personal hardship
and constant danger. The scholar Flagg Miller has insightfully detailed how Bin
Laden and like-minded jihadis extolled the virtues of asceticism.[33] The denial
of worldly pleasures is a classic indicator of a conscious rejection of the fruits
of modernity and added to Bin Laden's charismatic credentials. Polling in the
Muslim world consistently showed greater respect for Bin Laden individually
than for al-Qa'ida as a group, with the latter typically receiving single- or low-
double-digit favorability ratings.

It is fair to argue that Bin Laden's ideology was apocalyptic, as he sought
to create a global war against the United States and its allies. He argued that
Muslims had no choice but to fight, since that war had already begun, given
America's total war on Islam. His was an existential fear of annihilation
of Islam by the West, led by the United States. He believed that victory in
such a global war—defined as driving the United States out of the Muslim
world—was possible and would allow for the defeat of local apostate regimes
in Riyadh, Cairo, and throughout the region. Most obviously, Bin Laden employed a strategy of nihilistic violence. His violence was both unconstrained
and compartmentalized. It was unconstrained in that Bin Laden called for
the mass murder of hundreds of millions of people. His 1998 *fatwa* was un-
equivocal: Muslims were obligated to kill Americans, military and civilian,
everywhere in the world, anytime it was possible. While his call for murder
was very large, it was also compartmentalized, including Americans, other
Christians ("crusaders"), Jews (sometimes referred to as Zionists), near-enemy
targets, and their allies. On September 11, 2001, Bin Laden killed about as many
human beings as is physically possible with four airplanes as weapons. Access
to greater technologies of destruction would have led to a higher body count.

The Third Wave as a Movement of Rage

The ISIS state-building wave of global jihad strongly fits the model of movements of rage. Charismatic leaders of different types helped carry the movement forward. Abu Musab al-Zarqawi was not charismatic in the same way
Bin Laden was; rather, he embodied the idea of "jihadi cool"—a populist more

than charismatic approach to leadership. He did not appeal to clerics and others learned in Islam: quite the opposite, actually. Even his mentor, the famous Palestinian-Jordanian jihadi cleric Abu Muhammad al-Maqdisi, ultimately denounced his student.[34] But Zarqawi aimed at a different audience: young Muslim men looking for adventure and meaning in life. The murderous exploits and "coolness" of Zarqawi, advanced in numerous videos posted on the Internet, provided a thuggish but very real appeal, a Rambo for jihadis.

Abu Bakr al-Baghdadi, the self-proclaimed caliph, helped resuscitate a movement that had largely been extinguished after Zarqawi's death in 2006. Baghdadi's charisma emanated from a more traditional source: military victories in the swift conquest of northwestern Iraq in 2014 to go along with ISIS's hold over eastern Syria and Baghdadi's dramatic declaration of the restored caliphate from the Grand al-Nuri Mosque in Mosul. Again, it did not much matter that not a single ranking cleric anywhere in the Muslim world recognized this caliphate as legitimate. For the passionate followers of the cause, it was a mesmerizing and monumental achievement. Baghdadi's charismatic authority flowed from these "miraculous" achievements more than from his religious credentials or birthright.

Brookings scholar William McCants has convincingly demonstrated the apocalyptic nature of ISIS's ideology.[35] Tying into an Islamic history of apocalyptic sayings, many emanating from opposition to the Umayyad capture of the mantle of Muslim leadership in Damascus in the seventh century CE, ISIS conjured up a millenarian End Times narrative. It represented itself as the embodiment of the apocalyptic sayings about true and pure Muslims, riding under the black flags of Islam from Khorasan (at the time, the eastern edge of the Muslim empire) to save the true believers, smite the corrupt, and defeat the gathering Roman hordes in an Armageddon-like battle in Dabiq (today, a small village in northern Syria). In fact, when the ISIS British jihadi Mohammed Emwazi (aka Jihadi John) savagely decapitated ISIS's first American hostage, aid worker Peter Kassig, they brought him to Dabiq to kill him, with Emwazi intoning in his thick cockney accent: "Here we are, burying the first American Crusader in Dabiq, eagerly waiting for the remainder of your armies to arrive."[36]

ISIS even named its slick English-language propaganda magazine *Dabiq*, at least until it no longer controlled this hapless village. ISIS emphasized that the coming apocalypse was not sometime far off in the future; it was happening today, right now, and all true Muslims must answer the call and gather inside its state. The End Times narrative of ISIS mirrors similar religio-ideological strands from other cultural settings, most especially the Rapture literature in American evangelical writings of the late twentieth and early twenty-first centuries.[37] As a practical matter, once ISIS captured Mosul and northwestern Iraq in 2014 and had to seriously consider the actual state-building enterprise—collecting taxes, providing electricity, administering schools and courts, making the buses run on time, and so on—it tended to tone down the apocalyptic rhetoric, but it never ever fully abandoned the millenarian grandiloquence.

ISIS also employed a strategy of nihilistic violence. Both in making territory ungovernable in order to take it over and as a form of rule-by-terror, ISIS used a strategy of *idarat al-tawahhush* (the management of savagery).[38] Its gruesome violence against its perceived enemies was extensive and deliberate, and often posted online. Similar to al-Qa'ida, its enemies list was long (discussed in chapter 3). It included enemies within Syria and Iraq: Shia, Alawis, Yazidis and other Kurds, Sunnis who had worked with the post-2003 regime in Iraq, police, and certain tribes who had cooperated with Baghdad. Most chillingly, its enemies list included all "apostates," which ended up being any Muslim who disagreed with the goals of ISIS. This was ISIS's version of gnosicide: killing off or driving into exile any of the "best and brightest" who did not share its apocalyptic ideology. While ISIS did not initially call for acts of violence against civilians in Europe and North America, it did so with gusto once US and allied airstrikes against ISIS began in August 2014. ISIS's embrace of nihilistic violence, along with its apocalyptic ideology, clearly made it a movement of rage.

As an ironic last note on ISIS: Iran also began an armed campaign against ISIS at the same time the United States did, both working with their Iraqi government allies, and thus making the United States and Iran implicit allies in the fight against ISIS, in defense of the embattled regime in Baghdad.

The Fourth Wave as a Movement of Rage

The current *jihad fardi* (personal jihad) wave of global jihad lacks a specific charismatic leader, and instead relies on networks of like-minded radicals connected online and through social media to create a wiki-narrative of global jihad. Although there are well-known leaders of jihadi violence, no one or two individuals can be said to be global leaders today of this form of violence. It is not likely that Abu Musab al-Suri is still alive and, in any case, he has not been heard from since 2005. His ideas about networked global jihad for the twenty-first century, however, are still very much alive. It may be possible to think about the Internet itself as a form of authority, insofar as people can be mesmerized and compelled to act violently in the name of some cause merely through their online interactions. Again, authority-through-the-Internet is less Weberian charisma and more populist appeal. It is through that networked but impersonal connectivity that some lone wolves and small cells become radicalized enough to carry out acts of violence and terror.

Because personal jihad is so dependent on the radicalization of specific individuals without a direct connection to ISIS, al-Qa'ida, or any other violent group, their specific ideological goals and rationales will vary. Although these lone wolf attacks are carried out in the name of global jihad (in some form), their motivations can be significantly different. Omar Mateen, the Orlando nightclub shooter, had no logistical connection with ISIS yet claimed his murderous rampage in their name. Later evidence suggests that Mateen had deep psychological problems related to his apparent latent homosexuality. Syed Farook and Tashfeen Malik, the married couple in San Bernadino, California, who murdered fourteen people before being killed in a shootout with police, also had no known connection with any violent group and instead self-radicalized online. While texts between them made it clear that their violence was done to advance the global jihadi cause, they left no public message to explain or justify their ideological goals. The same can be said for nearly all of the lone wolf attacks in the West in recent years: the perpetrators generally self-radicalized online without direct logistical support from any jihadi group and undertook their violence to advance the global jihadi cause—but rarely left much evidence beyond perhaps simpleminded jargon about their ideological views.

Fourth wave jihadi violence is *stochastic* in nature. That is, it has been inspired by some individual or group—Abu Musab al-Suri, ISIS, Anwar al-Awlaki, al-Qa'ida, and so on—but has no logistical ties to a larger group or leader. The planning and financing of the attack is entirely self-generated by that lone wolf or small cell. Stochastic terror is not unique to jihadis; it is a growing form of violence for many causes in the world today. Violence from white nationalists, for example, is almost always stochastic: inspired by, but not logistically tied to, political leaders, groups, and ideologues. Anders Breivik murdered seventy-seven Norwegian youth in 2011 and in a written document cited inspiration from several leading anti-Muslim ideologues in the United States. But those ideologues only inspired Breivik; they did not assist him. Brenton Tarrant's murderous rampage against Muslims in New Zealand in 2019 was inspired in part by the American president Donald Trump ("a symbol of white identity and renewed purpose," according to Tarrant), but Trump played no direct role in the attack. This is what stochastic violence means: inspired by others but carried out wholly on one's own. It is the predictable outcome of encouragement to violence by leaders but without actual assistance for the attack.

With the caveat about often insufficient data on some specific fourth wave attacks aside, it is clear that Abu Musab al-Suri—the chief ideologue of the fourth wave—viewed the present danger in cataclysmic terms. When he wrote the *Call for Global Islamic Resistance* in 2004, he understood that the very existence of the jihadi cause was in peril. In Suri's view, the loss of the Afghan emirate was a catastrophic defeat for global jihad, and he needed to develop a strategy for the survival of global jihad. Personal jihad (*jihad fardi*) was his interim strategy; not enough force to defeat the enemy, but sufficient to keep hope alive for global jihad until better days were at hand. According to Suri's world view, these were apocalyptic times for the Muslim community, and Islam itself was in danger.

Finally, the fourth wave of global jihad undoubtedly represents a strategy of nihilistic violence. Suri, more than many jihadi ideologues, valued attacks on soft targets: terrorism, in the view of most. Indeed, all of the fourth wave jihadi attacks in Europe and North America have targeted noncombatants. Lone wolves and cells of two or three individuals simply do not have the capacity and wherewithal to attack hard military targets, so they turn their trucks down streets filled with civilian pedestrians instead. Fourth wave attacks are in some ways more nihilistic (if less lethal) than those from earlier waves of global jihad. Other than huge categories such as "Westerners," "Americans," "Jews," or "apostates," there are no restrictions on who gets targeted, no 'Azzam-like attempt to identify legitimate versus illegitimate targets of violence in the name of global jihad. Everyone within enormous groups (e.g., "Westerners") is a potential target as there is no leadership to identify and specify objectives. Radicalizing Internet sites and social media are not known for their discretion and careful judgment about just-war theory.

As this discussion makes clear, a movement-of-rage model better captures the nature of global jihad and similar nihilistic groups—both religious and secular—than the competing frameworks noted at the outset of this conclusion. While not every detail fits every case, the broader and insightful explanatory power of the movement-of-rage model sheds a great deal of light on the fundamental nature of global jihad, and why it is not a sui generis form of political violence. It is fair to conclude that most forms of global jihad to date represent a variant, global form of movement of rage. The combination of apocalyptic ideology and strategies of nihilistic violence set movements of rage apart as a distinctive form of political violence that can be seen in various political and cultural settings around the world over the course of the past century. National movements of rage seek to eliminate the sources of cultural contamination in their own capital cities, usually resulting in some form of gnosicide; global movements of rage, including most forms of global jihad, seek to attack the *global* centers of cultural corruption. The good news is that movements of rage tend to be weak and marginal, rarely actually coming to power. The bad news? When they do come to power alone or as part of a coalition, the results can be horrific. But even outside of issues of political power, with modern technologies, it does not take many people to create a very deadly outcome, and global jihadis, like other movements of rage, are all too willing to go down that path of destruction and annihilation.

Epilogue

WHO WON?

FOR ITS TITLE, THIS EPILOGUE ASKS THE PROVOCATIVE QUESTION "Who won?"—a rather imprecise and even banal question outside the field of sports. But I do so to raise the point that global jihad appears to have had an outsized and disproportionate impact on powerful countries, especially the United States, given its rather low level of actual strategic threat. The level of threat any actor represents to another is typically defined by the combination of intentions and capabilities. Significant capabilities without malintent— such as the relationship between the United States and the UK—is a benign outcome. Malintent without significant capabilities is less benign but not a significant problem, assuming that actor does not greatly enhance its capabilities (for example, get its hands on a nuclear weapon).

The ideologues described in this book are a pretty motley crew of nasty actors, many of whom would gladly use the worst weapons in the world if they could get their hands on them. Fortunately, they have not been able to obtain those weapons over the past four decades, and there are good reasons to believe it is highly unlikely that they ever will. By contrast, the Soviet Union represented a truly existential threat to North America and Europe, what with tens of thousands of nuclear warheads poised to annihilate the Western world. The reverse was also true, hence the Cold War concept of Mutually Assured Destruction (MAD). Today, and over the past forty years, there have been many significant strategic threats, or at least potential strategic perils, in the world: China, as a rising power, is increasingly flexing its muscle on the regional and global arenas to shape the world order to its advantage; Russia, as a declining power, aggressively uses cyberweapons to interfere in the elections of European and American democracies, and hybrid warfare to bully its neighbors; Weapons of Mass Destruction, and especially the proliferation of nuclear weapons around the world; and, most of all, a rapidly changing climate that threatens catastrophic impacts if left unchecked, just to name a few.[1]

But it has been global jihadis that have disproportionately driven the news and policy formulations in Washington, DC. Certainly the terror attacks of 9/11 were a major issue, representing the largest assault on American territory since the Japanese attack on Pearl Harbor in 1941. The US response, assisted by countries around the world, was proper: the overthrow of the Taliban regime that had harbored al-Qa'ida, and the killing and capturing of as many al-Qa'ida militants as possible. But what should have been an appropriate and fairly narrowly constructed response to Usama Bin Laden's bloody sucker punch, immediately grew into a nonsensical "Global War on Terror" (GWOT). Terrorism is a *tactic*, often used by weak parties because they are not strong enough to take on great powers frontally. Declaring war on a tactic such as terror is a bit like declaring war on the tactic of outflanking an enemy in battle: it makes no rational sense and seemed to morph into a justification for many varied military activities around the Muslim world. The GWOT was used as a rationale for the United States to remain in Afghanistan for far too long, making the war there—in a country that has little strategic value to the United States—the longest war in US history.

Global jihadism proved central to America's next war, when al-Qa'ida's purported links to Saddam Hussein's regime were used to justify the invasion of Iraq. Abu Musab al-Zarqawi became globally famous overnight when US Secretary of State Colin Powell showed his mug shot to the UN Security Council as part of making the case for al-Qa'ida's involvement in 9/11. It was a ludicrous argument that flew in the face of deep, known, historical animosity between Saddam's regime and Islamists of all stripes. Zarqawi's presence in the Kurdish region of Iraq (which was outside of Baghdad's control) was part of his scheme to overthrow all apostate regimes of the *Mashriq*, including Saddam Hussein's. The mistaken war in Iraq based in part on the GWOT against global jihadis led to the death of thousands of Americans, the wounding of tens of thousands more, at a total direct and indirect cost in the trillions of dollars. Needless to say, the cost to Iraqi society was far higher, including the launching of ISIS.

Global jihadism and the GWOT were next used to inform any number of brutish actions by Middle Eastern regimes, which justified those actions under the rubric of fighting terrorism. More often than not, such actions were accepted or even encouraged by American administrations—from the crushing of the second Palestinian uprising (which was so extensive that Israeli sociologist Baruch Kimmerling referred to it as "politicide," the attempted destruction of the Palestinians as a national group) in 2002 and 2003, to the Egyptian military's coup against Muhammad Morsi, the democratically elected president, in 2013, which the US government refused to even label a coup.[2] Even the illegal embargo by Saudi Arabia and the United Arab Emirates against US ally Qatar—where ten thousand US military personnel were stationed—was outrageously and publicly encouraged by President Donald Trump as a means to stamp out "terrorism." The bloody humanitarian disaster of the Saudi-UAE–led war in Yemen beginning in 2015 was likewise justified under the rubric of combatting terror.

But the threat of global jihadism has not only had an outsized influence on American foreign policy; it has also had a disproportionate impact on American democracy. The events of 9/11 caused such a reaction that they led to a serious increase in what is often called the "national security state."[3] Not only did Congress pass the so-called Patriot Act, which significantly restricted civil liberties in America, but various US intelligence agencies constructed far-flung capabilities that allowed them to engage in vast electronic domestic spying.[4] The public only became aware of this enterprise with the revelations made by whistleblower Edward Snowden. All of these measures and more were justified by the threat of global jihadism and the terrorism associated with it. Even more recently, the Trump administration's various bans on Muslims entering the United States were justified on national security grounds due to the threat of jihadi terror. In reality, it was bigotry disguised as national security.[5]

A cold and sober analysis of the level of threat that global jihadism represents would suggest a modest danger of seriously brutal intentions but limited capabilities. This is a danger that must not be ignored but likewise should not dominate policy formulation. Instead, the reality has been to frame global jihadism and its terrorism as an existential threat that justifies far-reaching changes to both foreign and domestic policies. To be sure, global jihadi ideologues are open in their contempt for democracy, and their actions have led to significant changes to civil liberties and democratic governance in the West, although not necessarily in the manner that the jihadis had envisioned. While waves of global jihadism have been destroyed or degraded, perhaps in some ways global jihadis are well on their way to accidentally achieving one of their goals after all: the internal degradation of Western democracy.

Notes

INTRODUCTION: THE BIRTH OF ISLAMISM AND JIHADISM

1. Jama'at-i Islami, founded in 1941 in British India by Abu A'la Mawdudi, was similarly influential in South Asia and espoused an ideology comparable to the Muslim Brotherhood.

2. See the distinction the late Sadik Jalal al-Azm often made between the lived religion of Islam, which often practiced a type of secularism, and the "dogmatic no" with regard to the written texts of Islam. See, for example, Sadik J. al-Azm, *Is Islam Secularizable? Challenging Political and Religious Taboos* (Berlin: Gerlach Press, 2014).

3. Support for Islamism has varied from country to country, and within the same country over time, so that 25 percent figure must be weighed accordingly. But if one examines support for Islamist parties in Muslim-majority countries, particularly since the 1990s when good polling data became widely available, about one in four adults supported Islamist parties. That number could rise considerably under certain circumstances, particularly when marginal potential supporters joined with core supporters to form a majority—as happened in Egypt in 2012, narrowly allowing the Muslim Brotherhood's Muhammad Morsi to win the presidency. Alternatively, it could narrow to just the true believers under other circumstances, a figure closer to 15 percent in most Muslim-majority countries.

4. For a good, early discussion of Islamist social movements in the Middle East, see Quintan Wiktorowicz, ed., *Islamic Activism: A Social Movement Theory Approach*

(Bloomington: Indiana University Press, 2003). The beginning section of my chapter "Hamas as Social Movement" in that volume contains a concise introduction to social movement theory.

5. The merger of Salafi ideas to political radicalism and violence is historically new, as Salafism tended to be the most nonpolitical of all Islamic tendencies. Most Salafis today still practice apolitical piety, but a subset has adopted an activist and violent bent, described later in this book. This new ideological innovation is known as Salafi-jihadism, a term coined by Abu Musab al-Suri (see chapter 4).

6. See, for example, Nasser's speech mocking the leader of the Muslim Brotherhood for demanding that Nasser make veiling mandatory for all Egyptian women while he was not even able to get his own daughter to veil. A subtitled clip from this speech can be found on YouTube at https://www.youtube.com/watch?v=TX4RK8bj2Wo (last accessed April 30, 2020). A more complete video of this same critical commentary on the Muslim Brotherhood, but without English subtitles, can be found at https://www.youtube.com/watch?v=iYrZUwa_2EM (accessed April 30, 2020).

7. For an early and brilliant assessment of the failure of Islamism, see Olivier Roy, *The Failure of Political Islam* (Cambridge: Harvard University Press, 1998).

8. For an excellent discussion of political discourses within modern Shi'ism, see Vali Nasr, *The Shia Revival: How Conflicts within Islam Will Shape the Future* (New York: W.W. Norton, 2007).

9. The earliest extensive study of the Muslim Brotherhood was Richard P. Mitchell's classic book *The Society of the Muslim Brothers* (Oxford: Oxford University Press, 1969). For excellent recent histories of the Muslim Brotherhood, see Carrie Rosefsky Wickam, *The Muslim Brotherhood: Evolution of an Islamist Movement* (Princeton, NJ: Princeton University Press, 2013), and Khalil al-Anani, *Inside the Muslim Brotherhood: Religion, Identity and Politics* (Oxford: Oxford University Press, 2016). A good analysis of the early years of the Brotherhood can be found in Brynjar Lia, *The Society of the Muslim Brothers in Egypt: The Rise of an Islamic Mass Movement, 1928–1942* (Reading, UK: Ithaca Press, 1999).

10. Perhaps embarrassed by this particular cultural appropriation, later Muslim Brothers claimed that the "Be Prepared" slogan came instead from the Qur'an (chapter 8, verse 60): "And prepare against them what force you can and horses tied at the frontier."

11. Khalil al-Anani, "The Power of the Jama'a: The Role of Hasan al-Banna in Constructing the Muslim Brotherhood's Collective Identity," *Sociology of Islam* 1, nos. 1–2

(2013): 43 and passim. An updated version of this essay can be found in al-Anani's book, *Inside the Muslim Brotherhood.*

12. Al-Anani, "Power of the Jama'a," 58.

13. The issue of violence also informs policy debates over the Muslim Brotherhood in many Western capitals to this day. Should the Muslim Brotherhood be banned because it encourages violence (the argument made by the Sisi regime in Cairo), or should it be accepted as a legitimate political group? The question can be situated as: Is the Muslim Brotherhood a "gateway drug" or stepping-stone to further radicalization and violence, or is it a "satisficing" organization that captures and organizes Islamist sentiment in a way that discourages further radicalization and encourages working within the system? That is, is the Muslim Brotherhood a firewall of sorts that diminishes further extremism and violence? While there is no simple answer that explains all of the data on this question, it is fair to say that most evidence supports the "satisficing" argument. Certainly, the most extreme jihadis routinely condemn the Muslim Brotherhood for being sellouts who end up legitimizing apostate regimes. Al-Qa'ida's Ayman al-Zawahiri wrote an entire book, *al-Hisad al-Murr (Bitter Harvest),* blasting the Muslim Brotherhood in Egypt for renouncing violence in the 1970s and vowing to work within the political and social systems for incremental change. Zawahiri wanted the Brotherhood to join in armed jihad against the Mubarak regime instead. Unfortunately the 2013 military coup against the elected Muslim Brotherhood president of Egypt, Muhammad Morsi, and the subsequent outlawing of the Brotherhood, means that there is no more Islamist firewall against greater extremism. This suggests greater violence in Egypt (and likely beyond) in the future from radicalized Islamists who must choose between submission or violence. There is already evidence that this transition has begun to occur. The middle way of nonviolent Islamist political activity has been outlawed by the Sisi regime in Cairo.

14. Greeley prohibited alcohol sales until 1972.

15. *Social Justice in Islam* was translated into English by John B. Hardie in 1953 and was revised with an introduction by Hamid Algar in 2000. Sayyid Qutb, *Social Justice in Islam,* revised edition (Oneonta, NY: Islamic Publications International, 2000).

16. A translation of *The America I Have Seen* by Qutb, written in 1951, can be found at: https://www.cia.gov/library/abbottabad-compound/3F/3F56ACA473044436B 4C174oF65D5C3B6_Sayyid_Qutb_-_The_America_I_Have_Seen.pdf (accessed April 30, 2020). For an academic treatment of Qutb's stay in the United States that emphasizes his dichotomy between the "spiritual East" and the "material West," see John

Calvert, "'The World is an Undutiful Boy!': Sayyid Qutb's American Experience," *Islam and Christian-Muslim Relations* 11, no. 1 (2000): 87–103. See as well Calvert's *Sayyid Qutb and the Origins of Radical Islamism* (New York: Columbia University Press, 2010), which is the best book-length treatment of Sayyid Qutb. I have yet to come across a true Freudian analysis of the overtly sexual writing that Qutb employs (as do some other jihadi ideologues), nor of two life experiences that Qutb apparently had: unrequited love from a wealthier, Westernized Egyptian young woman, and a topless passenger on his ship to America who drunkenly appeared at his stateroom door late one night, much to his horror . . . and delight? This is an article best left for an aspiring psychoanalyst to write!

17. Nasser emerged as the clear political leader of the Free Officers by 1954.

18. For a fascinating treatment of the long and complicated relationship between Qutb and Nasser, see Fawaz A. Gerges, *Making the Arab World: Nasser, Qutb, and the Clash That Shaped the Middle East* (Princeton, NJ: Princeton University Press, 2018).

19. For an excellent and nuanced analysis of how Qutb revised *Social Justice in Islam* to reflect his growing radicalism, see William E. Shepard, "The Development of Thought of Sayyid Qutb as Reflected in Earlier and Later Editions of 'Social Justice in Islam,'" *Die Welt des Islams* 32, no. 2 (1992): 196–236. Much of *In the Shade of the Qur'an* was also written from prison and has been translated into English as well. All eighteen volumes can be found online in both Arabic and English, including the translation and publication by The Islamic Foundation (2009).

20. *Milestones* is widely available online in both Arabic and English and can be found in paperback at Sayyid Qutb, *Milestones* (New Delhi, India: Islamic Book Service, 2006).

21. William E. Shepard, "Sayyid Qutb and Modern Islamist Violence," *Seasons* (Summer 2007): 26.

22. The charge was technically Qutb's relationship to the "1965 Organization" and its plot to overthrow Nasser, but it was Qutb's publication of *Milestones* (still an illegal book in Egypt today) that landed him at the gallows. Indeed, Barbara Zollner has argued that *Milestones* was designed as a "guidebook" for this violently antiregime organization. See Zollner, "Prison Talk: The Muslim Brotherhood's Internal Struggle during Gamal Abdel Nasser's Persecution, 1954 to 1971," *International Journal of Middle East Studies* 39, no. 3 (August 2007): 411–33.

23. The best concise treatment of Qutb's theory of *jahiliyya* is found in William E. Shepard, "Sayyid Qutb's Doctrine of Jahiliyya," *International Journal of Middle East*

Studies 35, no. 4 (2003): 521–45. For an interesting treatment of Qutb from a sociological perspective, including short translations of some of his many writings, see Albert J. Bergesen, ed., *The Sayyid Qutb Reader* (New York: Routledge, 2007).

24. *Takfir* has a much graver consequence, at least in theory, than excommunication in the Catholic Church. The latter is an act of censure that leads to the denial of rights, such as sacraments. The former means one is guilty of apostasy, of voluntarily leaving Islam, which in the *hudud* is a capital crime.

25. Dr. Shepard's work makes this point, although not as baldly as I put it here. My thanks to him for allowing me to pester him in his retirement to discuss Qutb's views on *jahiliyya* and *takfir*.

26. Qutb did not cite Lenin as his inspiration for this concept and instead suggested his view of armed jihad was consistent with the Prophetic tradition, whereby cycles of small provocations, repression, and exile could become stronger over time, leading to the ultimate victory of the vanguard, much like Muhammad's ultimate conquest of Mecca. My own sense is that this reading of Prophetic tradition was likely reading Lenin back into Islamic history, as it comports with Lenin's theory much more than it comports with actual Prophetic history.

27. Many of Shariati's books and lectures have been translated into English and can be found online. For an excellent biography of Shariati and his ideas, see Ali Rahnema, *An Islamic Utopian: A Political Biography of Ali Shari'ati* (London: IB Tauris, 2014).

28. The back corner of the great Umayyad mosque in the old city of Damascus (formerly a Byzantine church) still marks the place where Husayn's head was displayed in the Ra's al-Husayn (literally "head of Husayn") room. By tradition, his head was reunited with the rest of his body. Several locations around the Muslim world claim to have Husayn's remains.

29. A similar interpretive transformation occurred in the Black church in the southern United States after World War II. An emphasis on keeping one's head down and focusing on justice in the next life gave rise to a focus on following the example of Jesus to rabble-rouse when justice required it, even at the risk of one's life and liberty. Dr. Martin Luther King Jr. embodied this interpretive transformation and paid the price with his life.

30. Khomeini's lectures on Islamic government were put together in a book, which (along with other writings) has been translated and annotated by Hamid Algar, *Islam and Revolution: Writings and Declarations of Imam Khomeini* (Berkeley, CA: Mizan Press, 1981).

31. An excellent analysis of Khomeini's reinterpretation of *velayat-i faqih* can be found in Gregory Rose, "Velayat-e Faqih and the Recovery of Islamic Identity in the Thought of Ayatullah Khomeini," in *Religion and Politics in Iran*, edited by Nikki Keddi, 166–88 (New Haven, CT: Yale University Press, 1983).

32. In the main branch of Shi'ism, the twelfth leader of the community following the Prophet Muhammad, Muhammad Ibn al-Hasan al-Mahdi, went into spiritual hiding ("Occultation") circa 941 CE and will return during End Times to bring justice to the world and lead the righteous. He is known as the Hidden Imam, al-Imam al-Gha'ib. This Shia End Times prophecy is strikingly similar to the Christian belief in the second coming of Jesus during End Times.

33. Jalal Al-i Ahmad, *Occidentosis: A Plague from the West* (Berkeley, CA: Mizan Press, 1983).

34. The document was designed for internal use and not for publication. It was first published by the *al-Ahrar* newspaper in Cairo in December 1981. It has been translated in full, with considerable annotation and analysis by Johannes J. G. Jansen, *The Neglected Duty: The Creed of Sadat's Assassins* (New York: RVP Press, 2013). This is a reprint of the original 1986 book.

35. To understand the rise and evolution of Islamism, an excellent place to start is to read almost anything by Gilles Kepel, Olivier Roy, and Fawaz Gerges—all of whom have studied this issue deeply and published widely on it. Please see the bibliography for some of their specific works.

36. I use the term *waves* instead of *iterations* or similar word simply because it is a more accessible term for the reader. The word is not designed to denote evenly spaced timing (e.g., waves three and four greatly overlapped) but rather to suggest a set of distinctive forms of global jihad, each different from the other, much like each wave in the ocean is different from the next and are rarely evenly spaced apart. In addition, my use of the term *wave* should not be confused with David C. Rappaport's well-known argument about the four waves of modern terrorism, of which his fourth wave—religious terrorism—would necessarily include all four waves of global jihad.

37. For a detailed analysis of the first Palestinian intifada, see Glenn E. Robinson, *Building a Palestinian State: The Incomplete Revolution* (Bloomington: Indiana University Press, 1997).

38. World Islamic Front, "Jihad Against Jews and Crusaders: Statement, 23 February 1998," Federation of American Scientists, https://fas.org/irp/world/para/docs/980223-fatwa.htm (accessed April 30, 2020).

39. Arabic has words for both an infidel or nonbeliever (*kafir*) and an apostate (*murtadh*), but the delineation between these two concepts is not strictly observed. The process that leads to a finding of apostasy is *tafkir*, using the same root as the word for infidel, not apostate. Many of the Sunni jihadis discussed in this book would agree to a *takfir* finding of apostasy for all Shia but would tend to refer to them using other names, such as rejectionists. *Safawi* simply means Safavid, a reference to the Shia Persian Empire that began in 1501. But the connotation is negative, that Iraq's Shia were simply pawns in the hands of their masters in Tehran and therefore not even really Iraqis at all.

40. For more on these two terror events and their likely planning processes, see chapters 2 and 8 in Bruce Hoffman and Fernando Reinares, eds., *The Evolution of the Global Terrorist Threat: From 9/11 to Osama bin Laden's Death* (New York: Columbia University Press, 2014).

41. Jowitt has published only a few short descriptions of his concept of movements of rage, beginning with a few pages in Ken Jowitt, *New World Disorder: The Leninist Extinction* (Berkeley: University of California Press, 1992). During my graduate studies at Berkeley (1986–92), I was a teaching assistant for Professor Jowitt and he was the co-chair of my dissertation committee, so some of my discussion on movements of rage invariably come from those experiences and discussions, in addition to his brief published discussions on the topic.

42. On Bin Laden's asceticism, see Flagg Miller, *The Audacious Ascetic: What the Bin Laden Tapes Reveal about al-Qa'ida* (Oxford: Oxford University Press, 2015).

CHAPTER 1: THE JIHADI INTERNATIONAL

1. There had been instances of regional or transnational armed jihad undertaken by the Muslim Brotherhood against Israel both during the 1948 war and following the 1967 war, and by the Syrian preacher Izz al-Din al-Qassam in his recruitment of regional fighters against both British and Zionist targets before his death in 1935. These were fairly small efforts, however, and were not global in their orientations.

2. For a good analysis of these early jihadi groups, see Gilles Kepel, *Muslim Extremism in Egypt: The Prophet and Pharaoh,* 2nd ed. (Berkeley: University of California Press, 2003).

3. Thomas Hegghammer details the rise of more transnational Muslim identity ideologies in the 1970s that helped generate a much higher level of foreign fighters in Afghanistan and elsewhere in the 1980s; see Hegghammer, "The Rise of Muslim

Foreign Fighters: Islam and the Globalization of Jihad," *International Security* 35, no. 3 (Winter 2010–11): 53–94.

4. For more biographical details of 'Azzam's life, see Thomas Hegghammer, "Abdullah Azzam, the Imam of Jihad," in *Al Qaeda in Its Own Words*, ed. Gilles Kepel and Jean-Pierre Milelli, 81–143 (Cambridge, MA: Harvard University Press, 2008). Hegghammer's monumental biography of 'Azzam was published in 2020, as this book went to press, and will likely be the definitive account of 'Azzam's life. Hegghammer was generous in sharing with me some of his findings on 'Azzam to inform this book, even before his book was published. See his *The Caravan: Abdallah Azzam and the Rise of Global Jihad* (Cambridge, UK: Cambridge University Press, 2020).

5. Hegghammer, "Abdullah Azzam," 87.

6. In the 1990s, it was made clear to me in numerous interviews and conversations in Jordan that the Hashemites were concerned about 'Azzam parlaying his position as a leader of the Muslim Brotherhood in Jordan into the position of Supreme Guide in Jordan, particularly given his position on the Shura (or consultative council), his charismatic leadership, and his large following.

7. The Bin Laden family claims that 'Azzam played a personal role in Usama's radicalization while in Saudi Arabia, but this claim should not be taken at face value given that it was only made in 2018 and may be seen as a politically useful device. See Martin Chulov's interview with the Bin Laden family in *The Guardian*, August 3, 2018, https://www.theguardian.com/world/2018/aug/03/osama-bin-laden-mother -speaks-out-family-interview.

8. Ahmed Rashid's estimate of thirty-five thousand foreign fighters represents the high end of all credible estimates, while Mohammed M. Hafez estimates ten thousand foreign fighters. See Ahmed Rashid, *Taliban: Militant Islam, Oil and Fundamentalism in Central Asia* (New Haven, CT: Yale University Press, 2010), 129; and Mohammed M. Hafez, "Jihad after Iraq: Lessons for the Arab Afghans Phenomenon," *CTC Sentinel* 1, no. 4 (March 2008): 1–4. Hegghammer also estimates ten thousand foreign fighters in Afghanistan, split between seven thousand Arabs and three thousand South Asians (personal communication with the author, October 30, 2019).

9. Thomas Hegghammer, personal communication with the author, October 30, 2019.

10. Even this use came years after 'Azzam had begun speaking of the "solid base" (*al-qa'ida al-sulba*) of jihad. By itself, the word "al-qa'ida" has no intrinsic or necessary relationship with the idea of jihad; it is a secular, pedestrian word. But the word was adopted by jihadis who imbued it with a more religious and revolutionary sense.

11. See Patricia Crone, "Jihad: Idea and History," *Open Democracy*, April 30, 2007, https://www.opendemocracy.net/faith-europe_islam/jihad_4579.jsp.

12. By contrast, Sayyid Qutb specifically accepted the idea of offensive jihad.

13. The Arabic word *dunya* has a broader definition than territory or land, which is usually denoted as *ard* (pl.: *arad*)—the word that 'Azzam used. *Dunya* refers to all worldly items—from land to houses to valuable possessions. Taymiyya's mandate to Muslims to defend all that is theirs from hostile attack by infidels is thus more expansive than 'Azzam's call.

14. 'Azzam's short answer was yes, the greater good calls for such a sacrifice. This reticence of Arab Salafis to consider mostly Pashtun Afghans as true Muslims also perplexed and infuriated Abu Musab al-Suri. Although the tribal code of the Pashtuns, the *Pashtunwali*, contains within it much Islamic doctrine and custom, there are local and cultural differences that made many true-believing Salafis pause in their support of Afghan mujahideen. For 'Azzam, it was a greater sin to not fight the Soviet occupation of Muslim Afghanistan than it was to be tainted by fighting alongside imperfect Muslims.

15. I am of the view that Qutb would have certainly been familiar with various Marxist thinkers from the early twentieth century, including Lenin and Trotsky, as such thinking was widely read and debated throughout the Arab world during this period. An educated man such as Qutb would not have had such a huge gap in his studies. Lenin and Trotsky (and other Marxist thinkers) wrote and spoke precisely when Qutb would have been most impressionable, as a teenager and a young man in his early twenties. Russia's October Revolution that brought communism to power in Moscow occurred when Qutb was eleven years old, and it was a major international story for years after. Qutb never credited Marxist thinkers for inspiring some of his major concepts, including notions of vanguards and permanent revolution, but that may have been for reputational reasons (not wanting to credit atheists for ideas reworked as Islamist). And it is possible that Qutb was inculcated into these ideas from multiple exposures to Marxist thought but simply did not consciously draw the connection from those general exposures to his own writing. The proposition that Qutb had no exposure to Marxist thought or that such thought did not influence Qutb's thinking about jihadism is not persuasive.

16. The *hadith* about greater jihad–lesser jihad is classified as weak by all classical *hadith* compilers, so it is not just 'Azzam and Salafis who reject it. It gained prominence more as a result of modern political apologetics rather than historical *hadith* scholarship. That said, the distinction is so widely accepted by Muslims today as to be orthodoxy.

17. This paragraph draws on Shiraz Maher's excellent discussion on the relationship between *jihad* and *tawhid* for 'Azzam and other jihadi ideologues. See chapter 9 in Maher's *Salafi-Jihadism: The History of an Idea* (New York: Penguin Books, 2017).

18. See Fred M. Donner, *Muhammad and the Believers: At the Origins of Islam* (Cambridge, MA: Belknap Press, an Imprint of Harvard University Press, 2010).

19. Later in his article "Al-Qa'ida Al-Sulba" (in the April 1988 issue of *Al-Jihad*), Azzam uses the fuller definitional phrase of "the faithful fraternity and pioneering vanguard" (*al-'asaba al-mu'mina w' al-tali'a al-ra'ida*).

20. As Thomas Hegghammer has shown, extremist ideology was accompanied by a network of people in the Hijaz region of Saudi Arabia that helped encourage and facilitate the migration of foreign fighters to Afghanistan. See Hegghammer, "The Rise of Muslim Foreign Fighters: Islam and the Globalization of Jihad," *International Security* 35, no. 3 (Winter 2010–11), 53–94.

21. This line of argument was replicated later by Abu Musab al-Suri (see chapter 4).

22. The word *tali'a* for vanguard only appears three times in *Milestones*, while *jama'a* appears frequently. The word *'usba*, also meaning group, was periodically used by Qutb for the same vanguard meaning. William Shepard, private communication with the author, February 2019.

23. See Jeremy Simons, "Dureza's Betrayal and Duterte's Hypocrisy in Marawi," *Plowing Peace*, September 13, 2017.

24. For a good discussion of the meaning and evolution of martyrdom in Islamic history, see Asma Afsaruddin, *Striving in the Path of God: Jihad and Martyrdom in Islamic Thought* (Oxford: Oxford University Press, 2013).

25. See David Cook, *Martyrdom in Islam* (Cambridge, UK: Cambridge University Press, 2007).

26. Hegghammer, "Abdullah Azzam," 101. *Al-Farida Al-Gha'iba* has been translated in various ways, including by Hegghammer as "The Absent Imperative" or by Johannes Jansen as "The Neglected Duty." The key to understand is that a *fard* or *farida* is something that is obligatory for Muslims to do, hence the discussion about a *fard 'ayn*, or an obligation that is the duty of all able-bodied Muslims to carry out. *Gha'iba* means absent, neglected, or hidden. The Shia use the same word to mean in occultation and specifically for the Twelfth Imam who is currently in occultation waiting to return to earth to bring justice and the victory of Islam. He is known as the Imam al-Gha'ib, or the Imam in Occultation. By using the title he does, Faraj was being deliberately provocative, implying that the obligation of armed jihad has been

neglected by Muslims and needs to be reasserted. The text of Faraj's book has been translated in full, with annotation, by Johannes J. G. Jansen, in *The Neglected Duty: The Creed of Sadat's Assassins and Islamic Resurgence in the Middle East* (New York: McMillan, 1986).

27. For various competing translations of this verse in the Qur'an, see http://corpus.quran.com/translation.jsp?chapter=9&verse=111. For a detailed discussion of the words *jihad* and *martyrdom* in the Qur'an and broader Islamic interpretation, see Afsaruddin, *Striving in the Path of God*.

28. *Houris* have been defined is various ways, including inaccurately as "virgins." The best English word to understand what is being promised is "nymph." This is quoted by 'Azzam in *Join the Caravan*. The book can be found in both the original Arabic and in English translation at https://archive.org/.

29. Robert A. Pape, "The Strategic Logic of Suicide Terrorism," *American Political Science Review* 97, no. 3 (August 2003): 343–61. The University of Chicago, where Pape is based, keeps a searchable database of all suicide attacks around the world at http://cpostdata.uchicago.edu/search_new.php.

30. For a good discussion of how the discourse and representation of martyrdom among Palestinian groups evolved over time, see Attila Kovacs, *Martyrdom and Visual Representations of the Palestinian Islamic Movements*, at https://fphil.uniba.sk/fileadmin/fif/katedry_pracoviska/kvas/SOS_9_2/N5-22kovacs-form_1_.pdf (accessed May 1, 2020).

31. The Iranian revolution and especially the group Hizbullah (which Iran founded in response to Israel's invasion and occupation of Lebanon in 1982) also developed a similar Shia version of the importance of martyrdom during the same time frame. It is not clear which discourse influenced the other, or if they emerged independently from each other.

32. For an excellent discussion of how jihadi defenders of suicide operations deal with the prohibition in Islam against suicide, see Mohammed M. Hafez, "Apologia for Suicide: Martyrdom in Contemporary Jihadist Discourse," in *Martyrdom, Self-Sacrifice, and Self-Immolation: Religious Perspectives on Suicide*, ed. Margo Kitts, 126–39 (Oxford: Oxford University Press, 2018).

33. And here is where the comparison to Catholic excommunication breaks down. The penalty for excommunication is denial of sacraments, not death.

34. That said, slandering a theological opponent with the claim of apostasy was a more common occurrence in intellectual debates, as Al-Ghazali famously did with

philosophers in his famous book *Tahafut al-Falasifa* ("The Incoherence of the Philosophers").

35. A small caveat should be noted here. Ibn Taymiyyah did believe categories of people could be considered infidels (as did 'Azzam), including the presumably Muslim Shia, so that would constitute a form of collective excommunication. However, punishment could not be made collectively but was to be done on an individual basis with appropriate due process.

36. For an interesting discussion on this issue, see the open letter to ISIS leader Abu Bakr al-Baghdadi written by fellow Muslim clerics from around the world, especially point 9: http://www.lettertobaghdadi.com.

37. For an excellent analysis of the use and misuse of *takfir* by jihadis, see Mohammed M. Hafez, "Tactics, *Takfir* and Anti-Muslim Violence," in *Self-Inflicted Wounds: Debates and Divisions within al-Qa'ida and Its Periphery*, ed. Assaf Moghadam and Brian Fishman, 19–44 (West Point, NY: Combatting Terrorism Center, 2010). A version of this book, including Hafez's essay, was published the following year as *Fault Lines in Global Jihad: Organizational, Strategic and Ideological Fissures,* ed. Assaf Moghadam and Brian Fishman, 25–46 (New York: Routledge, 2011).

38. For an excellent introduction to Qutb's idea of *jahiliyya*, see William E. Shepard, "Sayyid Qutb's Doctrine of *Jahiliyya*," *International Journal of Middle East Studies* 35, no. 4 (2003): 521–45.

39. For an inside account of what little difference the foreign fighters made in the Afghan jihad, see Abdullah Anas, *To the Mountains: My Life in Jihad, from Algeria to Afghanistan* (New York: Oxford University Press/Hurst, 2019). Anas was an ally of 'Azzam and married his daughter.

40. This is a major theme in Thomas Heggahammer's monumental new book, *The Caravan: Abdallah Azzam and the Rise of Global Jihad* (Cambridge: Cambridge University Press, 2020).

41. Bin Laden made his Somalia claim to Peter Bergen, but with no real corroboration. See Peter L. Bergen, *Holy War, Inc.,: Inside the Secret War of Osama Bin Laden* (Touchstone, 2002).

CHAPTER 2: AMERICA FIRST!

1. For a brief history and analysis of Hamas during its early years, see Glenn E. Robinson, "Hamas as Social Movement," in *Islamic Activism: A Social Movement Theory Approach*, ed. Quintan Wiktorowicz, 112–42 (Bloomington: Indiana University

Press, 2004). Although some analysts date the formation of Hamas to a December 1987 meeting in Gaza of the leaders of the Muslim Brotherhood, I use the year 1988 when the formal announcement was made and its *mithaq* (charter) was published.

2. Alison Mitchell, "Letter Explained Motive in Bombing, Officials Now Say," *New York Times*, March 28, 1993, https://www.nytimes.com/1993/03/28/nyregion/letter -explained-motive-in-bombing-officials-now-say.html.

3. For the early history of al-Jama'a's regional focus, see Mamoun Fandy, "Egypt's Islamic Group: Regional Revenge?" *Middle East Journal* 48, no. 4 (Autumn 1994): 607–25.

4. Cassandra, "The Impending Crisis in Egypt," *Middle East Journal* 49, no. 1 (Winter 1995): 9–27.

5. For a good overview of this truly remarkable evolution by al-Jama'a al-Islamiyya as an organization and many important leaders of al-Jihad, see Amr Hamzawy and Sarah Grebowski, *From Violence to Moderation: Al-Jama'a al-Islamiya and al-Jihad,* Carnegie Paper 20 (Washington, DC: Carnegie Endowment for International Peace, 2010), http://carnegieendowment.org/files/Hamzawy-Grebowski-EN.pdf.

6. Sharif's book is *Wathiqat Tarshid al-'Aml al-Jihadi fi Misr w'al-'Alam*, which may be translated as *Guidance on the Proper Place of Jihad in Egypt and the World*. For a detailed account of the renunciation of violence, including translated original documents by al-Jama'a al-Islamiyya, see Sherman A. Jackson, *Initiative to Stop the Violence (Mubadarat Waqf al-'Unf)* (New Haven, CT: Yale University Press, 2015).

7. World Peace Foundation, "Algeria: Civil War," August 7, 2015, part of the Tufts University project on Mass Atrocity Endings, https://sites.tufts.edu/atrocityendings/2015/08/07/72/.

8. Indeed, there was an official branch of the Brotherhood in Algeria that adopted the name Hamas. But the FIS, as a broad coalition and not a tight organization, was a far more important Islamist political actor in Algeria than the Brotherhood's formal organization.

9. For more on the Algerian civil war, see Luis Martinez, *The Algerian Civil War, 1990–1998* (New York: Columbia University Press, 2000). For an interesting account of the lessons learned from the violence in the Algerian civil war, see Jacob Mundy, *Imaginative Geographies of Algerian Violence: Conflict Science, Conflict Management, Antipolitics* (Palo Alto, CA: Stanford University Press, 2015).

10. Gilles Kepel, *Jihad: The Trail of Political Islam* (Cambridge, MA: Belknap Press, an imprint of Harvard University Press, 2003).

11. A great many books and articles have been written about Usama Bin Laden, many of which are sensationalist and unreliable. For solid and reliable histories of his life, see Lawrence Wright, *The Looming Tower: Al-Qaeda and the Road to 9/11* (New York: Vintage Books, 2007); and Fawaz A. Gerges, *The Rise and Fall of al-Qaeda* (Oxford: Oxford University Press, 2014).

12. There is some speculation, obliquely fueled by Usama Bin Laden himself, that his parents were not actually ever married. See Jonathon Randal, *Osama: The Making of a Terrorist* (New York: Knopf, 2004).

13. For more on this family dynamic, see Martin Chulov, "My Son, Osama: The al-Qaida Leader's Mother Speaks for the First Time," *The Guardian,* August 2, 2018, https://www.theguardian.com/world/2018/aug/03/osama-bin-laden-mother-speaks -out-family-interview.

14. For an overview of both major rounds of the civil war in Syria, see Glenn E. Robinson, "Syria's Long Civil War," *Current History* 111, no. 749 (December 2012): 331–36.

15. Thomas Hegghammer, personal communication with the author, October 30, 2019; and Hegghammer, *The Caravan: Abdallah Azzam and the Rise of Global Jihad* (Cambridge, UK: Cambridge University Press, 2020).

16. Turki bin Faysal al-Saud, the longtime intelligence chief in Saudi Arabia, tells the fainting story in *The Guardian* story cited in note 13.

17. While I have used the CDLR's chosen English translation of its name, there is ambiguity in Arabic over the meaning of the word *shar'iyya*. While it does mean "legitimate," it is closely related to the word shari'a and thus can also mean "pertaining to the shari'a." In this way the CDLR could make a nonreligious appeal for support to English speakers, while simultaneously confirming to Arabic speakers the underlying religious nature of the organization.

18. Flagg Miller shows that through 1993, the public speeches Bin Laden gave in Saudi Arabia and Yemen were carefully constructed not to be openly confrontational with the Saudi state. See Flagg Miller, *The Audacious Ascetic: What the Bin Laden Tapes Reveal about al-Qa'ida* (Oxford: Oxford University Press, 2015), chapters 2–4.

19. F. Gregory Gause III, private communication with the author. Gause has the CDLR faxes as part of his files.

20. For detailed analyses of the evolution of the near enemy–far enemy concept, see Fawaz A. Gerges, *The Far Enemy: Why Jihad Went Global,* 2nd ed. (Cambridge, UK: Cambridge University Press, 2009); and Steven Brooke, "Strategic Fissures: The Near and Far Enemy Debate," in *Self Inflicted Wounds: Debates and Divisions within al-Qa'ida and Its Periphery,* ed. Assaf Moghadam and Brian Fishman, 47–68 (West Point, NY:

Combatting Terrorism Center, 2010). See the revised chapter in the 2011 reissue by Routledge, *Fault Lines in Global Jihad: Organizational, Strategic and Ideological Fissures*, 47–68. The entire text of Faraj's manifesto has been translated and annotated in Johannes J. G. Jansen, *The Neglected Duty: The Creed of Sadat's Assassins* (New York: Macmillan, 1986; reissued by New York: RVP Press, 2013).

21. This Egyptian group has many names that all refer to the same organization, including at least two in Arabic (al-Jihad al-Islami and Tanzim al-Jihad) and three in English: Egyptian Islamic Jihad (EIJ), Islamic Jihad, and the Jihad (or al-Jihad) group or organization. Any reference that is not to the Islamic Group (al-Jama'a al-Islamiyya) is almost certainly to this organization.

22. Brooke, "Strategic Fissures," 47. Shiqaqi was assassinated by Israeli commandoes in Malta in 1995.

23. See the UNICEF dataset for the Iraq Country Profile, https://data.unicef.org/country/irq/.

24. See Tim Dyson, "Child Mortality in Iraq since 1990," *Economic and Political Weekly* 41, no. 42 (October 21–27, 2006).

25. "Land of the Two Holy Mosques" (*bilad al-haramayn*) is a commonly used phrasing for Saudi Arabia, particularly by jihadis who reject both the legitimacy of the Saudi regime and the fact that the clan gave its family name to the entire country.

26. The story of Bin Laden's speech and its various transcriptions and translations is covered in fascinating detail by Miller in *The Audacious Ascetic*, chapter 9. For the following discussion, I rely on the Arabic document posted on the website of the US Military Academy's Combating Terrorism Center (CTC), which appears to be the most complete and widely used of the transcriptions of Bin Laden's speech, https://ctc.usma.edu/app/uploads/2013/10/Declaration-of-Jihad-against-the-Americans-Occupying-the-Land-of-the-Two-Holiest-Sites-Original.pdf. A good translation is at the same CTC site, https://ctc.usma.edu/app/uploads/2013/10/Declaration-of-Jihad-against-the-Americans-Occupying-the-Land-of-the-Two-Holiest-Sites-Translation.pdf.

27. One could argue that the *fatwa* was issued by an organization, the World Islamic Front, as opposed to the five men who signed it (Bin Laden, Zawahiri, a leader of the Al-Jama'a Al-Islamiyya in Egypt, and Islamists from Pakistan and Bangladesh). But that would be inconsistent with Islamic history where *fatwas* are issued by people, not institutions (although there have been several instances in recent years that violate this tradition). Institutions, unlike individuals, have not earned the religious credentials to issue a *fatwa*. Bin Laden's use of the honorific *shaykh* was a fraudulent attempt to assert those credentials.

28. The Arabic honorific *shaykh* has multiple uses, beyond referring to a credentialed member of the Muslim clergy. A tribal head, for example, is also referred to as a *shaykh*. Indeed, it is common usage to address any elderly man, particularly one wearing traditional clothing or religious garb as *shaykh* or *hajji*. But in the context of a *fatwa*, using the title *shaykh* definitively connotes a member of the clergy.

29. The original Arabic text was printed in *Al-Quds Al-Arabi* newspaper on February 23, 1998. Many English-language translations are available, including this "Jihad against Jews and Crusaders," February 23, 1998, at https://fas.org/irp/world/para/docs/980223-fatwa.htm.

30. Peter Bergen dates the birth of al-Qa'ida to 1988, a year that others quote. But this dating conflates Bin Laden's Afghan jihad work, including his compiling a database of Arab volunteers, with Bin Laden's concept of a global jihad organization, which did not happen until 1996. Even by 1998, al-Qa'ida as an organization with a well-trained fighting force was illusory, although it was definitely trying to gear up by that point. This conflation of two enterprises aside, Bergen is a highly recommended source on all things jihadi. See his book *Holy War, Inc.*

31. One could fill a library with books about the 9/11 attacks. For accessible and credible accounts, see Wright, *Looming Tower*, cited in note 11, any one of the books by either Peter Bergen or Steve Coll, or, for a denser, more detailed account, see the National Commission on Terrorist Attacks, *9/11 Commission Report: Final Report of the National Commission on Terrorist Attacks Upon the United States* (New York: Norton, 2004). The numerous and absurd conspiratorial accounts of 9/11 as being an "inside job" hatched by the Bush administration are best ignored.

32. There is substantial speculation about whether there was supposed to be a twentieth hijacker, making five hijackers per plane. Many names about the supposed twentieth hijacker have been suggested, including Ramzi bin al-Shibh, Muhammad al-Qahtani, Zacarias Moussaoui, and Fawaz al-Nashimi.

33. *9/11 Commission Report*, 147.

34. Presidential Daily Brief, "Bin Ladin Determined to Strike in US," National Security Archive, George Washington University, August 6, 2001, https://nsarchive2.gwu.edu/NSAEBB/NSAEBB116/pdb8-6-2001.pdf.

35. Gadahn was killed in a US drone strike in Pakistan in 2015.

36. Marc Sageman takes up this argument about the sharp degrading of al-Qa'ida's leadership and capabilities following 9/11 in *Leaderless Jihad: Terror Networks in the 21st Century* (Philadelphia: University of Pennsylvania Press, 2008).

37. For an excellent discussion of Saudi jihadism and its suppression by the regime in 2003 through 2005, see Thomas Hegghammer, *Jihad in Saudi Arabia: Violence and Pan-Islamism since 1979* (Cambridge, UK: Cambridge University Press, 2010).

38. "The War in Yemen," New America database, https://www.newamerica.org/in-depth/americas-counterterrorism-wars/us-targeted-killing-program-yemen/.

39. The best discussion of the rise of al-Qa'ida in Yemen is found in Gregory D. Johnsen, *The Last Refuge: Yemen, al-Qaeda, and America's War in Arabia* (New York: W. W. Norton, 2014).

40. For a discussion of the evolution of both the political and criminal motivations of AQIM, see Richard Chelin, "From the Islamic State of Algeria to the Economic Caliphate of the Sahel: The Transformation of al Qaeda in the Islamic Maghrib," *Terrorism and Political Violence* (June 2018): 1–20, https://www.tandfonline.com/doi/abs/10.1080/09546553.2018.1454316. AQIM did not neglect broader jihadi goals entirely, including helping in the initial takeover of northern Mali by jihadis in 2012 and leading an attack on a large oil facility near Amenas, Algeria, in 2013 that led to the death of thirty-seven foreigners.

CHAPTER 3: CALIPHATE NOW!

1. Demographic statistics are hotly contested in Iraq, made more complicated by some degree of intermarriage across sectarian lines (although generally not across ethnic lines). Shia-friendly sources use the figure of 70 percent; others go as low as 60 percent.

2. Samuel Helfont effectively demolishes the argument that Sunni radicalism was encouraged in the 1990s by Saddam Husayn's regime through its cynical "Faith Campaign." Rather, Sunni extremism was greatly exacerbated in the aftermath of the 2003 invasion. See his *Compulsion in Religion: Saddam Hussein, Islam, and the Roots of Insurgencies in Iraq* (New York: Oxford University Press, 2018).

3. See Nikolaos van Dam, *The Struggle for Power in Syria: Politics and Society under Asad and the Ba'th Party*, 4th ed. (London: IB Tauris, 2011).

4. Even some pious Twelver Shia share the view that 'Alawis are not fully Muslim, labeling them as *ghulat* (extremists). Extremism in this case refers to the 'Alawi deification of Ali, not 'Alawi politics.

5. Glenn E. Robinson, "Syria's Long Civil War," *Current History* 111, no. 749 (December 2012): 331–36.

6. In colloquial use today, "Sham" is used for "Damascus" more often than not.

7. Zarqawi's sweetheart deal was a result of intra-jihadi competition between Bin Ladin and Abu Musab al-Suri. Bin Ladin saw the Jordanian Zarqawi as a means to undermine the appeal of the Syrian al-Suri among new recruits from the Levant. See Brian Fishman, "Revising the History of al-Qa'ida's Original Meeting with Abu Musab al-Zarqawi," *CTC Sentinel* 9, no. 10 (October 2016): 28–33, https://ctc.usma.edu/revising-the-history-of-al-qaidas-original-meeting-with-abu-musab-al-zarqawi/.

8. The best book on Maqdisi's life and ideas is Joas Wagemakers, *A Quietist Jihadi: The Ideology and Influence of Abu Muhammad al-Maqdisi* (Cambridge: Cambridge University Press, 2012).

9. Zawahiri's letter to Zarqawi was captured in transit and published by the Americans. The original Arabic letter as well as an English translation can be found at https://ctc.usma.edu/harmony-program/zawahiris-letter-to-zarqawi-original-language-2/.

10. This letter, both in Arabic and in English translation, can be found at https://ctc.usma.edu/harmony-program/atiyahs-letter-to-zarqawi-original-language-2/.

11. See ISI, *Strategic Plan*, December 2009, summary translation done by Mohammed M. Hafez, https://www.academia.edu/36180899/A_Strategic_Plan_for_the_Islamic_State_of_Iraq_-_Summary_Translation. Also, personal communication with Hafez.

12. Stephen Biddle, Jeffrey A. Friedman, and Jacob N. Shapiro give the troop escalation strategy more credit for reducing violence outside of the Anbar province (at least temporarily) than I do, and their argument is well worth reading: Biddle, Friedman, and Shapiro, "Testing the Surge: Why Did Violence Decline in Iraq in 2007? *International Security* 37, no. 1 (Summer 2012): 7–40, https://www.mitpressjournals.org/doi/abs/10.1162/ISEC_a_00087.

13. For a good example of the argument about how the Asad regime and ISIS work together in a marriage of convenience, see Sarah Hunaidi, "ISIS Has Not Been Defeated. It's Alive and Well in Southern Syria," *Foreign Policy* (April 3, 2019), https://foreignpolicy.com/2019/04/03/isis-has-not-been-defeated-its-alive-and-well-in-southern-syria/?utm_source=PostUp&utm_medium=email&utm_campaign=12013&utm_term=Editor's%20Picks%20OC.

14. Ten million is a maximum figure based on population estimates before the civil war. Given the number of refugees and forced expulsions of populations both before ISIS took over and in the early months of its rule, the actual population under ISIS control was probably closer to half that figure. Rukmini Callimachi, "The ISIS

Files," *New York Times*, April 4, 2018, https://www.nytimes.com/interactive/2018/04/04/world/middleeast/isis-documents-mosul-iraq.html

15. Although the authenticity of the 2004 letter has been challenged, it is consistent with many other sources of information on Zarqawi's views, particularly those regarding the Shia, including the statements from Zarqawi interlocuter Hassan Ghul. The letter can be found in English translation at the US State Department archives, https://2001-2009.state.gov/p/nea/rls/31694.htm.

16. Zarqawi's 2004 letter.

17. Zarqawi's 2004 letter. I have lightly edited the translation to make for clearer reading.

18. The book has been translated by William McCants. See Abu Bakr Naji, *Idarat al-Tawahhush* [The management of savagery], translated by William McCants, John M. Olin Institute for Strategic Studies, Harvard University, May 2006, http://media.leeds.ac.uk/papers/pmt/exhibits/2800/Management_of_Savagery.pdf.

19. The importance and extent of al-Anbari in the early radicalization process of what became ISIS has only recently come to light through the research of Hassan Hassan. See his article "The True Origins of ISIS: A Secret Biography Suggests That Abu Ali al-Anbari Defined the Group's Radical Approach More Than Any Other Person," *The Atlantic*, November 30, 2018, https://www.theatlantic.com/ideas/archive/2018/11/isis-origins-anbari-zarqawi/577030/. For more on Suri, see chapter 4 in this book.

20. Hassan, "True Origins of ISIS."

21. Brian H. Fishman's excellent book, although with hyperbolic title, is *The Master Plan: ISIS, al-Qaeda, and the Jihadi Strategy for Final Victory* (New Haven: Yale University Press, 2016).

22. The video was titled *Clanging of the Swords II*. My thanks to Craig Whiteside for calling my attention to this video.

23. Ned Parker, Isabel Coles, and Raheem Salman, "Special Report: How Mosul Fell: An Iraqi General Disputes Baghdad's Story," *Reuters*, October 14, 2014, https://uk.reuters.com/article/uk-mideast-crisis-gharawi-special-report/special-report-how-mosul-fell-an-iraqi-general-disputes-baghdads-story-idUKKCN0I30ZA20141014.

24. I have mostly used McCants's translation of Naji's *Idarat al-Tawahhush* (The management of savagery), although I have made a small number of changes that make Naji's meaning clearer in context. I have also added the emphasis in one sentence.

25. See the discussion on these three men in Hassan, "True Origins of ISIS."

26. This argument comes from the invaluable work of Hassan Hassan, in this case in his essay "The Sectarianism of the Islamic State: Ideological Roots and Political Context," Carnegie Endowment for International Peace, Washington, DC, June 13, 2016.

27. For a longer discussion of bumper-sticker ideological framing by social movements, see Glenn E. Robinson, "Hamas as Social Movement," in *Islamic Activism: A Social Movement Theory and Islamic Fundamentalism*, ed. Quinten Wiktorowicz, 112–42 (Bloomington: Indiana University Press, 2003).

28. Graeme Wood, "What ISIS Really Wants," *The Atlantic*, March 2015, https://www.theatlantic.com/magazine/archive/2015/03/what-isis-really-wants/384980/.

29. For a good example of detailed Muslim clerical rejection of Baghdadi's claims with regard to a caliphate, see http://www.lettertobaghdadi.com.

30. In my personal experience, US military analysts routinely exaggerated the goal of a caliphate by jihadis, including Usama Bin Ladin, in the post-9/11 environment. Focusing on the "digital caliphate" and related notions was a means to take all politics and policies out of the global jihadi movement, as though only a yearning for a new caliphate, instead of US policies, had an impact on al-Qa'ida's calculations. This was obviously false. It was not until the rise of ISIS years later that the notion of a caliphate became central.

31. On the issue of foreign fighters in ISIS, see Sean C. Reynolds and Mohammed M. Hafez, "Social Network Analysis of German Foreign Fighters in Syria and Iraq," *Terrorism and Political Violence* 31, no. 4 (February 14, 2017): 661–86, https://www.tandfonline.com/doi/full/10.1080/09546553.2016.1272456; and Richard Barrett, "Beyond the Caliphate: Foreign Fighters and the Threat of Returnees," The Soufan Center, October 2017, https://thesoufancenter.org/wp-content/uploads/2017/11/Beyond-the-Caliphate-Foreign-Fighters-and-the-Threat-of-Returnees-TSC-Report-October-2017-v3.pdf.

32. A translation of his speech may be found at https://scholarship.tricolib.bryn mawr.edu/bitstream/handle/10066/14272/ABB20140705.pdf. ISIS issued a formal statement on the proclamation of the caliphate by Abu Muhammad al-Adnani, the official spokesman of ISIS, through its Furqan Institute, titled "Hadha wa'd Allah" [This is the promise of God], which can be found in English translation at https://ia902505.us.archive.org/28/items/poa_25984/EN.pdf.

33. Wood, "What ISIS Really Wants," and William McCants, *The ISIS Apocalypse: The History, Strategy and Doomsday Vision of the Islamic State* (New York: St. Martin's Press, 2015).

34. Milo Comerford, "What ISIS Lost in Dabiq," *New Statesman America*, October 18, 2016, https://www.newstatesman.com/politics/staggers/2016/10/what-isis-lost-dabiq.

35. There is some debate among scholars and others about whom "Rome" refers to in this prophecy. At the time, in the seventh century CE, it would have applied to the Byzantine Empire based in Istanbul. Today, perhaps it means American forces, as Emwazi implied, or even Western forces in general; there is no consensus.

36. The best sources for ISIS's day-to-day administrative records are the documents taken by a *New York Times* team after the fall of Mosul. However, the removal of these ISIS administrative records from Iraq to the United States sparked controversy: for some, it reflected a modern type of cultural theft by an outside power without the permission of the internationally recognized government in Baghdad. In any case, see Callimachi, "ISIS Files." For an overview of the controversy with links to various letters, see Elizabeth Redden, "Controversy over an ISIS Archive," *Inside Higher Education*, September 27, 2018, https://www.insidehighered.com/quicktakes/2018/09/27/controversy-over-isis-archive.

37. Aisha Ahmad, *Jihad & Co.: Black Markets and Islamist Power* (New York: Oxford University Press, 2017).

38. This quotation and other information in the paragraph is taken from Kinana Qaddour, "Inside ISIS' Dysfunctional Schools: The Failure of the Group's Educational System," *Foreign Affairs* (October 13, 2017), https://www.foreignaffairs.com/articles/syria/2017-10-13/inside-isis-dysfunctional-schools. See as well Quilliam International, "Quilliam Releases Report on Children in the Caliphate," March 7, 2016, summarized at https://www.quilliaminternational.com/quilliam-releases-report-on-children-in-the-caliphate/.

39. Hosam al-Jablawi, "A Closer Look at the Educational System of ISIS," Atlantic Council, April 26, 2016, https://www.atlanticcouncil.org/blogs/syriasource/a-closer-look-at-isis-s-educational-system.

40. For a fuller discussion of ISIS's early state-building activities, see Aaron Zelin, "The Islamic State of Iraq and Syria Has a Consumer Protection Office," *The Atlantic* (June 13, 2014), https://www.theatlantic.com/international/archive/2014/06/the-isis-guide-to-building-an-islamic-state/372769/.

41. For this discussion, I draw on the data found in Stefan Heissner, Peter R. Neumann, John Holland-McCowan, and Rajan Basra, *Caliphate in Decline: An Estimate of Islamic State's Financial Fortunes* (London: International Centre for the

Study of Radicalisation and Political Violence, 2017), https://icsr.info/wp-content/
uploads/2017/02/ICSR-Report-Caliphate-in-Decline-An-Estimate-of-Islamic-States-Fi-
nancial-Fortunes.pdf.

42. Mara Revkin, "The Non-Economic Logic of Rebel Taxation: Evidence from an
Islamic State-Controlled District," Project on Middle East Political Science, September
2017, https://pomeps.org/wp-content/uploads/2017/09/POMEPS_Studies_27_Web.pdf.

43. Wood, "What ISIS Really Wants."

44. There is a debate as to whether the watch is a Rolex or an Omega Seamaster,
but both are high-end watches.

45. Jonathon Landay, Warren Strobel, and Phil Stewart, "Islamic State Ruling Aims
to Settle Who Can Have Sex with Female Slaves," *Reuters*, December 29, 2015, https://
www.reuters.com/article/usa-islamic-state-sexslaves-idUSKBN0UC0DZ20151229.

46. "The Failed Crusade," *Dabiq*, October 11, 2014, https://clarionproject.org/docs/
islamic-state-isis-magazine-Issue-4-the-failed-crusade.pdf.

47. Samuel Oakford, "Counting the Dead in Mosul," *The Atlantic*, April 5, 2018,
https://www.theatlantic.com/international/archive/2018/04/counting-the-dead-in
-mosul/556466/.

48. See Hugh Kennedy, *Caliphate: The History of an Idea* (New York: Basic Books,
2016).

49. See Cole Bunzel, "The Kingdom and the Caliphate: Duel of the Islamic States,"
Carnegie Endowment for International Peace, Washington, DC, February 2016. See
also Bunzel's report for the Brookings Institution, "From Paper State to Caliphate: The
Ideology of the Islamic State," Washington, DC, March 2015.

CHAPTER 4: PERSONAL JIHAD

1. Suri's book, more than sixteen-hundred pages long, can be found in the original Arabic at https://archive.org/details/The-call-for-a-global-Islamic-resistance/
page/n13. Parts of it have been translated into English by various sources, the best
of which by far is by Brynjar Lia as an appendix in his book *Architect of Global Jihad:
The Life of Al-Qaeda Strategist Abu Mus'ab al-Suri* (Oxford: Oxford University Press,
2009). Unless otherwise noted, all quotations from Suri in this chapter are from Lia's
excellent translation of *The Call for Global Islamic Resistance*, although I have made
some minor adjustments for clarity.

2. I strongly recommend Lia's book, *Architect of Global Jihad*, for a much fuller
treatment, as well as the other articles and book chapters Lia has devoted to analyzing
Suri's work (see the bibliography).

3. Marc Sageman, *Leaderless Jihad: Terror Networks in the 21st Century* (Philadelphia: University of Pennsylvania Press, 2008).

4. For an excellent discussion of Suri's feud with puritanical Salafis, see Brynjar Lia, "Destructive Doctrinarians: Abu Mus'ab al-Suri's Critique of the Salafis in the Jihadi Current," *Global Salafism: Islam's New Religious Movement*, ed. Roel Meijar, 281–300 (New York: Columbia University Press, 2009).

5. This form of informational and networked warfare was first made famous by John Arquilla and David Ronfeldt in "Cyberwar Is Coming!" *Comparative Strategy* 12, no. 2 (Spring 1993): 141–65.

6. French Army General Paul Aussaresses vigorously defended France's system of torture in Algeria, first in an interview in *Le Monde* and then in his book, *The Battle of the Casbah: Terrorism and Counter-Terrorism in Algeria, 1955–1957* (New York: Enigma Books, 2004). Aussaresses's admissions launched a vigorous public debate in France, leading ultimately to French president Emmanuel Macron formally apologizing in 2018 for France's "system" of torture in Algeria.

7. Abu Muhammad al-Adnani as quoted in Mark S. Hamm and Ramon Spaaij, *The Age of Lone Wolf Terrorism* (New York: Columbia University Press, 2017), Kindle edition.

8. The best general treatment to date of the phenomenon of stochastic and lone wolf violence is by Hamm and Spaaij, *Age of Lone Wolf Terrorism*.

9. Chauncey DeVega, "Author David Neiwert on the Outbreak of Political Violence: Expect 'an Intense Period of Terrorism,'" *Salon*, November 1, 2018, https://www .salon.com/2018/11/01/author-david-neiwert-on-the-outbreak-of-political-violence -expect-an-intense-period-of-terrorism/.

10. For a good, brief analysis of Awlaki's influence, see Scott Shane, "The Enduring Influence of Anwar al-Awlaki in the Age of the Islamic State," *CTC Sentinel* 9, no. 7 (July 2016): 15–19, https://ctc. usma. edu/the-enduring-influence-of-anwar-al-awlaki -in-the-age-of-the-islamic-state/.

11. A handful of attacks in the Middle East and North Africa targeted Europeans, including three during 2015: the attack on the Bardo museum in Tunis (23 dead); the slaughter of beachgoers in Sousse, Tunisia (38 dead, mostly British; and the downing of a Russian commercial airliner in the Sinai Peninsula (224 dead).

12. See Mohammed M. Hafez, "The Ties That Bind: How Terrorists Exploit Family Bonds," *CTC Sentinel* 9, no. 2 (February 2016): 15–17, https://ctc. usma. edu/the-ties -that-bind-how-terrorists-exploit-family-bonds/.

13. For lists of ISIS attacks, see List of Terrorist Incidents Linked to ISIL," https:// en.wikipedia.org/wiki/List_of_terrorist_incidents_linked_to_ISIL (accessed May 2,

2020); and Tim Lister et al., "ISIS Goes Global: 143 Attacks in 29 Countries Have Killed 2,043," CNN.com, https://edition.cnn.com/2015/12/17/world/mapping-isis-attacks -around-the-world/index.html (accessed February 12, 2018). See also the up-to-date database on terrorism in America kept by the New America Foundation, "Terrorism in America After 9/11," at https://www.newamerica.org/in-depth/terrorism-in-america/.

14. US Consumer Product Safety Commission, https://www. cpsc. gov/PageFiles /129419/nonpoolsub2012. pdf (accessed March 12, 2019).

15. Major Nidal Hasan's 2009 shooting rampage at the Fort Hood Army base that left thirteen dead should likely be classified as an earlier instance of stochastic violence. Hasan's opposition to the US war in Iraq and his growing jihadi sympathies provide plenty of evidence of self-radicalization. The sticking point is Hasan's email communications with Anwar al-Awlaki, a leading al-Qa'ida ideologue from the United States who was then living in Yemen. That direct tie with a jihadi group detracts from the stochastic argument in this case, although there is no evidence that Awlaki actually helped plan the shooting.

16. Seth G. Jones, "The Evolution of the Salafi-Jihadist Threat," Center for Strategic & International Studies, November 20, 2018, https://www. csis. org/analysis/ evolution-salafi-jihadist-threat.

CONCLUSION: MOVEMENTS OF RAGE

1. What are now independent countries in Central Asia were in the 1980s still a part of the Soviet Union, including Kazakhstan, Kyrgyzstan, Tajikistan, Turkmenistan, and Uzbekistan. Because they were ruled by Moscow, 'Azzam viewed them as occupied by a foreign, infidel power.

2. For critical analyses of the expanding global footprint of US military bases— and not just in the Middle East—see David Vine, *Base Nation: How US Military Bases Abroad Harm America and the World* (New York: Metropolitan Books/Henry Holt, 2015); and a trilogy of books by Chalmers Johnson, especially *The Sorrows of Empire: Militarism, Secrecy and the End of the Republic* (New York: Metropolitan Books/Henry Holt, 2004).

3. As noted in the introduction, Ken Jowitt introduced the concept of "movements of rage" in his book *New World Disorder: The Leninist Extinction* (Berkeley: University of California Press, 1992) and again in his short monograph, *Notes on National Weakness* (Washington, DC: National Council for Soviet and East European Research, 1995). Unfortunately, Jowitt did not much expand on the idea in his publications. However, as he was on my dissertation committee, I had the opportunity to discuss the concept

in more detail with him. What follows in this concluding chapter is largely my interpretation and expansion of his concept.

4. See chapter 2 for a discussion of the 1996 Declaration of War.

5. James C. Scott, *Seeing Like a State: How Certain Schemes to Improve the Human Condition Have Failed* (New Haven, CT: Yale University Press, 1999).

6. Eric Hobsbawm, *The Age of Extremes: A History of the World, 1914–1991* (New York: Vintage, 1996).

7. Bruce Hoffman, *Anonymous Soldiers: The Struggle for Israel, 1917–1947* (New York: Knopf, 2015).

8. See Douglass C. North, John Joseph Wallis, and Barry R. Weingast, *Violence and Social Orders: A Conceptual Framework for Interpreting Recorded Human History* (Cambridge University Press, 2012).

9. Robert Springborg, *Political Economies of the Middle East and North Africa* (Cambridge, UK: Polity Press, 2020).

10. Mark Juergensmeyer, *Terror in the Mind of God: The Global Rise of Religious Violence*, 4th ed. (Berkeley: University of California Press, 2017).

11. The article has been published in several iterations, but perhaps the best is David C. Rapoport, "The Four Waves of Modern Terrorism," in *Attacking Terrorism: Elements of a Grand Strategy*, ed. Audrey Kurth Cronin and James Ludes, 46–73 (Washington, DC: Georgetown University Press, 2004). My use of the "waves" metaphor is unrelated to Rapoport's work.

12. Walter Laqueur, "Postmodern Terrorism: New Rules for an Old Game," *Foreign Affairs* 75, no. 5 (September–October 1996), https://www.foreignaffairs.com/articles /1996-09-01/postmodern-terrorism-new-rules-old-game. For an early statement on "new terrorism," see Ian O. Lesser et al., *Countering the New Terrorism* (Santa Monica, CA: RAND, 1999). For Hoffman's widely used textbook on terrorism, see Bruce Hoffman, *Inside Terrorism*, 3rd ed. (New York: Columbia University Press, 2017).

13. See, for example, Ersun N. Kurtulus, "The New Terrorism and Its Critics," *Studies in Conflict and Terrorism* 34, no. 6 (2011): 476–500. See also Heather Selma Gregg, *The Path to Salvation: Religious Violence from the Crusades to Jihad* (Lincoln: Potomac Books, an imprint of the University of Nebraska press, 2014).

14. Juergensmeyer, *Terror in the Mind of God*, 146.

15. Juergensmeyer, *Terror in the Mind of God*, 146.

16. For an interesting discussion comparing al-Qa'ida with earlier secular groups, including anarchists, see Mark Sedgwick, "Al-Qaeda and the Nature of Religious Terrorism" in *Terrorism and Political Violence* 16, no. 4 (Winter 2004): 795–814.

17. Mark Thompson, "The Legacy of IEDs: The $500,000+ Jeep," *Time*, September 3, 2015, https://time.com/4022300/the-legacy-of-ieds-the-500000-jeep/.

18. There are many good books that cover this terrain but a particularly useful read is Joel S. Migdal, *Strong Societies and Weak States: State-Society Relations and State Capabilities in the Third World* (Princeton, NJ: Princeton University Press, 1988).

19. Franz Fanon, *The Wretched of the Earth* (New York: Penguin Modern Classics, 2001). Fanon's book was first published in 1961.

20. Jeff Goodwin's notion of "categorical" violence is similar but does not easily apply to violence undertaken globally, as opposed to the theory of in-country rebel violence against civilians that he develops. See Jeff Goodwin, "A Theory of Categorical Terrorism," *Social Forces* 84, no. 4 (2006): 2027–46.

21. Diego Gambetta and Steffen Hertog, *Engineers of Jihad: The Curious Connection between Violent Extremism and Education* (Princeton, NJ: Princeton University Press, 2017).

22. The Kepel-Roy debate has taken a nasty personal turn. See Adam Nossiter, "'That Ignoramus': 2 French Scholars of Radical Islam Turn Bitter Rivals," July 12, 2016, https://www.nytimes.com/2016/07/13/world/europe/france-radical-islam.html.

23. This discussion is based on the two Jowitt publications cited in note 3 above, as well as on communications with him during my graduate studies at the University of California–Berkeley.

24. Francis Fukuyama, *The End of History and the Last Man* (New York: Free Press, 1992). This book was based on his 1989 essay "The End of History?" *The National Interest* 16 (Summer 1989): 3–18.

25. An early and especially insightful book on the topic is Daniel Bell, *The Cultural Contradictions of Capitalism*, 20th anniversary edition (New York: Basic Books, 1996).

26. The classic scholarly book on the Khmer Rouge is Ben Kiernan, *The Pol Pot Regime: Race, Power, and Genocide in Cambodia under the Khmer Rouge, 1975–1979*, 3rd ed. (New Haven, CT: Yale University Press, 2008). As Kiernan notes, the Pol Pot regime was not without foreign support, particularly from China.

27. With the fall of Angkor in 1431, the area became even more Buddhist, with Hinduism largely disappearing.

28. *Haram* is Arabic for *forbidden* or *sinful*. *Boko* is often thought to be a Hausa loanword from the English word *book*. Hausa language specialist Paul Newman disputes the English loanword origins of *boko*, however. He argues that it was derived from the Hausa word for *fake*, *fraudulent*, or *inauthentic*, and was commonly used in

the early twentieth century to describe the new British secular school system in north-ern Nigeria. See Paul Newman, "The Etymology of Hausa *Boko*," Mega Chad Research Network, 2013, https://scholarworks.iu.edu/dspace/bitstream/handle/2022/20965/Etymology%20of%20Hausa%20Boko.pdf?sequence=1&isAllowed=y.

29. Lauren Ploch Blanchard and Katia T. Cavigelli, "Boko Haram and the Islamic State's West Africa Province," CRS Report No. IF10173, Congressional Research Service, Washington DC, 2018, https://crsreports.congress.gov/product/pdf/IF/IF10173/6.

30. Abdullahi Abubakar Lamido, "Debating Boko Haram," *CCI Occasional Papers* 2 (March 2019): 4.

31. "Global Terrorism Index 2019: Measuring the Impact of Terrorism," Institute for Economics and Peace, 2019, http://visionofhumanity.org/app/uploads/2019/11/GTI-2019web.pdf.

32. For example, Yusuf's interview with the BBC at Joe Boyle, "Nigeria's 'Taliban' Enigma," *BBC News*, July 13, 2009, http://news.bbc.co.uk/2/hi/africa/8172270.stm.

33. Flagg Miller, *The Audacious Ascetic: What the Bin Laden Tapes Reveal about al-Qa'ida* (Oxford: Oxford University Press, 2015).

34. For an excellent treatment of Maqdisi, including his relationship with Zarqawi, see Joas Wagemakers, *A Quietest Jihadi: The Ideology and Influence of Abu Muhammad al-Maqdisi* (Cambridge, UK: Cambridge University Press, 2012).

35. William McCants, *The ISIS Apocalypse: The History, Strategy, and Doomsday Vision of the Islamic State* (New York: St. Martin's Press, 2015).

36. Rick Noack, "The ISIS Apocalypse Has Been Postponed but the Militants Might Still Believe in It," *Washington Post*, October 17, 2016, https://www.washingtonpost.com/news/worldviews/wp/2016/10/17/the-isis-apocalypse-has-been-postponed-but-the-militants-might-still-believe-in-it/. In a change, the actual beheading was not shown on the video, only the moments after the execution with Emwazi standing over Kassig. Since this did not fit the ISIS pattern, there is some speculation that Kessig may have been executed for other reasons and then used as a prop with his head severed.

37. The pervasive American evangelical notion that the End Times are imminent was reinvigorated in 1970 with the publication of *The Late Great Planet Earth* by Hal Lindsey (Grand Rapids, MI: Zondervan Press, 1970), and has been a staple of evangelical belief ever since. The turn of the year 2000 ("Y2K") was widely thought by some to be a mark that the Second Coming was nigh. Needless to say, if you are reading this, none of the predictions of the End of the World have come to fruition. For a broader historical depiction of the use of millenarian ideology by European Christians, see

Norman Cohn, *The Pursuit of the Millennium: Revolutionary Millenarians and Mystical Anarchists of the Middle Ages*, revised and expanded edition (Oxford: Oxford University Press, 1970).

38. This 2004 text published in Arabic online was translated into English in 2006 by William McCants with the title "The Management of Savagery" by Abu Bakr Naji. In Arabic, *idara* can mean both "administration" and "management." The English text can be found at http://media.leeds.ac.uk/papers/pmt/exhibits/2800/Management_of_Savagery.pdf.

EPILOGUE: WHO WON?

1. Climate change can easily be classified as not just a major strategic threat but indeed an existential threat to humanity if it is not seriously and expeditiously addressed.

2. Baruch Kimmerling, *Politicide: Ariel Sharon's War against the Palestinians* (New York: Verso, 2003).

3. For an excellent scholarly discussion of the meaning and evolution of the national security state, particularly after 9/11, see Andreas Busch, "The Changing Architecture of the National Security State," *The Oxford Handbook of Transformations of the State*, ed. Stephan Leibfried et al. (June 2015), http://www.oxfordhandbooks.com/view/10.1093/oxfordhb/9780199691586.001.0001/oxfordhb-9780199691586-e-29.

4. This is not to suggest that all aspects of the Patriot Act were improper. Indeed, it provided some necessary tools to law enforcement that properly updated capabilities for the twenty-first century. It is to suggest that the Patriot Act and similar legislation have tipped the security-freedom scales significantly toward the former.

5. See, for example, David Cole, "It's Still a Muslim Ban," *New York Review of Books*, March 11, 2017, https://www.nybooks.com/daily/2017/03/11/its-still-a-muslim-ban-trump-executive-order/.

Bibliography

Abd al-Rahman, Atiyah. "Atiyah's Letter to Zarqawi." Combating Terrorism Center, 2005. https://ctc.usma.edu/harmony-program/atiyahs-letter-to-zarqawi-origin al-language-2/.

al-Adnani, Abu Muhammad. "Hadha Wa'd Allah" [This is the promise of God]. Al-Hayat Media Center of the al-Furqan Institute, 2014. Found in multiple languages at https://ia902505.us.archive.org/28/items/poa_25984/EN.pdf.

Afsaruddin, Asma. *Striving in the Path of God: Jihad and Martyrdom in Islamic Thought.* Oxford: Oxford University Press, 2013.

Ahmad, Aisha. *Jihad & Co.: Black Markets and Islamist Power.* New York: Oxford University Press, 2017.

Ahmad, Jalal Al-i. *Occidentosis: A Plague from the West.* Berkeley, CA: Mizan Press, 1983.

Algar, Hamid. *Islam and Revolution: Writings and Declarations of Imam Khomeini.* Berkeley, CA: Mizan Press, 1981.

al-Anani, Khalil. *Inside the Muslim Brotherhood: Religion, Identity and Politics.* Oxford: Oxford University Press, 2016.

———. "The Power of the Jama'a: The Role of Hasan al-Banna in Constructing the Muslim Brotherhood's Collective Identity." *Sociology of Islam* 1, no. 1–2 (2013): 41–63.

Anas, Abdullah. *To the Mountains: My Life in Jihad, from Algeria to Afghanistan.* New York:: Oxford University Press/Hurst, 2019.

Arquilla, John, and David Ronfeldt. "Cyberwar Is Coming!" *Comparative Strategy* 12, no. 2 (Spring 1993): 141–65.

Aussaresses, Paul. *The Battle of the Casbah: Terrorism and Counter-Terrorism in Algeria, 1955–1957.* New York: Enigma Books, 2004.

'Azzam, Abdullah. "Al-Qa'ida al-Sulba" [The solid base]. *Al-Jihad*, April 1988 (in Arabic).

'Azzam, Abdullah. *Al-Difa' 'an Aradi al-Muslimin: Aham Farud al-'Amin* [The defense of Muslim lands: The first obligation after faith]. 1985 (in Arabic). Found in English translation at https://archive.org/details/Defense_of_the_Muslim_Lands.

'Azzam, Abdullah. *Ilhaq bi'l-Qafila* [Join the caravan]. Peshawar, Pakistan: Rayah Publications, 1987 (in Arabic). In Arabic and English at https://archive.org; in English translation at https://ebooks.worldofislam.info/ebooks/Jihad/Join%20the %20Caravan.pdf.

al-Azm, Sadik J. *Is Islam Secularizable? Challenging Political and Religious Taboos.* Berlin: Gerlach Press, 2014.

Barrett, Richard. "Beyond the Caliphate: Foreign Fighters and the Threat of Returnees." The Soufan Center. October 2017. https://thesoufancenter.org/wp-content/uploads/2017/11/Beyond-the-Caliphate-Foreign-Fighters-and-the-Threat-of-Returnees-TSC-Report-October-2017-v3.pdf.

Bell, Daniel. *The Cultural Contradictions of Capitalism.* 20th anniversary edition. New York: Basic Books, 1996.

Bergen, Peter L. *Holy War, Inc.: Inside the Secret War of Osama Bin Laden.* New York: Touchstone, 2002.

Bergesen, Albert J., ed. *The Sayyid Qutb Reader.* New York: Routledge, 2007.

Biddle, Stephen, Jeffrey A. Friedman, and Jacob N. Shapiro. "Testing the Surge: Why Did Violence Decline in Iraq in 2007?" *International Security* 37, no. 1 (Summer 2012): 7–40.

Bin Laden, Usama. "Declaration of Jihad against the Americans Occupying the Land of the Two Holy Mosques." Combating Terrorism Center, 1996. https://ctc.usma.edu/app/uploads/2013/10/Declaration-of-Jihad-against-the-Americans-Occupying-the-Land-of-the-Two-Holiest-Sites-Original.pdf (in Arabic); https://ctc.usma.edu/app/uploads/2013/10/Declaration-of-Jihad-against-the-Americans-Occupying-the-Land-of-the-Two-Holiest-Sites-Translation.pdf (in English).

Bin Laden, Usama Bin Mohammed, Ayman al-Zawahiri, Abu-Yasir Rifa'i Ahmad Taha, Mir Hamzah, and Fazlur Rahman (as The World Islamic Front). "Jihad against Jews

and Crusaders." February 23, 1998. Federation of American Scientists. https://fas
.org/irp/world/para/docs/980223-fatwa.htmm.

Blanchard, Lauren Ploch, and Katia T. Cavigelli. "Boko Haram and the Islamic State's
West Africa Province." CRS Report No. IF10173. Washington, DC: Congressional
Research Service, 2018.

Boyle, Joe. "Nigeria's 'Taliban' Enigma." *BBC News*. July 13, 2009. http://news.bbc.co.uk/2
/hi/africa/8172270.stm.

Brooke, Steven. "Strategic Fissures: The Near and Far Enemy Debate." In *Self Inflicted
Wounds: Debates and Divisions within al-Qa'ida and Its Periphery*, edited by Assaf
Moghadam and Brian Fishman, 47–68. West Point, NY: Combatting Terrorism
Center, 2010.

Bunzel, Cole. "From Paper State to Caliphate: The Ideology of the Islamic State." Brookings Institution, Washington, DC, March 2015.

———. "The Kingdom and the Caliphate: Duel of the Islamic States." Carnegie Endowment for International Peace, Washington, DC, February 2016.

Busch, Andreas. "The Changing Architecture of the National Security State." In *The
Oxford Handbook of Transformations of the State*, edited by Stephan Leibfried,
Evelyne Huber, Matthew Lange, Jonah D. Levy, and John D. Stephens. Oxford
Handbooks Online. June 2015. https://www.oxfordhandbooks.com/view/10.1093
/oxfordhb/9780199691586.001.0001/oxfordhb-9780199691586-e-29.

Byman, Daniel. *Al-Qaeda, the Islamic State and the Global Jihadist Movement*. New
York: Oxford University Press, 2016.

Callimachi, Rukmini. "The ISIS Files." *New York Times*, April 4, 2018. https://www.ny
times.com/interactive/2018/04/04/world/middleeast/isis-documents-mosul-iraq
.html?searchResultPosition=1.

Calvert, John. *Islam and Christian-Muslim Relations* 11, no. 1 (2000): 87–103.

———. *Sayyid Qutb and the Origins of Radical Islamism*. New York: Columbia University Press, 2010.

Cassandra. "The Impending Crisis in Egypt." *Middle East Journal* 49, no. 1 (Winter
1995): 9–27.

Chelin, Richard. "From the Islamic State of Algeria to the Economic Caliphate of the
Sahel: The Transformation of al Qaeda in the Islamic Maghrib." *Terrorism and
Political Violence* (June 2018): 1–20. https://www.tandfonline.com/doi/abs/10.1080
/09546553.2018.1454316.

Chulov, Martin. "My Son, Osama: The al-Qaida Leader's Mother Speaks for the First Time." *The Guardian,* August 2, 2018. https://www.theguardian.com/world/2018/aug/03/osama-bin-laden-mother-speaks-out-family-interview.

Cole, David. "It's Still a Muslim Ban." *New York Review of Books.* March 11, 2017. https://www.nybooks.com/daily/2017/03/11/its-still-a-muslim-ban-trump-executive-order/.

Cohn, Norman. *The Pursuit of the Millennium: Revolutionary Millenarians and Mystical Anarchists of the Middle Ages.* Revised and expanded edition. Oxford: Oxford University Press, 1970.

Comerford, Milo. "What ISIS Lost in Dabiq." *New Statesman America.* October 18, 2016. https://www.newstatesman.com/politics/staggers/2016/10/what-isis-lost-dabiq.

Cook, David. *Martyrdom in Islam.* Cambridge, UK: Cambridge University Press, 2007.

Crone, Patricia. "Jihad: Idea and History." Open Democracy. April 30, 2007. https://www.opendemocracy.net/faith-europe_islam/jihad_4579.jsp.

Dam, Nikolaos van. *The Struggle for Power in Syria: Politics and Society under Asad and the Ba'th Party.* 4th edition. London: IB Tauris, 2011.

DeVega, Chauncey. "Author David Neiwert on the Outbreak of Political Violence: Expect 'an Intense Period of Terrorism.'" *Salon.* November 1, 2018. https://www.salon.com/2018/11/01/author-david-neiwert-on-the-outbreak-of-political-violence-expect-an-intense-period-of-terrorism/.

Donner, Fred M. *Muhammad and the Believers: At the Origins of Islam.* Cambridge, MA: Belknap Press, an Imprint of Harvard University Press, 2010.

Dyson, Tim. "Child Mortality in Iraq since 1990." *Economic and Political Weekly* 41, no. 42 (October 21–27, 2006).

"The Failed Crusade." *Dabiq.* October 11, 2014. Accessed at Clarion Project. https://clarionproject.org/docs/islamic-state-isis-magazine-Issue-4-the-failed-crusade.pdf.

Fandy, Mamoun. "Egypt's Islamic Group: Regional Revenge?" *Middle East Journal* 48, no. 4 (Autumn 1994): 607–25.

Fanon, Franz. *The Wretched of the Earth.* 1961; reprint, New York: Penguin Modern Classics, 2001.

Fishman, Brian H. *The Master Plan: ISIS, al-Qaeda, and the Jihadi Strategy for Final Victory.* New Haven, CT: Yale University Press, 2016.

———. "Revising the History of al-Qa'ida's Original Meeting with Abu Musab al-Zarqawi." *CTC Sentinel* 9, no. 10 (October 2016): 28–33. https://ctc.usma.edu/revising-the-history-of-al-qaidas-original-meeting-with-abu-musab-al-zarqawi/.

Fukuyama, Francis. "The End of History?" *The National Interest* 16 (Summer 1989): 3–18.

———. *The End of History and the Last Man*. New York: Free Press, 1992.

Gambetta, Diego, and Steffen Hertog. *Engineers of Jihad: The Curious Connection between Violent Extremism and Education*. Reprint edition. Princeton, NJ: Princeton University Press, 2017.

Gerges, Fawaz A. *The Far Enemy: Why Jihad Went Global*. 2nd edition. Cambridge, UK: Cambridge University Press, 2009.

———. *ISIS: A History*. Princeton, NJ: Princeton University Press, 2017.

———. *Making the Arab World: Nasser, Qutb, and the Clash That Shaped the Middle East*. Princeton, NJ: Princeton University Press, 2018.

———. *The Rise and Fall of al-Qaeda*. Oxford: Oxford University Press, 2014.

Global Policy Forum. "Half Million Child Deaths, 1991–1998." https://www.globalpolicy.org/component/content/article/102/32796.html (accessed May 3, 2020).

"Global Terrorism Index 2019: Measuring the Impact of Terrorism." Institute for Economics and Peace. 2019. http://visionofhumanity.org/app/uploads/2019/11/GTI-2019web.pdf.

Goodwin, Jeff. "A Theory of Categorical Terrorism." *Social Forces* 84, no. 4 (2006): 2027–2046.

Gregg, Heather Selma. *The Path to Salvation: Religious Violence from the Crusades to Jihad*. Lincoln: Potomac Books, an imprint of the University of Nebraska Press, 2014.

Hafez, Mohammed M. "Apologia for Suicide: Martyrdom in Contemporary Jihadist Discourse." In *Martyrdom, Self-Sacrifice, and Self-Immolation: Religious Perspectives on Suicide*, edited by Margo Kitts, 126–39. Oxford: Oxford University Press, 2018.

———. "Jihad after Iraq: Lessons for the Arab Afghans Phenomenon." *CTC Sentinel* 1, no. 4 (March 2008): 1–4.

———. "Tactics, *Takfir* and Anti-Muslim Violence." In *Self-Inflicted Wounds: Debates and Divisions within al-Qa'ida and Its Periphery*, edited by Assaf Moghadam and Brian Fishman. West Point, NY: Combatting Terrorism Center, 2010

———. "*Takfir* and Violence Against Muslims." In *Fault Lines in Global Jihad: Organizational, Strategic and Ideological Fissures*, edited by Assaf Moghadam and Brian Fishman, 25–46. New York: Routledge, 2011.

———. "The Ties That Bind: How Terrorists Exploit Family Bonds." *CTC Sentinel* 9, no. 2 (February 2016): 15–17. https://ctc.usma.edu/the-ties-that-bind-how-terrorists-exploit-family-bonds/.

————, trans. "A Strategic Plan to Strengthen the Political Position of the Islamic State of Iraq." *Academia*. December 2009. https://www.academia.edu/36180899/A _Strategic_Plan_for_the_Islamic_State_of_Iraq_-_Summary_Translation.

Hamm, Mark S., and Ramon Spaaij. *The Age of Lone Wolf Terrorism*. New York: Columbia University Press, 2017. Kindle edition.

Hamzawy, Amr, and Sarah Grebowski. "From Violence to Moderation: Al-Jama'a al-Islamiya and al-Jihad." Carnegie Paper 20. Carnegie Endowment for International Peace, Washington, DC, 2010. http://carnegieendowment.org/files/Hamzawy -Grebowski-EN.pdf.

Hassan, Hassan. "The Sectarianism of the Islamic State: Ideological Roots and Political Context." Carnegie Endowment for International Peace, Washington, DC, June 13, 2016.

————. "The True Origins of ISIS: A Secret Biography Suggests That Abu Ali al-Anbari Defined the Group's Radical Approach More Than Any Other Person." *The Atlantic*, November 30, 2018. https://www.theatlantic.com/ideas/archive/2018/11/isis-origins -anbari-zarqawi/577030/.

Hegghammer, Thomas. "Abdullah Azzam, the Imam of Jihad." In *Al Qaeda in Its Own Words*, edited by Gilles Kepel and Jean-Pierre Milelli, 81–143. Cambridge, MA: Harvard University Press, 2008.

————. *The Caravan: Abdallah Azzam and the Rise of Global Jihad.* Cambridge, UK: Cambridge University Press, 2020.

————. *Jihad in Saudi Arabia: Violence and Pan-Islamism since 1979.* Cambridge, UK: Cambridge University Press, 2010.

————. "The Rise of Muslim Foreign Fighters: Islam and the Globalization of Jihad." *International Security* 35, no. 3 (Winter 2010–11): 53–94.

Heissner, Stefan, Peter R. Neumann, John Holland-McCowan, and Rajan Basra. *Caliphate in Decline: An Estimate of Islamic State's Financial Fortunes.* London: International Centre for the Study of Radicalisation and Political Violence, 2017. https:// icsr.info/wp-content/uploads/2017/02/ICSR-Report-Caliphate-in-Decline-An -Estimate-of-Islamic-States-Financial-Fortunes.pdf.

Helfont, Samuel. *Compulsion in Religion: Saddam Hussein, Islam, and the Roots of Insurgencies in Iraq.* New York: Oxford University Press, 2018.

Hobsbawm, Eric. *The Age of Extremes: A History of the World, 1914–1991.* New York: Vintage, 1996.

Hoffman, Bruce. *Anonymous Soldiers: The Struggle for Israel, 1917–1947*. New York: Knopf, 2015.

———. *Inside Terrorism*. 3rd edition. New York: Columbia University Press, 2017.

Hoffman, Bruce, and Fernando Reinares, eds. *The Evolution of the Global Terrorist Threat: From 9/11 to Osama bin Laden's Death*. New York: Columbia University Press, 2014.

Hunaidi, Sarah. "ISIS Has Not Been Defeated. It's Alive and Well in Southern Syria." *Foreign Policy* (April 3, 2019). https://foreignpolicy.com/2019/04/03/isis-has-not-been-defeated-its-alive-and-well-in-southern-syria/?utm_source=PostUp&utm_medium=email&utm_campaign=12013&utm_term=Editor's%20Picks%20OC.

al-Jablawi, Hosam. "A Closer Look at the Educational System of ISIS." Atlantic Council. April 26, 2016. https://www.atlanticcouncil.org/blogs/syriasource/a-closer-look-at-isis-s-educational-system.

Jackson, Sherman A. *Initiative to Stop the Violence* [Mubadarat Waqf al-'Unf]. New Haven, CT: Yale University Press, 2015.

Jansen, Johannes J. G. *The Neglected Duty: The Creed of Sadat's Assassins*. New York: RVP Press, 2013.

Johnsen, Gregory D. *The Last Refuge: Yemen, al-Qaeda, and America's War in Arabia*. New York: W. W. Norton, 2014.

Johnson, Chalmers. *The Sorrows of Empire: Militarism, Secrecy and the End of the Republic*. New York: Metropolitan Books/Henry Holt, 2004.

Jones, Seth G. "The Evolution of the Salafi-Jihadist Threat." Center for Strategic and International Studies. November 20, 2018. https://www.csis.org/analysis/evolution-salafi-jihadist-threat.

Jowitt, Ken. *New World Disorder: The Leninist Extinction*. Berkeley: University of California Press, 1992.

Jowitt, Kenneth. *Notes on National Weakness*. Washington, DC: National Council for Soviet and East European Research, 1995.

Juergensmeyer, Mark. *Terror in the Mind of God: The Global Rise of Religious Violence*. 4th edition. Berkeley: University of California Press, 2017.

Kennedy, Hugh. *Caliphate: The History of an Idea*. New York: Basic Books, 2016.

Kepel, Gilles. *Jihad: The Trail of Political Islam*. Cambridge, MA: Belknap Press, an imprint of Harvard University Press, 2003.

———. *Muslim Extremism in Egypt: The Prophet and Pharaoh*. 2nd edition. Berkeley: University of California Press, 2003.

Kiernan, Ben. *The Pol Pot Regime: Race, Power, and Genocide in Cambodia under the Khmer Rouge, 1975–1979*. 3rd edition. New Haven, CT: Yale University Press, 2008.

Kimmerling, Baruch. *Politicide: Ariel Sharon's War against the Palestinians*. New York: Verso, 2003.

Kovacs, Attila. "Martyrdom and Visual Representations of the Palestinian Islamic Movements." 2010. https://fphil.uniba.sk/fileadmin/fif/katedry_pracoviska/kvas/SOS_9_2/N5-22kovacs-form_1_.pdf\.

Kurtulus, Ersun N. "The New Terrorism and Its Critics." *Studies in Conflict and Terrorism* 34, no. 6 (2011): 476–500.

Lamido, Abdullahi Abubakar. "Debating Boko Haram," *CCI Occasional Papers* 2 (March 2019): 1–36.

Landay, Jonathan, Warren Strobel, and Phil Stewart. "Islamic State Ruling Aims to Settle Who Can Have Sex with Female Slaves." Reuters. December 29, 2015. https://www.reuters.com/article/us-usa-islamic-state-sexslaves-exclusive-idUSKBN0UC0AO20151230.

Laqueur, Walter. "Postmodern Terrorism: New Rules for an Old Game." *Foreign Affairs* 75, no. 5 (September–October 1996). https://www.foreignaffairs.com/articles/1996-09-01/postmodern-terrorism-new-rules-old-game.

Lesser, Ian O., Bruce Hoffman, John Arquilla, David Ronfeldt, Michele Zanini, and Brian Michael Jenkins. *Countering the New Terrorism*. Santa Monica, CA: RAND, 1999.

Lia, Brynjar. *Architect of Global Jihad: The Life of Al-Qaeda Strategist Abu Mus'ab al-Suri*. Oxford: Oxford University Press, 2009.

———. "Destructive Doctrinarians: Abu Mus'ab al-Suri's Critique of the Salafis in the Jihadi Current." In *Global Salafism: Islam's New Religious Movement*, edited by Roel Meijar, 281–300. New York: Columbia University Press, 2009.

———. *The Society of the Muslim Brothers in Egypt: The Rise of an Islamic Mass Movement, 1928–1942*. Reading, UK: Ithaca Press, 1999.

Lindsey, Hal. *The Late Great Planet Earth*. Grand Rapids, MI: Zondervan Press, 1970.

Lister, Tim, Ray Sanchez, Mark Bixler, Sean O'Key, Michael Hogenmiller, and Mohammed Tawfeeq. "ISIS Goes Global: 143 Attacks in 29 Countries Have Killed 2,043." CNN. Last modified February 12, 2018. https://edition.cnn.com/2015/12/17/world/mapping-isis-attacks-around-the-world/index.html.

Maher, Shiraz. *Salafi-Jihadism: The History of an Idea*. New York: Penguin Books, 2017.

Mandaville, Peter. *Islam and Politics*. 2nd edition. New York: Routledge, 2014.

Martinez, Luis. *The Algerian Civil War, 1990–1998*. New York: Columbia University Press, 2000.

McCants, William. *The ISIS Apocalypse: The History, Strategy, and Doomsday Vision of the Islamic State*. New York: St. Martin's Press, 2015.

Migdal, Joel S. *Strong Societies and Weak States: State-Society Relations and State Capabilities in the Third World*. Princeton, NJ: Princeton University Press, 1988.

Miller, Flagg. *The Audacious Ascetic: What the Bin Laden Tapes Reveal about al-Qaʾida*. Oxford: Oxford University Press, 2015.

Mitchell, Alison. "Letter Explained Motive in Bombing, Officials Now Say." *New York Times*. March 28, 1993. https://www.nytimes.com/1993/03/28/nyregion/letter-explained-motive-in-bombing-officials-now-say.html.

Mitchell, Richard P. *The Society of the Muslim Brothers*. Oxford: Oxford University Press, 1969.

Mundy, Jacob. *Imaginative Geographies of Algerian Violence: Conflict Science, Conflict Management, Antipolitics*. Palo Alto, CA: Stanford University Press, 2015.

Naji, Abu Bakr. *Idarat al-Tawahhush* [The management of savagery]. Translated by William McCants. 2006. https://archive.org/stream/TheManagementOfBarbarismAbuBakrNaji/The+Management+of+Barbarism+-+Abu+Bakr+Naji_djvu.txt.

Nasr, Vali. *The Shia Revival: How Conflicts within Islam Will Shape the Future*. New York: W. W. Norton, 2007.

Nasser, Gamal Abdel. "Gamal Abdel Nasser on the Muslim Brotherhood." YouTube video, 2:12. https://www.youtube.com/watch?v=TX4RK8bj2Wo.

———. "Gamal Abdel Nasser, on the Muslim Brotherhood." YouTube video, 12:58. https://www.youtube.com/watch?v=iYrZUwa_2EM.

National Commission on Terrorist Attacks. *9/11 Commission Report: Final Report of the National Commission on Terrorist Attacks upon the United States*. New York: W. W. Norton & Company, 2004.

New America. "Drone Strikes: Yemen." Database. https://www.newamerica.org/in-depth/americas-counterterrorism-wars/us-targeted-killing-program-yemen.

Newman, Paul. "The Etymology of Hausa *Boko*." Mega Chad Research Network. 2013. https://scholarworks.iu.edu/dspace/bitstream/handle/2022/20965/Etymology%20of%20Hausa%20Boko.pdf?sequence=1&isAllowed=y.

Noack, Rick. "The ISIS Apocalypse Has Been Postponed, but the Militants Might Still Believe in It." *Washington Post*. October 17, 2016. https://www.washingtonpost

.com/news/worldviews/wp/2016/10/17/the-isis-apocalypse-has-been-postponed
-but-the-militants-might-still-believe-in-it/.

North, Douglass C., John Joseph Wallis, and Barry R. Weingast. *Violence and Social Orders: A Conceptual Framework for Interpreting Recorded Human History.* Reprint edition. Cambridge, UK: Cambridge University Press, 2012.

Nossiter, Adam. "'That Ignoramus': 2 French Scholars of Radical Islam Turn Bitter Rivals." *New York Times.* July 12, 2016. https://www.nytimes.com/2016/07/13/world/europe/france-radical-islam.html.

Oakford, Samuel. "Counting the Dead in Mosul." *The Atlantic.* April 5, 2018. https://www.theatlantic.com/international/archive/2018/04/counting-the-dead-in-mosul/556466/.

"Open Letter to Al-Baghdadi." September 19, 2014. http://www.lettertobaghdadi.com.

Pape, Robert A. "The Strategic Logic of Suicide Terrorism." *American Political Science Review* 97, no. 3 (August 2003): 343–61.

Parker, Ned, Isabel Coles, and Raheem Salman. "Special Report: How Mosul Fell: An Iraqi General Disputes Baghdad's Story." Reuters. October 14, 2014. https://uk.reuters.com/article/uk-mideast-crisis-gharawi-special-report/special-report-how-mosul-fell-an-iraqi-general-disputes-baghdads-story-idUKKCN0I30ZA20141014.

Presidential Daily Brief. "Bin Ladin Determined to Strike in US." August 6, 2001. National Security Archive, George Washington University. https://nsarchive2.gwu.edu/NSAEBB/NSAEBB116/pdb8-6-2001.pdf.

Qaddour, Kinana. "Inside ISIS' Dysfunctional Schools: The Failure of the Group's Educational System." *Foreign Affairs.* October 13, 2017. https://www.foreignaffairs.com/articles/syria/2017-10-13/inside-isis-dysfunctional-schools.

"Quilliam Releases Report on Children in the Caliphate." Quilliam International. March 7, 2016. https://www.quilliaminternational.com/quilliam-releases-report-on-children-in-the-caliphate/.

"Quranic Arabic Corpus." http://corpus.quran.com.

Qutb, Sayyid. *The America I Have Seen.* N.p.: Kashful Shubuhat Publications, 1951. https://www.cia.gov/library/abbottabad-compound/3F/3F56ACA473044436B4C1740F65D5C3B6_Sayyid_Qutb_-_The_America_I_Have_Seen.pdf.

———. *In the Shade of the Qur'an.* Markfield, Leicestershire, UK: Islamic Foundation, 2009.

———. *Milestones.* New Delhi, India: Islamic Book Service, 2006.

————. *Social Justice in Islam*. Translated by John B. Hardie, with an introduction by Hamid Algar. Revised edition. Oneonta, NY: Islamic Publications International, 2000.

Rahnema, Ali. *An Islamic Utopian: A Political Biography of Ali Shari'ati*. London: IB Tauris, 2014.

Randal, Jonathon. *Osama: The Making of a Terrorist*. New York: Knopf, 2004.

Rapoport, David C. "The Four Waves of Modern Terrorism." In *Attacking Terrorism: Elements of a Grand Strategy*, edited by Audrey Kurth Cronin and James Ludes, 46–73. Washington, DC: Georgetown University Press, 2004.

Rashid, Ahmed. *Taliban: Militant Islam, Oil and Fundamentalism in Central Asia*. New Haven, CT: Yale University Press, 2010.

Redden, Elizabeth. "Controversy over an ISIS Archive." *Inside Higher Education*. September 27, 2018. https://www.insidehighered.com/quicktakes/2018/09/27/controversy-over-isis-archive.

Revkin, Mara. "The Non-Economic Logic of Rebel Taxation: Evidence from an Islamic State-Controlled District." Project on Middle East Political Science. September 2017. https://pomeps.org/wp-content/uploads/2017/09/POMEPS_Studies_27_Web.pdf.

Reynolds, Sean C., and Mohammed M. Hafez. "Social Network Analysis of German Foreign Fighters in Syria and Iraq." *Terrorism and Political Violence* 31, no. 4 (February 14, 2017): 661–86. https://www.tandfonline.com/doi/full/10.1080/09546553.2016.1272456.

Robinson, Glenn E. *Building a Palestinian State: The Incomplete Revolution*. Bloomington: Indiana University Press, 1997.

————. "Hamas as Social Movement." In *Islamic Activism: A Social Movement Theory Approach,* edited by Quintan Wiktorowicz, 112–42. Bloomington: Indiana University Press, 2004. https://www.researchgate.net/publication/292494431_Hamas_as_social_Movement.

————. "Syria's Long Civil War." *Current History* 111, no. 749 (December 2012): 331–36. http://www.joshualandis.com/blog/wp-content/uploads/Robinson-Current-History.pdf.

Rose, Gregory. "Velayat-e Faqih and the Recovery of Islamic Identity in the Thought of Ayatullah Khomeini." In *Religion and Politics in Iran: Shi'ism from Quietism to Revolution*, edited by Nikki R. Keddi, 166–88 New Haven, CT: Yale University Press, 1983.

Roy, Olivier. *The Failure of Political Islam*. Cambridge, MA: Harvard University Press, 1998.

———. *Globalized Islam: The Search for a New Umma*. New York: Columbia University Press, 2006.

———. *Jihad and Death: the Global Appeal of Islamic State*. New York: Oxford University Press, 2017.

Sageman, Marc. *Leaderless Jihad: Terror Networks in the 21st Century*. Philadelphia: University of Pennsylvania Press, 2008.

Scott, James C. *Seeing Like a State: How Certain Schemes to Improve the Human Condition Have Failed*. New Haven, CT: Yale University Press, 1999.

Sedgwick, Mark. "Al-Qaeda and the Nature of Religious Terrorism." *Terrorism and Political Violence* 16, no. 4 (Winter 2004): 795–814.

Shane, Scott. "The Enduring Influence of Anwar al-Awlaki in the Age of the Islamic State." *CTC Sentinel* 9, no. 7 (July 2016): 15–19. https://ctc.usma.edu/the-enduring -influence-of-anwar-al-awlaki-in-the-age-of-the-islamic-state/.

Shepard, William E. "The Development of Thought of Sayyid Qutb as Reflected in Earlier and Later Editions of 'Social Justice in Islam.'" *Die Welt des Islams* 32, no. 2 (1992): 196–236.

———. "Sayyid Qutb and Modern Islamist Violence." *Seasons* 26 (Summer 2007).

———. "Sayyid Qutb's Doctrine of *Jahiliyya*." *International Journal of Middle East Studies* 35, no. 4 (2003): 521–45.

Simons, Jeremy. "Pagdaro Sa Kalinaw: Dureza's Betrayal and Duterte's Hypocrisy in Marawi." MindaNews. September 8, 2017. https://www.mindanews.com/minda views/2017/09/pagdaro-sa-kalinaw-durezas-betrayal-and-dutertes-hypocrisy-in -marawi.

Soufan, Ali. *Anatomy of Terror: From the Death of bin Laden to the Rise of the Islamic State*. New York: W. W. Norton, 2017.

Springborg, Robert. *Political Economies of the Middle East and North Africa*. Cambridge, UK: Polity Press, 2020.

al-Suri, Abu Mus'ab. *The Call for a Global Islamic Resistance* [Da'wat al-Muqawama al-Islamiyya al-'Alamiyya]. November 12, 2008. https://archive.org/details/The -call-for-a-global-Islamic-resistance/page/n13.

Tahrir Institute for Middle East Policy. Egypt Security Watch. Database. https://timep .org/esw/.

"Terrorism in America after 9/11." New America database. https://www.newamerica
.org/in-depth/terrorism-in-america/.

Thompson, Mark. "The Legacy of IEDs: The $500,000+ Jeep." *Time.* September 3, 2015.
http://time.com/4022300/the-legacy-of-ieds-the-500000-jeep/.

Trotsky, Leon. *The Permanent Revolution.* 1929.

Vine, David. *Base Nation: How US Military Bases Abroad Harm America and the World.*
New York: Metropolitan Books/Henry Holt, 2015.

Wagemakers, Joas. *A Quietist Jihadi: The Ideology and Influence of Abu Muhammad
al-Maqdisi.* Cambridge, UK: Cambridge University Press, 2012.

Whiteside, Craig. "The Islamic State and the Return of Revolutionary Warfare." *Small
Wars and Insurgencies* 26 (2016): 743–76.

———. *Lighting the Path: The Evolution of the Islamic State Media Enterprise.* The
Hague: International Centre for Counter-Terrorism, 2016.

Wickham, Carrie Rosefsky. *The Muslim Brotherhood: Evolution of an Islamist Movement.* Princeton, NJ: Princeton University Press, 2013.

Wikipedia. S.v. "List of Terrorist Incidents Linked to ISIL." Last modified December 24,
2019. https://en.wikipedia.org/wiki/List_of_terrorist_incidents_linked_to_ISIL.

Wiktorowicz, Quintan. *Islamic Activism: A Social Movement Theory Approach.* Bloomington: Indiana University Press, 2003.

Wood, Graeme. "What ISIS Really Wants." *The Atlantic.* March 2015.

Wright, Lawrence. *The Looming Tower: Al-Qaeda and the Road to 9/11.* New York: Vintage Books, 2007.

———. *The Terror Years: From al-Qaeda to the Islamic State.* New York: Knopf, 2016.

al-Zarqawi, Abu Musab. "Zarqawi Letter." US Department of State Archive, February
2004. https://2001-2009.state.gov/p/nea/rls/31694.htm.

al-Zawahiri, Ayman. "Zawahiri's Letter to Zarqawi." Combating Terrorism Center, October 11, 2005. https://ctc.usma.edu/harmony-program/zawahiris-letter-to-zarqa
wi-original-language-2/.

Zelin, Aaron. "The Islamic State of Iraq and Syria Has a Consumer Protection Office."
The Atlantic. June 13, 2014. https://www.theatlantic.com/international/archive
/2014/06/the-isis-guide-to-building-an-islamic-state/372769/.

Zollner, Barbara. "Prison Talk: The Muslim Brotherhood's Internal Struggle during
Gamal Abdel Nasser's Persecution, 1954 to 1971." *International Journal of Middle
East Studies* 39, no. 3 (2007): 411–33.